CLOSE AIR SUPPORT AND THE BATTLE FOR KHE SANH

by
Lieutenant Colonel Shawn P. Callahan
U.S. Marine Corps

Occasional Paper

HISTORY DIVISION
UNITED STATES MARINE CORPS
QUANTICO, VIRGINIA
2009

Published by Books Express Publishing Copyright@ Books Express, 2010
ISBN 978-1-907521-82-9 Booksellers, libraries and the military may order
at deiscounted prices by contacting info@books-express.com.

TABLE OF CONTENTS

Foreword 5
List of Tables and Illustrations 7
Introduction 9
Close Air Support Doctrines 13
Khe Sanh Background 39
The Hill Battles of 1967 45
The Siege of 1968 53
Operation Pegasus and the Relief of Khe Sanh 85
The Deep Air Battle and the B-52 103
Radar Controlled Tactical Air Support 115
Close Air Support 123
Conclusions 145
Appendix A: Glossary of Acronyms and Terms 147
Appendix B: Orders of Battle 151
Appendix C: Fratricide and Near Fratricide Aviation Incidents at Khe Sanh .153
Bibliography 155

Foreword

The History Division has undertaken the publication for limited distribution of various studies, theses, compilations, bibliographies, monographs, and memoirs, as well as proceedings at selected workshops, seminars, symposia, and similar colloquia, which it considers to be of significant value for audiences interested in Marine Corps history. These "Occasional Papers," which are chosen for their intrinsic worth, must reflect structured research, present a contribution to historical knowledge not readily available in published sources, and reflect original content on the part of the author, compiler, or editor. It is the intent of the Division that these occasional papers be distributed to selected institutions, such as service schools, official Department of Defense historical agencies, and directly concerned Marine Corps organizations, so the information contained therein will be available for study and exploitation.

This manuscript was developed from a master's thesis written by then-Major Shawn P. Callahan while an Advanced Degree Program student at George Washington University. The research was financially supported by the Naval Historical Center's Rear Admiral Samuel Eliot Morison Naval History Supplemental Scholarship Program and the Marine Corps Heritage Foundation's Lieutenant Colonel Lily H. Gridle Memorial Master's Thesis Fellowship Program.

As an occasional paper, this work is presented with limited stylistic correction and essentially stands as the author's revised thesis. Book layout and design by Emily D. Funderburke and W. Stephen Hill.

Dr. Charles P. Neimeyer
Director of Marine Corps History

LIST OF TABLES AND ILLUSTRATIONS

Figure 1. Map of Key Locations in Northern Quang Tri Province in the Northern I Corps Tactical Zone 39

Figure 2. Map of Khe Sahn and Key locations in the Immediate Vicinity 40

Figure 3. Map of Positions of U.S. Marine Units Defending the Key Hill Outposts around Khe Sanh Combat Base 63

Figure 4. Graph of Aerial Logistics Deliveries to Khe Sanh and its Outposts 76

Figure 5. Diagram of Command Relationships Between Major Units and Headquarters of the I Corps Tactical Zone during (and after) Operation Pegasus in 86

Figure 6. Graph of Daily Attack Sorties Devoted to Operations Around Khe Sanh 87

Figure 7. Diagram of Interface between the U.S. Marine Air Command and Control System Agencies of the 1st Marine air Wing and its Supported Units (1st and 3d Marine Divisions) 91

Figure 8. Diagram of Airspace Divisions in the Vicinity of Khe sanh for Operation Niagara 98

Table 1. Comparative strengths of U.S. Marine and Army Infrantry Divisions in Vietnam 94

Table 2. MACV Cumulative Bomb Damage Assessment for Operation Niagara 112

Table 3. Total Sortie and Ordnance Contributions to the Defense of Khe Sanh 124

Except for those noted here, all photographs in this work are official U.S. Marine Corps images. Photographs on the following pages appear courtesy of the listed individuals. Cover and page 9: Robert Donoghue. Page 23: David Steinberg. Pages 72 (top), 75, 78, 118, 128, 131, 135 (top): Joanne Schneider. Page 108: Ronald Smith. Page 109: Richard Dworsky. Page 134 (top), 136: David Powell. Page 134 (bottom): John Sabol.

INTRODUCTION

In the 77 days from 20 January to 18 March of 1968, two divisions of the North Vietnamese Army (NVA) surrounded a regiment of U.S. Marines on a mountain plateau in the northwest corner of South Vietnam known as Khe Sanh. The episode was no accident; it was in fact a carefully orchestrated meeting in which both sides got what they wanted. The North Vietnamese succeeded in surrounding the Marines in a situation in many ways similar to Dien Bien Phu, and may have been seeking similar tactical, operational, and strategic results. General William C. Westmoreland, the commander of the joint U.S. Military Assistance Command Vietnam (COMUSMACV), meanwhile, sought to lure the NVA into the unpopulated terrain around the 26th Marines in order to wage a battle of annihilation with air power. In this respect Khe Sanh has been lauded as a great victory of air power, a military instrument of dubious suitability to much of the Vietnam conflict. The facts support the assessment that air power was the decisive element at Khe Sanh, delivering more than 96 percent of the ordnance used against the NVA.[1]

Most histories of the battle, however, do not delve much deeper than this. Comprehensive histories like John Prados and Ray Stubbe's *Valley of Decision*, Robert Pisor's *End of the Line*, and Eric Hammel's *Siege in the Clouds* provide excellent accounts of the battle, supported by detailed analyses of its strategic and operational background but tend to focus on the ground battle and treat the application of air power in general terms. Official Marine Corps histories predictably focus on the experience of the 26th Marines at the expense of the contributions of air forces. Air Force histories, including those written by historians well acquainted with both the U.S. Air Force and U.S. Marine Corps like Bernard C. Nalty, do analyze the application of air power in detail. They do not, however, make significant distinction between the contributions of the two primary air combat elements in this air-land bat-

An A-4 drops two "snake-eye" bombs on a target close to the southern perimeter of Khe Sanh Combat Base.

tle: the 7th Air Force and the 1st Marine Air Wing. An analysis of their respective contributions to the campaign reveals that they each made very different contributions that reflected very different approaches to the application of air power.

There is a fundamental cultural difference between the U.S. Marine Corps and U.S. Air Force that affects many, if not all, aspects of their approaches to preparing for and fighting the nation's wars. One of the most distinct manifestations is their individual treatments of close air support (CAS), defined as air action by fixed- and rotary-wing aircraft against hostile targets that are in close proximity to friendly forces and that require detailed integration of each air mission with the fire and movement of those forces.[2] Khe Sanh presents an opportunity to compare the different approaches of these two institutions since it was one of the few times during the Vietnam War during which the two services were united in their operational objectives, in this case the destruction of NVA forces around Khe Sanh. Detailed analysis shows that even within this unified objective, the institutional differences between the services yielded different approaches and different results. The Air Force sought to fight the battle using various sensors to locate targets around the fixed defensive positions of the 26th Marines, which constituted little more than bait for the NVA. Once large NVA units were detected, the Air Force sought to unleash air power for their destruction, using fearsome weapons like the B-52 to attrite the NVA as they approached Khe Sanh. The Marines, meanwhile, sought to use air power to accomplish the more immediate objectives of the 26th Marines. While they acknowledged the utility of air power for a more distant battle of attrition when the situation permitted, the priority was for the destruction of enemy forces in the immediate vicinity of Khe Sanh that presented an imminent threat to the Marines attempting to maneuver or occupy defensive positions. In this respect, it can be said that the Air Force was more interested in engaging in Deep Air Support (DAS) rather than CAS.

The close confines of Khe Sanh and the threat imposed by enemy forces often prevented the two services from pursuing their preferred operational approaches to the battle. Instead, Marine and Air Force aircraft were often mixed, along with Navy aircraft, in both the deep and close battles. Even when this occurred, they each brought different strengths to the fight. The primary asset contributed by the Air Force was the massive firepower of the Strategic Air Command's B-52, which has been lauded as the decisive weapon of Khe Sanh. The sheer volume of this firepower, however, made it unsuitable for close battles, and the NVA sought to exploit this limitation by drawing close to Marine positions. When this occurred, the decisive element was the close air support provided by the tactical aviators of the 1st Marine Aircraft Wing (1st MAW), who were trained, equipped, and motivated to provide precision delivery of ordnance in ways and places where Air Force crews often proved untrained, ill-equipped, or unwilling. When Air Force crews did attempt to duplicate the close application of air power that the Marines specialized in, they sometimes met with disastrous results. The final conclusion is that although these distinct institutional approaches to close air support persist to this day, a careful examination of Khe Sanh reveals a victory not only of air power, but of complementary air forces: a strategically-oriented Air Force based on heavy firepower, and a tactical Marine air force that emphasized the close integration of air power with the fire and movement of friendly forces.

This work focuses mainly on fixed-wing close air support, or the support provided by jet and propeller-driven conventional aircraft, to the general exclusion of rotary-wing aircraft, also known as helicopters. There are several reasons for this, none of which are meant to belittle the contributions or heroism of the Marine, Army, and Air Force helicopter pilots who fought in the hills around Khe Sanh. First, until the arrival of the AH-1G Cobra in April 1969, there was no helicopter designed for dedicated close air support of Marines in Vietnam.[3] The primary gunship during the battle of Khe Sanh was the UH-1E outfitted with machine guns and rocket launchers for the escort of unarmed helicopters. These helicopters were sometimes used for the direct support of ground troops with suppressive fires and were frequently used as forward air controllers, spotting and marking targets for fixed-wing aircraft with heavier ordnance. These roles are appropriately discussed alongside the contributions of the fixed-wing aircraft, but as a general rule, analysis remains focused on the heavier attack aircraft.

Perhaps an even more important reason for the general exclusion of helicopters as CAS aircraft, however, is that outside of the Marine Corp helicopters were considered organic assets of the Army divisions in Vietnam and as such were completely external to the U.S. Air Force command and control system. They were not part of the massed firepower the Air Force sought to concentrate at Khe Sanh. Marine helicopters, meanwhile, fit nicely alongside the fixed-wing aircraft in the Marine Air Command and Control System (MACCS), so that no distinction needs to be made when discussing air request and control procedures.

The research methodology behind this paper reflects a broad approach. The main focus has been to reexamine the analysis of official operational and institutional historians and popular commemorative histories in order to develop an overlooked distinction. In order do so, the author has examined the working notes upon which several of these histories have been written and returned to the primary sources, including official documents, memoirs, and oral histories, in search of nuances ruled insignificant by other historians. In cases where the records contain gaps or necessitate further explanation, the author has corresponded with veterans of the battle to seek their clarification on important issues.

This research has admittedly delved deeper into Marine Corps sources than Air Force sources for two reasons. Recognizing that all research is subject to time and resource limitations, official historians like Donald J. Mrozek and John Schlight have already developed excellent histories on the Air Force's culture and doctrine. Air Force histories of the battle of Khe Sanh also generally do a good job of detailing Air Force participation in the campaign, facilitating comparison with the performance of Marine aviation in the battle. As a very infantry-centric service, however, the Marine Corps had tended to overlook the details of the performance of its air arm throughout the history of Marine aviation, and the battle of Khe Sanh is no exception. In order to develop a picture of the culture of the Marine Corps with respect to aviation, the author has had to reconstruct some of the picture. Finally, since this paper focuses on close air support (both the Air Force and Marine conceptions), it is less important what aviators thought about their performance than what opinions the infantrymen had on the support they were receiving. At Khe Sanh, therefore, the most important judgments on performance were the Marines of the combat base and its outposts. These men were naturally subject to some institutional prejudice in favor of Marine aviation, but their comments tend to be remarkably unbiased. The demands and personal risk of combat tended to quickly overwhelm parochialism. Marine infantrymen have historically been some of the harshest critics of the Marine air arm they demand so much of, and depend so heavily upon, and Khe Sanh was no exception.

For brevity's sake, the Marine Corps convention for identifying units has generally been maintained. The highest echelon of ground combat element typically identified by name is the regiment, which in Marine Corps parlance is referred to as the 26th Marines, instead of the 26th Marine Regiment. Individual battalions within each regiment are always identified with the parent regiment, so the 2d Battalion, 26th Marines becomes "2/26." The lettered companies within each regiment do not repeat within battalions, so technically Company F of the 2d Battalion, 26th Marines could be identified as F/26, since there is no Fox Company in 1/26 or 3/26. For clarity's sake, however, F/2/26 has been used in this paper, making it easier to keep track of parent units. The structure of aviation units discussed within this work can be especially confusing, but the appendices include both a Glossary of Acronyms and Terms (GOAT) and a listing of Orders of Battle for various friendly and enemy units that may help clarify the matter. Again, for brevity's sake, unless otherwise specified, all of the military servicemen identified in this paper are U.S. Marines.

CLOSE AIR SUPPORT DOCTRINES

What is Close Air Support?

Part of the reason for such wide differences in institutional approaches to close air support (CAS) is that this term means different things to different organizations. Essential to any detailed study of CAS, then, is a working definition. Such a definition is harder to come by than may be imagined since the only common feature the various military services agreed upon was that CAS involved the support of ground troops. By the early 1960s, even before the major U.S. involvement in Vietnam, the Joint Chiefs had agreed on a working definition of CAS as "Air action against hostile targets in close proximity to friendly forces and which requires detailed integration of each air mission with the fire and movement of those forces."[4] This consensus, however, was purely one of form, certainly not of function.

In his study as a senior research fellow for the U.S. Air Force's Airpower Research Institute, *Air Power and the Ground War in Vietnam,* Donald J. Mrozek did an excellent job showing how various factors prevented a true consensus on what CAS really was and how it fit into operational plans. Between the services and civil authority, there was no consensus on the effectiveness of air power in World War II and Korea. Varying expectations for air power in Vietnam, also combined with an absence of clear political and strategic goals, all against a backdrop of interservice rivalry, only confused the situation.[5] In combination, the vegetation, terrain, and weather, and the counterinsurgency mission to which air power was applied for the first time in Vietnam, presented new challenges which further altered service approaches to CAS.[6] The two major CAS providers in Vietnam, the U.S. Marine Corps and U.S. Air Force, may have shared a common definition, but they had radically different approaches to CAS.

The U.S. Air Force Approach to CAS

In order to understand the radical difference between the services with regard to close air support, it is necessary to go back at least as far as World War II. This high intensity conflict demonstrated the potential of air power as foreseen by a number of prewar air power theorists and provided opportunities for developing equipment, tactics, and doctrine. The most significant development was the realization of the vision that airspace existed as a separate medium through which military force could be directed to win wars and accomplish national policy. Although air support had proven critical to the successful conduct of air and sea campaigns, strategic bombing campaigns convinced many policy makers that the potential of air power could never be fully realized until it was unleashed from a subordinacy to land and sea forces. As a result, the U.S. Air Force was established as a separate service in 1947, and its leadership was populated by men who focused on the potential of air power as a strategic force, not as a military arm to serve the interests of the Army or Navy.[7]

Of course air power had many different applications, and the early leaders of the Air Force did not reject its importance in support of ground campaigns. As a result, in the postwar period the Air Force maintained a tactical air component alongside the strategic and air mobility components of the Air Force. Exactly how these tactical air forces would be employed, however, was open to significant debate. Tactical air forces were associated with three main mission areas: air superiority, interdiction, and close air support. Air superiority is defined as the control of airspace by denying its use to the enemy and the suppression of enemy air defense systems. With regard to priority, military theorists generally agreed that air superiority had to be first, since tactical air forces could not carry out their other missions while the use of the airspace was contested. Close air support was another mission, defined by the Air Force as the application of air power to attack enemy forces in order to assist friendly ground forces in attaining their objectives. The third mission, air interdiction, came between CAS and strategic bombing directed against enemy industry and morale. Interdiction is the application of air power in order to deny the enemy the material and human resources it needs to win a battle or campaign by preventing its forces from reaching the battlefield. This may mean isolating the battlefield by destroying critical transportation links like railways and bridges, or it may mean attacking the military forces and supplies en route to the battlefield.[8] Even before the Air Force was established as a separate service, in 1943 the Army defined an explicit priority for the use of tactical air forces: 1) air superiority, 2) interdiction, and 3) close air support.[9] With the establishment of a separate air service, interdiction remained a much more attractive mission than CAS to air-centric leaders because it allowed them much greater latitude in the application of air power. It was also seen as capable of producing decisive results while not being mired in coordination with ground forces, and without having to acknowledge the subordinacy of air power or directly share credit for victory. In summary, in the post-World War II era, the Air Force sought to focus its tactical air forces on air superiority and interdiction, leaving close air support as an ancillary mission despite the concerns of the army it supported.[10]

This conflict in prioritization was manifest in the Korean War. When necessary, as in the early months of the war when the ground battle was so fluid, Air Force leaders were willing to focus on CAS, but the Army remained concerned about the responsiveness of the Air Force command and control system and was critical of the air service's efforts at meeting their needs.[11] Common was the complaint that the war was begun with only four tactical air control parties to coordinate air support in Korea, and only over time was this number built up to merely one team per regiment.[12]

In the late 1950s and early 1960s, the Air Force remained focused on its strategic missions, especially the nuclear forces that were being counted upon to deliver "more bang for the buck" under President Dwight D. Eisenhower's New Look at defense. This did not mean, however, that the value of tactical forces was completely overlooked. In 1956, for example, General Otto P. Weyland, who had recently returned from command of the Far East Air Forces, predicted that "the most likely conflict in the immediate future will be the peripheral type. In this event, it will be primarily a tactical air war."[13] The idea was seconded in 1957,[14] and the 1958 Quemoy and Matsu crisis convinced many that the Air Force had to maintain capabilities for non-nuclear conflicts. In practice, however, other than concluding the most basic joint agreements for Air Force support of Army ground operations,[15] close air support got remarkably little attention. As a result, the Air

A B-29 from the 19th Bomb Group, Far East Air Force, drops a stick of bombs over North Korea in February 1951. The heavy employment of these aircraft in a limited war reflected the Air Force's preference for strategic air power but did little to discourage the enemy from continuing to fight.

Force was unprepared for its initial involvement in Indochina.

The primary impetus for change within the Air Force was created by President John F. Kennedy's doctrine of flexible response. Regardless of the Air Force's lack of interest in "brush fire" wars, where strategic air power was of questionable utility, the new administration forced it to begin preparation. In April 1961, the 4400th Combat Training Squadron was formed at Eglin Air Force Base in Florida to begin training for the employment of air power in counterinsurgency. While the president's wishes were translated into a two-week course in counterinsurgency operations, there was no corresponding realignment of forces to provide the muscle. General Curtis E. LeMay was charged with conducting a review of the Air Force's suitability to meet the needs of the nation in the period from 1965 to 1975, but his project forecast yielded no substantive conclusions on the application of air power below the strategic level.[16] Air Force leaders were clearly focused on other things besides how to best support ground forces.

Within months of its formation, a detachment of the 4400th Combat Training Squadron was deployed to Vietnam to train the Vietnamese Air Force (VNAF) to fight the Viet Cong insurgency. The October 1961 arrival of the training detachment, under the code name Farm Gate, brought in small numbers of C-47s, T-28s, and B-26s, which began flying from Bien Hoa air base near Saigon. These aircraft were repainted with South Vietnamese insignia and were required to carry a Vietnamese Air Force crewmember since the mission of Farm Gate was to train the VNAF. The American aviators, however, were de facto doing the fighting.[17] The arrival of the 2d Advance Echelon of the 13th Air Force (based in the Philippines) in November formalized the U.S. involvement, as the new headquarters became the air component of the Military Assistance Advisory Group, Vietnam, established in February 1962. The unit continued to grow in size and was later reclassified the 2d Air Division.[18]

The experiences of the Air Force as its involvement grew should have inspired an increased emphasis on Close Air Support. This interdiction-minded force, for example, found it impossible to anticipate exactly where decisive military engagements would occur in insurgency operations and so could not use air power to cut off the flow of men and materials to these "battles."[19] Instead, air power could only be used reactively to support ground forces that had been met by the enemy at times and places of his choosing. The increasing involvement of the U.S. Air Force in a war where combat depended on contact by ground forces should have had a dramatic impact on its formation of a more effective CAS doctrine. Instead, the service dug in its heels in interservice disputes back in the United States, where the war was stressing already strained relationships.

In the interwar period, the U.S. Army was quick to perceive the diverging strategic viewpoints of the two services as it prepared for a major ground war in Europe. Since the Air Force was uninterested in supporting ground operations, the Army began strengthening its own air component, increasing the number of Army aircraft from 3,495 to 5,475 in the period from 1955 to 1959.[20] There were two consequences of the Army's willingness to provide for itself what the Air Force would not. First, it aroused Air Force leaders, who saw this fourth air force (the second and third being the aviation forces of the Navy and Marine Corps) as another competitor to challenge the senior air service's authority overall aviation matters.[21] Second, it caught the interest of the efficiency-minded secretary of defense, Robert S. McNamara, who constantly urged the Army and Air Force to work out their differences in joint training exercises and field tests.[22] While Air Force planners remained unconcerned with sub-strategic missions and considered counterinsurgency too low of a level of war for the application of air power,[23] they found themselves both conducting an escalating counterinsurgency mission in Vietnam and engaging in a turf battle over close air support at home.

The U.S. Army had been calling for a joint doctrine on close air support since 1960, advocating maximum responsiveness through decentralized command and control of tactical aviation at the field army/tactical air force level under Army command.[24] In April 1962, Secretary McNamara asked for a reassessment of land warfare doctrine. The resulting Howze Board recommended that the Army develop its own air arm to assure a basic level of close air support, but also recommended that the Air Force more fully commit to supporting the ground battle by developing a single-mission aircraft specifically designed for CAS. Additionally, the Howze Board recommended that the Air Force formally agree to support ground operations with discrete numbers of sorties for various theater.[25]

The Air Force's response was its Tactical Air Support Requirements Board, known as the Disoway Board, whose final report was published just one month later. The Disoway Board insisted on the consolidation of all air assets under a single Air Force commander, who would in turn answer to a joint task force commander and would respond to his directions regarding support for ground forces. Allowing the Army to pursue its own airmobility concept was declared to be a dangerous dispersion of air power, contradicting the principle that concentration and centralization maximized effectiveness in combat.[26] The Disoway Board also explicitly rejected the idea that the Air Force should develop a CAS-specific aircraft, insisting that multiple-use aircraft allowed greater flexibility for the application of air power.[27] Essentially, in response to McNamara's direction that the Army and the Air Force reevaluate their perspectives of air-ground cooperation, the two services restated their previous positions on the issue.[28]

Unsatisfied, McNamara ordered a joint Army and Air Force examination of close air support in February 1963. When the two services met in April, they again failed to produce any significant agreement and came to an impasse over the central issue of command and control. The Army argued for decentralized control of air assets under ground commanders, while the Air Force insisted that an air commander should prioritize targets and schedule strikes.[29] While there was little agreement, the joint exercises that soon followed were significant.

In the fall of 1964, the Army and Air Force participated in the largest joint exercise since World War II, known as Operation Desert Strike. In the deserts of Southern California it became apparent that the two services would have to compromise if they were to work effectively on the same battlefield. The Air Force admitted that its command and control system had become too disconnected from ground operations and developed new links to reconnect them. These improvements included a new agency that would provide a liaison team to the Army at the corps level, known as Air Support Operations Centers (ASOCs). The ASOCs changed the role of Air Liaison Officers (ALOs) from mere advisers to staff officers with operational responsibilities for seeing that air and ground operations were successfully integrated.[30] The Army gave in on its call for a hard commitment on sortie numbers, agreeing that the joint commander would decide how many sorties would be apportioned to CAS and interdiction missions on a daily basis. The Air Force, in turn, agreed that the ground commander would allocate the specified CAS sorties to subordinate commanders for the decentralized application of air power according to the needs of the lower echelon units in contact with the enemy. The Air Force also agreed to provide tactical air control parties down to the battalion level in order to provide a link between the lowest maneuver unit and the air power that would support it.[31] In short, the joint vision for the application of close air support between the Army and Air Force came to resemble the system the Marine Corps had already established in practice. Unfortunately, the Air Force was uncommitted to translating that vision into an air-ground team that was as capable as the Marine Corps.

The escalation in Vietnam was concurrent with the growing Army-Air Force cooperation and provided not only urgency to help them overcome their differences, but also a place to try out their new solutions. In 1965, the two services took the first steps by replacing the rudimentary air command and control system with a new one. At Tan Son Nhut Air Base near Saigon, the Air Operations Center (AOC) continued to serve as the primary control agency for all operations in South Vietnam, but now four ASOCs were established, one each in the I and II Corps Tactical Zones, one to cover III and IV Corps, and one final ASOC to float between regions and handle special operations as needed.[32]

When U.S. ground combat operations escalated, the number of CAS sorties increased dramatically, from 2,392 in January 1965 to more than 7,000 in June and 13,000 in December. By August 1966 they were averaging 15,000 a month.[33] These numbers can be deceiving, however, since they suggest that the Air Force was focusing its efforts on close air support. In fact, a key Air Force leader who arrived in July 1966, General William W. Momyer, was driving operations in the opposite direction. Momyer took command of the 2d Air Division, which was redesignated the 7th Air Force in March 1966 due to the increasing numbers of U.S. aircraft in South Vietnam. In this position, Momyer also served as MACV's deputy commander for air operations.[34] Momyer was a talented and aggressive leader who was an ardent believer in the supremacy of air power. His perspective of this unconventional war was that it had no front lines except the 17th parallel. North of that line, he considered anything that might support the enemy effort to be fair game for his aviators.[35] Within South Vietnam, Momyer admitted that his aviators would have to be more discriminating in the application of air power and would often have to work with ground forces. He considered the results of this cooperation to be disappointing, however focusing on problems like those encountered in October 1966 during an enemy assault on Loc Ninh, just three months after he took command. The Air Force supported the defense with 700 tactical sorties but was not rewarded with even a single confirmed casualty for these efforts.[36] Aircraft were used in conjunction with artillery to drive the enemy back, but it was noted that the aircraft found themselves restricted in their ability to support the defense because they had to wait for the artillery to stop firing before they could enter the airspace to attack. In light of these events, ardent air power advocates like Momyer saw cooperation, with ground forces as a hindrance. The easy solution was to not to solve the problems of integrating air and artillery attack, but to condemn it. Momyer developed a new view of air-ground cooperation, and saw the typical engagement as one in which ground forces found and made contact with the enemy until aircraft would arrive to destroy them. In his memoirs, Momyer went on to elaborate:

> All ground operations were designed to seek out the North Vietnamese and VC and to force an engagement in which our superior firepower, particularly air power, could be employed. It was our policy that after contact with the enemy was established, our ground forces would pull back a sufficient distance to allow artillery and air power to be used without restraint. Then the Army would follow up these attacks with reaction forces.[37]

Momyer was not alone. A contemporary Air Force study also overlooked the benefits of synergistic close cooperation, stating that "Air Power was used effectively in its traditional roles as well as in compensating for shortages or as a substitute for ground forces."[38]

It can be seen, then, that despite interservice agreements and CINCPAC's clear directive in April 1965 to focus tactical air forces on CAS, by the time Khe Sanh became a place of significance in 1967 and 1968, the U.S. Air Force still considered true close air support to be a secondary mission. Part of the reason for this was that the Air Force still operated under the unspecific 1956 definition of CAS, as air support or cooperation provided to friendly surface forces, consisting of air attacks with guns bombs, guided airborne missiles or rockets on hostile surface forces, their installations, or vehicles so close to surface operations as to require coordination between air and friendly surface forces.[39]

It is important to note that this definition is based on proximity to friendly ground forces. It does not imply a subordination of air power to objectives established by ground commanders, and suggests that coordination with ground forces was an incidental hindrance, rather than a tool for synergistically integrating supporting arms.

This very loose definition of CAS only blurred the already unclear line between CAS and interdiction, leaving the Air Force plenty of room to still fight the war the way is best thought fit. Because of the danger of attacking friendly forces and civilians within South Vietnam, the entire country was declared to be within the bombline[40] (today known as the Fire Support Coordination Line, or FSCL), and all operations within South Vietnam were technically classified as CAS. As such, the rules of engagement required that all air strikes be under the direction of a forward air controller, and that all targets be further approved by the Vietnamese province chief and by corps-level military officers of the U.S. and South Vietnam.[41] At any given time, however, the vast majority of South Vietnam did not fall within the tactical operating area of one ground unit or another, and so, there was no unit to be supported in these missions or FAC to coordinate them. To service these areas and get around the restriction, the Air Force sought to use mobile FAC(A)s in observation aircraft. Unfortunately, it had no aircraft suitable for the task despite the key roles observation aircraft had played in the Korean War, and in Indochina for the French. Following the Korean War, the Air Force had declared disinterest in the mission and had actually given all of its L-19 aircraft to the Army, which then had to provide its own aerial observation services.[42] With the Farm Gate deployment of aircraft and Air Force "advisors" to Vietnam in 1961, the Air Force suddenly found itself dependent on the small number of Vietnamese Air Force FAC(A)s for locating targets for its faster attack aircraft. As a result, in 1963, the Air Force took twenty-five L-19s (now redesignated as O-1s) back from the Army, and in June deployed them to Vietnam as the 19th Tactical Air Support Squadron.[43] Although the Air Force did its best to make it appear that this was a proactive decision made in the interest of providing better support to Army combat battalions, when backed into a corner by a congressional subcommittee investigation, it could not deny that the move was purely a reaction to unforeseen shortcomings in Vietnam.[44]

Prior to the deployment of U.S. ground combat forces in Vietnam in 1965, the Air Force erected a forward air control system centered on the FAC(A). Ideally, four to six Air Liaison Officers and FAC's were assigned to each of South Vietnam's 44 provinces. These became known as "area FACs" since their primary responsibility was territorial, rather than to ground units which might be operating in that province. These FACs were recruited from various Air Force commands to serve their entire overseas tours advising the province chiefs, and were provided with a checkout as an O-1 pilot, as well as FAC-specific training.[45] Their primary responsibility was reconnaissance,[46] although they could and did control attacks by strike aircraft when suitable targets could be found and approved by the province chief. As direct U.S. involvement in the war increased in 1965, General Westmoreland directed that this reconnaissance effort by area FAC's be organized for more comprehensive coverage. The country was then further divided into sectors, each of which could be inspected in two hours. Ideally, each sector would be covered by at least one O-1 each day, and the same FAC(A) would patrol the same sector day after day, gaining great familiarity with the terrain and its inhabitants. This goal proved problematic, since even after the formation and deployment of three more O-1 squadrons to Vietnam in 1965, such coverage proved beyond the capabilities of the Air Force. The efforts of the 110 Air Force O-1s were joined by 152 Army and 114 Vietnamese Air Force O-1s in a joint effort, but these still proved insufficient to meet Westmoreland's intent. In the densely vegetated or heavily populated area it sometimes took several O-1s up to eight hours to conduct a through search of a single sector, and a 1966 RAND study found that only 65 percent of the sectors were covered daily.[47] As far as directing offensive operations, the Army O-1 pilots were trained only to spot for artillery, and VNAF FAC(A)s were not permitted to control air support for the blossoming number of U.S. Army units appearing in the provinces after 1965.

By the end of 1965, the Air Force had erected its FAC(A)-based air control system. Each of the four corps tactical zones in South Vietnam were provided with a 30-aircraft O-1 squadron, and each corps headquarters was provided with a Direct Air Support Center (DASC) to control the application of air power within each zone.[48] While these "area FACs" were able to provide some coverage to each province, the Tactical Air Control Parties (TACPs) that had been promised by the Air Force to serve as the link between the Army's maneuver battalions and the Air Force support structure were rare. Despite an agreement in spring 1965 to provide two FACs to each Army combat unit from the battalion level on up to the field army, the Air Force simply did not have enough FAC's. The problem was exacerbated by the Air Force's insistence that these FACs be fighter attack pilots (designated as "Class A" FACs, in contrast to the full-time "Class C" FACs assigned to the provinces). The air service had the best of intentions with this policy, which was designed to provide highly qualified ground FACs to U.S. Army ground combat units, leaving the FAC(A)s to support ARVN units.[49] Unfortunately, the expanding air war was simultaneously placing very high demands on this same manpower pool. As a result, unlike Marine TACPs, which early in the war provided three FAC-qualified aviators to each battalion to enable two FACs to move with and control air support for the company-sized elements actually engaged in combat with the enemy, Air Force TACPs included only a single Air Liaison Officer (ALO). This officer remained in the battalion headquarters behind the companies and platoons engaging the enemy, with the only radio capable of talking to aircraft. As a result, when infantry units needed air support, they had to relay their request back to the battalion headquarters, where the ALO would submit the request for support to the air command and control system, and communicate with the aircraft to direct its attack.[50]

The manpower situation only got worse, forcing the Air Force to further compromise its commitments to both the quality and extent of FAC support it provided. By October 1965, the shortages were severe enough that the requirement for TACP (Class A) FACs to have one year of current fighter experience was waived.[51] Despite this compromise, the Air Force was unable to meet more than about half of its commitment to the Army, and one year later it began to pool its FACs at the brigade level,[52] reducing their familiarity and access to the battalion- and company-level units actually in contact with the enemy. In 1966, the rules of engagement for the control of air strikes were also modified. Under this revision, free-fire areas could be designated by MACV in which targets could be attacked without the permission of a province chief or higher military authority. If no U.S. Air Force FACs were available to support U.S. Army units, then Vietnamese FACs could be used, or ground commanders and U.S. pilots could direct attacks without the clearance of any FAC at all.[53] Ultimately, despite a series of compromises, the Air Force was never able to meet its obligations to the U.S. Army during the peak years of U.S. involvement on Vietnam. The first time 100 percent FAC manning was reached in South East Asia was in December 1970,[54] when U.S. ground combat unit deployments, and therefore FAC demands, had begun to decline precipitously. It is telling that even as the Air Force was compromising its policies for ground FAC assignments and still failing to meet its commitments, the air service found a means to establish a fifth observation squadron to provide FAC(A) coverage for aerial interdiction missions along the Ho Chi Minh Trail.[55] In Vietnam, the Air Force's peacetime neglect of its obligation to support the Army with ground FACs simply proved too difficult to overcome, especially when Air Force leaders believed they had new opportunities to win the war from the air.

The air service rationalized its failure to meet its commitment to support infantry units by increased reliance on FAC(A)s, which it believed could serve the dual purposes of supporting maneuver units and covering the regions not incorporated into the operations of ground units. The main reason for this emphasis, stated by General Momyer himself, was that, "As in Korea, the Vietnamese terrain seriously restricted the utility of FACs on the ground. The airborne FAC was the only effective way of controlling a strike."[56] The vegetation and terrain in Vietnam undoubtedly complicated a ground FAC's job—the Marine Corps' increased reliance on FAC(A)s is evidence that they were indeed useful. The Marine Corps, however, increased its reliance on Airborne FAC's as a supplement to the critical link that a ground FAC provided. The Air Force developed the airborne FAC as a replacement, and as a result, the Air Force FAC(A) often hunted independently within his assigned region, and directed "close air support" at his own discretion in interdiction-type missions, rather than in support of ground operations.[57]

For the Air Force, the primary requesting and controlling agency for air strikes within South Vietnam was not a ground FAC in a TACP assigned to an Army unit, but the airborne FAC roaming about to hunt independently, unless a ground unit happened to be in his area. By 1968, over 60 percent of all targets generated were products of the airborne reconnaissance effort, not the ground combat units which could sustain contact with the enemy and which should have been supported as the basic consumers of CAS.[58] Essentially, instead of dividing operations within South Vietnam into two separate categories, CAS when supporting ground units and interdiction when working independently of them, the Air Force lumped them all under the category of CAS and a single rules of engagement set that essentially left it up to the FAC(A)s to decide when and how much they wanted to cooperate with ground forces. The vast majority of these FAC(A)s were ready, willing, and anxious to render whatever assistance they could provide to ground forces, but the fact remains that there was no clear institutional distinction in air operations as to when air power became a subordinate, supporting effort to ground operations. As General Momyer related, "At all times, the [airborne] FAC was the final air authority on whether or not the strike would continue. He was, in fact, the local air commander for the conduct of air operations; and his authority was recognized by the ground force commander and flight leader alike."59

Significantly, the training these FACs received did little to disrupt the air-centric approach to CAS. As a result of the various policy changes, during the years of peak U.S. involvement in Vietnam, the typical Air Force FACs were young captains who had already completed the first six-months of their tours in Vietnam as pilots in fighter squadrons, and they provided forward air control from observation aircraft, not on the ground. Although some were attracted to FAC duty by more progressive views about the application of air power in support of the ground war, giving up one's seat in a high performance jet fighter aircraft at the pinnacle of the Air Force's warfighting hierarchy to fly a slow, low-flying, lightly armed observation aircraft was probably not seen as a prestigious assignment. Little was done to prepare these FAC(A)s to serve as the Air Force's primary link to the ground forces. They had no personal exposure to the challenges faced by ground commanders or other supporting arms like artillery, and retained the air power-centric viewpoints they had been indoctrinated with their entire careers. Even when they had the training required to adjust artillery fire, Air Force FAC(A)s usually flew solo, and there was a limit to how much coordination with ground forces a single pilot could do while flying his plane. Institutionally, the Air Force declared the coordination of ground fire to be simply too complicated to be done while simultaneously directing aircraft.60 Air Force FAC(A)s preferred the more familiar job of scouting out targets on their own, rather than having to deal with ground operations and the accompanying complications that they did not understand or consider vital to how the war was fought.

U.S. Air Force Aircraft

The Air Force's distaste for CAS operations was also reflected in the poor array of close air support equipment which it brought to Vietnam.

An F-84F Thunderstreak fires 5-inch rockets at ground targets in Korea. When pressed to fulfill its commitment to provide ground support forces for the U.S. Army, the Air Force's insistence on developing multi-role fighter bomber jet aircraft whose armament and high speeds and made them less than ideally suited for CAS when called upon to support the Army in that mission.

It has already been shown that the U.S. Army pushed for the Air Force to develop a single-mission CAS aircraft to ensure that its aircrews were not distracted by other missions in training and war. The Air Force, on the other hand, insisted on multi-role aircraft. In general, this meant a preference for versatile jet fighter-bombers which would be more survivable on dangerous missions striking deep into enemy territory. These aircraft were able to carry more ordnance than propeller-driven aircraft, were faster and therefore often more responsive, but on the whole they were not as suitable for CAS missions. Propeller driven aircraft had a longer loiter time to provide more coverage, and flew slower attacks, giving the pilots more time to acquire targets.[61] As a result of its multi-role focus, the Air Force did not develop a single aircraft designed even primarily for CAS after World War II,[62] until it learned some hard lessons in Vietnam, at the expense of the Army troops it had agreed to support. Although the Air Force had approximately 1,000 aircraft in Vietnam at the time of the siege of Khe Sanh in 1968 (as shown in Appendix B), and began augmenting this number with aircraft based in Thailand in January of that year,[63] the service was unable to support ground units as effectively as it would have had proactive action been taken to develop specialized CAS aircraft before the war escalated.

Once committed to the war, the Air Force came to the realization that it was somewhat unprepared, and in May 1964 it actually obtained a number of two-seat propeller-driven A-1E and A-1H Skyraiders from the U.S. Navy, along with a squadron of navy pilots to serve as training cadre for the new aircraft. With their long loiter times and heavy ordnance loads, these aircraft had proven well-suited for CAS missions in the Korean War, and the Navy had kept them in active use. They were effective enough that the Air Force kept them in service to provide close air support for the rescue of downed pilots—a CAS mission the Air Force was certainly committed to—until 1972, and even considered reopening the production line. By and large, however, the initial acquisition of this particular aircraft was probably motivated more by a political restriction against deploying jet aircraft to Vietnam than by a desire for more suitable CAS aircraft. A new provision in January 1965 permitted the use of jets in emergency situations and without a VNAF observer aboard, allowing the immediate employment of B-57s in South Vietnam. A rapid buildup and dominance of less-suitable multi-role F-100 Super Sabres and F-4 Phantoms followed shortly thereafter.[64]

Later in the war, the Air Force did employ aircraft specifically adopted for CAS, but the impetus for their adoption was not an altruistic motivation to provide better CAS service. Continued dissatisfaction with Air Force support in the wake of the 1964 and 1965 interservice agreements led the Army to make its attack helicopter a high priority. The Army's insistence on developing its own attack helicopter eventually reignited the turf battle and forced the Air Force to revise its position on multi-role aircraft. To justify its program the Army gave its aircraft's mission another name: Aerial Fire Support (AFS). Of note, the fact that the Army defined AFS as the application of "discriminatory firepower in close proximity to ground combat elements"[65] suggests that the Army did not consider the Air Force's application of firepower in CAS to be very discriminatory. The Army program came to fruition with the introduction of the Huey Cobra to combat service in Vietnam in November 1967. Although the Marines at Khe Sanh never benefited from the support of this weapon, it did cause the Air Force to respond by reversing its policy on purchasing CAS-optimized aircraft.

Since 1963, the Army had urged the Air Force to participate in the Navy's light attack aircraft (VAL) program, which later gave birth to the A-7A Corsair, A-6A Intruder, and A-4 Skyhawk. The Army tried to appeal to the Air Force's emphasis on multi-role aircraft by advocating the Vought A-7, which had been designed for CAS, but had the versatility to perform other missions as well. The A-7 was rejected by the Air Force because it was not supersonic, a feature with no application in the support of ground troops.[66] After the frustrated Army began to pursue its own CAS aircraft programs, however, the Air Force adopted the Navy design. It redesignated its version the A-7D, which was not operational in Vietnam until October 1972, after the withdrawal of ground combat forces.[67] The concession was made, once again, only when the Air Force's doctrinal turf was threatened. Of note, since it ultimately appeased the Army by purchasing the A-7, the Air Force also rejected some other fine multi-role products of the Navy's VAL program. Among them were the A-6 Intruder, a medium attack/CAS aircraft capable of bombing day or night in all weather conditions, and the A-4 Skyhawk, a light attack/CAS aircraft designed for visual bombing.[68] The robust all-weather attack capabilities on the A-6 were not obtained by the Air Force during the Vietnam War until the combat deployment of the F-111A in September 1972, after ground troops had been withdrawn.

The Air Force followed the A-7 precedent by participating in several other quick-fix aircraft programs as a result of its experience in Vietnam. In 1966, it contracted the Cessna Aircraft Company to modify an existing aircraft for counterinsurgency CAS missions. The most suitable airframe in the Air Force arsenal was a jet train-

The AC-47 Spooky, popularly known as "Puff the Magic Dragon" because of the huge volume of tracers its three 7.62mm gatling guns could be seen delivering at night, was an excellent CAS aircraft developed by the Air Force. It was, however, developed primarily as an interdiction platform, and the Air Force made the program a low priority until the weapon proved critical in several engagements on the eve of U.S. escalation in Vietnam.

ing aircraft adopted in 1952! Thirty-nine T-37Bs were improved with armor plating, upgraded avionics, and 7.62mm miniguns to create the A-37A Dragonfly. This aircraft however, did not see full combat deployment in Vietnam until 1968. As a multi-purpose ground support aircraft to replace the A-1's borrowed from the Navy, the A-37A and A-37B had a number of faults, and was considered effective only in the most permissive threat environments.[69]

The Air Force did develop one group of superior CAS platforms, the AC-47, AC-119, and AC-130 gunships, but in many ways the contribution was unintentional. C-47s had been used in ground support missions as early as World War II, when they were employed to drop flares to illuminate targets for B-26s flying night interdiction missions.[70] The Air Force developed a plan to mount heavy guns in the fuselage of the C-47s, which could deliver huge volumes of fire on ground targets as the aircraft orbited overhead. The platform was designed to be used on interdiction missions more than it was for CAS, but it was obvious that it could serve either role in supporting President Kennedy's low-intensity counterinsurgency vision for the United States in Vietnam in the early 1960s.[71] Despite the utility of the aircraft, the Air Force dragged its feet and the program was retarded from 1961 to 1964. As a ground support platform it did not have the support of Air Force leaders with more conventional views about the primacy of air power.[72]

Operational testing of the AC-47 "Spooky" finally began in Vietnam in 1964, and it was the experience of that year that solidified the gunship's role as a CAS platform. The slow-flying, relatively unmaneuverable, and poorly armored aircraft proved to be too vulnerable to ground fire for interdiction missions in high-threat areas like North Vietnam. On the other hand, the endurance of these slow propeller-driven aircraft proved to be a great asset. Their slow speed decreased their response time when launched from a ground alert, but once they arrived in a battle area, they could remain on station for six to ten hours. This made them available to immediately respond to requests for support and able to maintain a continual presence for follow-on attacks. The aircraft carried its own parachute flares which could be dropped to illuminate targets at night, and its slow orbit at low altitudes allowed its crews to careful discriminate enemy from friendly forces, and fire at these targets in close proximity with great accuracy. The aircraft's three SUU-11A 7.62 mm Gatling guns could deliver a total of up to 18,000 rounds per minute, so that in one minute a gunship could cover an area one-third the size of a regulation football field with a round in every square foot. One in every few bullets was a red tracer that could be seen from miles away at night, earning the aircraft the popular nickname "Puff the Magic Dragon" after the mythical fire breather.[73] The experiences of 1964 showed that the AC-47 was a decisive factor in the defense of a number of outposts, especially at night and during poor weather conditions, when other attack aircraft were unable to provide reliable and continuous support.[74] Only after this immense success and widespread acclaim of the C-47 emerged in 1964 did the gunship program get full support from within the Air Force. The next year, after the presence of U.S. ground forces was escalated significantly, the 4th Air Commando Squadron was deployed to Vietnam with the primary mission of ground support.[75] These 14 aircraft were mainly used in night CAS missions where they proved so superior to other CAS platforms, that within a few months they were operating out of numerous bases to cover all four of South Vietnam's corps tactical zones.[76]

The success of the AC-47 program led to the development of two other gunships, modified from the C-119 and C-130 aircraft. The AC-119 Shadow was optimized for the CAS mission with improved sensors for target acquisition. When it was deployed to Vietnam in late 1969, it included improved flares, two 20mm Gatling guns, and jet assistance for takeoff. The AC-130 Spectre was a parallel program, specifically designated not as a CAS weapon, but to fill in the AC-47s original intended mission as a long-range interdiction platform.[77] The Spectre included low-light TV and infrared sensors for improved target acquisition at night without having to drop flares which would make it more visible to the enemy. Although the Spectre did not see full operational deployment to Vietnam until late in 1968, prototypes were flying in combat in late 1967.[78] This interdiction platform proved to be a very capable CAS weapon, and it is possible that some of them flew in support of Khe Sanh.

In the observation roles, the Air Force also found jet aircraft unsuitable for use in South Vietnam, and depended on the propeller-driven O-1 and O-2A for FAC support.[79] It has already been shown that the USAF completely discarded the O-1, along with its commitment to provide forward air controllers to support ground forces, after the Korean War. By 1963 it had returned the O-1 to operational use, and its numbers were soon augmented by the higher performanc O-2A, which offered additional coverage at night. The Air Force did join the Light Armed Reconnaissance Aircraft program initiated by the Marine Corps in 1962 to replace the O-1, but did not become a strong supporter until late in 1965, two months after a Congressional subcommittee visited Vietnam and urged an acceleration of the program.[80] The OV-10 which resulted was a superb FAC(A) platform, but was not survivable enough for duty in North Vietnam on strike coordination and reconnaissance missions. Since operations north of the DMZ did not require the detailed target area situational awareness necessitated by the presence of friendly troops, the Air Force used the F-100F there as a TAC platform beginning in June 1967.[81]

The Marine Approach to Close Air Support

The Marine Corps' approach to close air support differed from the Air Force's because the Marines viewed ground combat forces as the primary instruments for winning battles. Air power was valued almost exclusively based on its contribution to the ground battle. For this reason, CAS was considered the most important mission of Marine aviation, and the Marine Corps focused the lion's share of its aviation effort on developing and refining its CAS capability. As the senior aviator in the Marine Corps put it just months before the siege of Khe Sanh, "Marine aviation is a tactical air arm. Its sole mission is to provide support to the ground forces." Because of this, CAS, he went on to elaborate "is a Marine hallmark."[82]

All three of the U.S. military services of the early 20th century began their interest in aviation as a new arm which could support surface operations. While the Navy and Army saw men like Billy Mitchell, who envisioned air power as a new, independent dimension of warfare, as a threat, the Marine Corps maintained the primacy of surface combat and embraced air power as a force multiplier. The pattern of close cooperation between Marine air and ground arms was recognized as a military virtue. In 1926, even as the other services were engaged in heated debates about the role of air power, Major Edwin H. Brainard, the Director of Marine Corps Aviation, stated,

"To obtain maximum results, aviation and the troops with which it operates should be closely associated with each other, and know each other, as well as have a thorough knowledge of each other's work.... Marine Aviation is not being developed as a separate branch of the service that considers itself too good to do anything else. Unlike the Army Air Service, we do not aspire or want to be separated from the line or to be considered as anything but regular Marines."[83]

Major Roy S. Geiger (left), a Marine pilot who would later command the III Amphibious Corps, and very briefly the U.S. Tenth Army in World War II, and five other officers in Port au Prince, Haiti, in 1926. Even before the battle of Ocotal, Nicaragua, in 1927, the event traditionally identified as the first time Marines conducted close air support, extensive cooperation between air and ground units in the "Banana Wars" encouraged the development of the Marine Corps' air arm as a tactical force multiplier for ground forces.

While both the Army and the Marine Corps experimented with aircraft in support of ground attacks during World War I, the Marine Corps was the first to truly integrate air operations in support of ground maneuver. As a combined arms tactic, CAS was successfully executed for the first time in Nicaragua in the defense of the town of Ocotal from Sandino Rebels on 16 July 1927.[84] What made this situation unique was the unprecedented control of dive bombing attacks by Marine riflemen who were conducting simultaneous attacks on the ground.[85] As the Marine Corps evolved from its colonial, counterinsurgency role to an amphibious assault force in the late 1930s, Marines continued to refine the use of aircraft in support of ground operations. From 1935 through the start of World War II, Marine squadrons participated in all of the annual fleet landing exercises, refining their close air support techniques. During this period they also became convinced that a specialized attack aircraft was needed for effective close air support, rather than depending on multi-role fighter and observation aircraft whose dramatically increasing performance made them too fast for proper observation and situational awareness of friendly and enemy positions on the ground.[86] Although the primary role of Marine aviation was the support of amphibious forces, the Marines continued to prepare for several types of ground combat, and kept Marine aviation a vital part of their planning for each. Heavy emphasis was placed on small wars (a classification in which Vietnam would later fit), and here aviation was recognized as a key, but subordinate, element. As the *Small Wars Manual* of 1940 stated, "The primary mission of combat aviation in a small war is the direct support of the ground forces. This implies generally that all combat aviation will be used for ground attack."[87] The manual went on to delineate specific procedures for the employment of aviation in support of fluid battlefield procedures, such as the use of colored panels on the ground to mark the location of friendly troops, as well as the direction and distance to the enemy.[88]

Although great progress was made by the start of World War II, serious obstacles remained in the employment of aircraft in close air support, such as a lack of communication between aircrews and ground troops. Although Marine aviators provided critical support for ground operations on Guadalcanal, Pelileiu, and Okinawa, in many famous Pacific battles Marine aviation was only able to provide limited support. In the assaults on Tarawa, the Marianas, and Iwo Jima, the landings took place at extended distances from ground bases, and most close air support came from navy squadrons embarked on aircraft carriers. Only late in the war were Marine Air Groups embarked on carriers dedicated to the close air support of amphibious forces. The vast majority of Marine aviation was left to secure rear areas, or supported the more gradual Southwest Pacific advance under General Douglas MacArthur. In this advance, the Army reaped the greatest benefits from Marine aviation's focus on supporting ground operations. In Army operations in the Philippines, the soldiers were followed closely by Marine Air Groups, and were provided with first rate communication and support. In many ways the Philippines advance was the most complete realization of the Marine Corps' vision for close air support, even though ironically no infantry Marines were involved.

The Marine Corps continued to refine its CAS capabilities by applying lessons learned in World War II. In the unification debates of the late 1940s, the Marine Corps jealously guarded its air arm from those who would have preferred to concentrate all Marine and navy air assets under the newly formed U.S. Air Force. By the start of the Korean War, the Marines were equipped with better communications, and the air-ground team was well rehearsed despite force and spending reductions. Fortunately, the Marine Corps pre-

Deck crew loading rockets on the wings of F4U-4 Corsairs aboard the carrier Badoeng Strait *off Korea in September 1950. Although a holdover from World War II, the relatively low-speed, long-endurance, and durable Corsair proved to be an indispensable CAS aircraft, most notably in the early stages of the war. Corsairs provided critical support for the defense of the Pusan Perimeter and in the extremely dense weather that complicated operations in the Chosin Reservoir.*

served the ability to operate off of the small "jeep" carriers that it had acquired toward the end of World War II. This proved critical when the First Marine Brigade was formed in response to the Korean crisis in the summer of 1950. Marine aircraft flying from the carriers provided CAS to the Marines stabilizing the Pusan Perimeter, and were critical to the success of that effort. Marine CAS was also critical in the Inchon landings and the campaign that followed. Army officers were envious of the support Marine infantrymen were receiving and began to argue that unified command of air and ground forces on the Marine model was the only way to realize the potential of air power for ground combat.[89] As a result of its early performance, the Marine air-ground team also earned public acclaim for its performance, which contrasted sharply with an Air Force facing criticism for neglecting its ground support responsibilities.[90] Unfortunately for the Marines, the air-ground team became disjointed as major combat forces were introduced into the theatre. The 1st Marine Division was made subordinate to the 8th Army, and its supporting air unit, the 1st Marine Air Wing, was absorbed by the 11th Air Force. Although an agreement was made that Marine aircraft would be used to support Marine forces whenever possible, this command arrangement interfered with the unity of command and close liaison that made the Marine air-ground team so effective.

When the United States began its active involvement in Vietnam, the Marine Corps had a working definition of CAS almost identical to that accepted as the joint definition today. Since at least 1955, Marine doctrinal publications had defined CAS as "the attack of hostile ground or naval targets which are so close to friendly forces as to require detailed integration of each air mission with the fire and movement of those forces and with supporting forces."[91] It can be seen, therefore, that in the 1960s the Marine Corps was focusing on the integration of close air support as a combined arms tactic in dynamic battlefield conditions. This definition further implied a subordination of air power to the ground operations if not by wording, then certainly by the permanency of ground forces relative to air units in the battle area. In other words, ground units defined air and ground maneuvers because they were the ones who remained in the battle area to hold contested terrain longer than the hour or so an aircraft might be on station to support them. The Marines adapted this philosophy over time, giving air power a greater role than acting merely as a substitute for artillery. As Marine units gained experience in search and destroy operations, for example, they learned how to use FAC(A)s as virtual blocking forces, able to monitor large sections of the battle area and call in CAS to stop the enemy from fleeing sweeps on the ground.[92]

There is much more to making an organization's doctrine a reality than merely publishing it in official manuals. One of the reasons Marines were able to maintain such a close connection between their air and ground arms is that the men who made up these different branches were all products of the same training—in short, as Marines they all shared a common ethos enabled only by common experiences. For the officers who led Marine units on the ground and in the air, the common background they shared was The Basic School. From the beginning of the 20th century, the Marine Corps had sought to increase the professionalism of its officers with common professional schools that all attended, regardless of their military specialty. Some of these schools in Quantico, Virginia, like the Senior Course for colonels and lieutenant colonels, and the Junior Course for majors and captains, served to bring officers together after they had the benefit of operational experience to reconnect the communities in their common culture. These schools were not unique, since they were paralleled by those of other services, like the Naval War College and the Army's War College. What made the Marine Corps unique, however, was that it had an entry-level school for commissioned officers in Quantico, known as The Basic School. The name was self-explanatory, accurately describing its function of ensuring that all newly commissioned second lieutenants, regardless of military specialty or commissioning source, all received a common instructional course of approximately six months duration in the basics of Marine Corps leadership and combat techniques. This course was heavily weighted in favor of infantry fundamentals and ensured that Marine aviators truly understood the Marine doctrine that defined air power as a supporting element for ground combat. They understood the problems faced by the infantry officers because they experienced these challenges first hand and learned to appreciate the nature of ground combat. Just as important, The Basic School ensured that air and ground officers shared a common ethos and it laid the foundation of teamwork which ultimately paid high dividends on the battlefield. As one senior Marine aviator put it, "the Marine Corps attempts to initiate the bulk of its officer personnel into service with a common background of training, friendship and mutual purpose. This tends to bond together air and ground organizations into an extremely close-knit striking force with reciprocal confidence of all elements, each with the other."[93]

There were occasions when the Marine Corps could not always meet the ideal of sending all its officers to The Basic School immediately upon commissioning. Exceptions were made in emergency situations, usually in time of time of war, when aviators were in especially high demand, or when enlisted Marines were awarded battlefield commissions. Once the crisis of meeting battlefield needs was over, however, as many of these officers as possible were sent back to The Basic School.[94] During these crisis periods, the peacetime policy of sending all officers to The Basic School still paid high dividends by creating a common culture of air-ground teamwork in the Corps, and a core of aviators who were committed to ground support.

The most critical link in the Marine air-ground team was the Forward Air Controller. A FAC not only had to be an aviator, but also one who had operational experience that often provided an informed expertise on CAS. All FACs were required

In this last role the FAC provided terminal control to CAS aircraft. There were several responsibilities as part of terminal control. First, the FAC had to help the attack pilot find the target he was to hit. Since many targets were well camouflaged and difficult to see from the air, this was usually accomplished through the use of a mark. The FAC arranged for a white phosphorus smoke round to be fired by mortars or artillery at the target, which created a large white smoke plume to use as a reference point when directing the pilot where to drop his bombs. The second and most critical responsibility of terminal control was to make sure that not only were the bombs being delivered on target, but also that they would not endanger friendly forces. In order to do this, the FAC would not issue a "cleared hot" (approval to drop ordnance) until the attack aircraft was ob-

Lieutenant Philbrook S. Cushing, the Air Officer for Battalion Landing Team 2/9, talks over a PRC-10 radio during a peacetime operation on Taiwan in 1964. The assignment of aviation officers to serve as Forward Air Controllers in ground combat units provided a vital link, maximizing the effectiveness of Marine aviation in support of ground forces.

to attend a five-week course in order to further prepare them for their duties,[95] after which they were assigned to a Marine ground unit for a limited duration, typically six months to a year long. Marine doctrine dictated that three FAC's be assigned to each infantry battalion: one to serve as the Air Liaison Officer, responsible for coordinating air support in the battalion Fire Support Coordination Center, and two to serve as FAC's with the infantry companies operating in the field. While supporting ground combat units, these FAC's were equipped with radios capable of communicating with aircraft. A FAC was responsible for understanding the ground scheme of maneuver, advising the ground commander on how aircraft could be used to support his plan, requesting air support, and directing CAS attacks.

Marines watch as an A-4 Skyhawk attacks a Viet Cong position that had been blocking their advance in Quang Ngai province in February 1967. A Forward Air Controller has coordinated the attack, and the white smoke billowing in the tree line is most likely the "mark," an artillery or mortar smoke round fired near the target to help the pilot find what the FAC needs him to hit. This picture also demonstrates that Marine aviators often made low-altitude bombing attacks to improve their accuracy because their training had given them a good appreciation of the needs of the infantry Marines they were supporting.

Brigadier General Frederick J. Karch, commander of the 9th Marine Expeditionary Brigade, welcomes Lieutenant Colonel William C. McGraw Jr., Commanding Officer of Marine Fighter Attack Squadron-531, to Da Nang in April 1965. The 9th MEB became the first U.S. ground combat force deployed to Vietnam when it landed on 8 March with the mission of protecting the airfield at Da Nang, which was swelling with the introduction U.S. aviation forces for Operation Rolling Thunder. Although Marine helicopters had already been operating from the base in support of the MEB and ARVN, the arrival of the first Marine fixed-wing squadron just a month after the MEB landed reflected the importance of Marine CAS assets to the air-ground team. General Westmoreland had requested the multi-role Phantom II jets to use as part of the larger air campaign and wanted to place them under the operation control of the Air Force, but he was overruled by CinCPac, Admiral U.S. Grant Sharp Jr.

served to be in a level dive pointed at the target which would not endanger friendly forces. The FAC, therefore, was the primary means of ensuring that close air support would effectively support the ground commander without the danger of fratricide.

The Marine Air-Ground Team in Vietnam

Marine aviation was an integral part of the Marine Corps presence in Vietnam from the start. In fact, Marine helicopters supported South Vietnamese ground forces long before the arrival of ground combat units. These squadrons were operating out of Da Nang alongside Air Force units, and the need to protect the base was actually the justification for President Lyndon B. Johnson's March 1965 introduction of ground combat forces in the ICTZ. As the ground presence grew and became the focal effort, the Marine Corps was careful to increase the size of its corresponding air units to ensure adequate support was maintained. The Marines had developed the capability to rapidly construct expeditionary airfields with aluminum matting, catapults, and arresting gear to ensure that Marine air units would be able to phase ashore quickly on a large scale and support ground operations after an amphibious landing.[96] As suitable airfield space ran out in 1965, the Marines validated the concept with the construction of such an expeditionary short airfield for tactical support (SATS) at Chu Lai. This SATS was operational just 45 days after the order to begin construction began, providing an airfield where only a sandy beach existed beforehand. Although these expeditionary fields were only designed to last for relatively brief periods, the Chu Lai SATS remained operational until the Marines left the base during their planned withdrawal in late 1970.[97]

By the 1968 battle of Khe Sanh, the Marine aviation presence in Vietnam (shown in Annex B) was considerable. The premier Marine CAS aircraft was the A-4 Skyhawk. Like the Air Force, the Marine Corps had discarded the AD Skyraider after the Korean War because many were lost to anti-aircraft fire in the last year of the war. Unlike the Air Force, however, the Marine Corps made sure that it developed a suitable CAS aircraft to replace the Skyraider. The result was the joint Marine-Navy program begun in 1952 to develop the A-4 as a purpose-built CAS and light attack aircraft. The Douglas aircraft company's engineers designed the plane literally from the ground up, consulting not only pilots on what improvements they wanted to see, but also FACs and ground

An A-4 Skyhawk about to take off from the expeditionary short airfield for tactical support (SATS) at Chu Lai. When it became apparent that another forward operating base was needed for the aircraft supporting the Marines in the ICTZ, this airfield was built on a sandy coastal strip in less than one month's time. The project was a feat of determination and engineering that validated the expeditionary airfield concept that the Marine Corps had developed to keep its air power accessible to its ground combat forces. Assembled from aluminum matting and less than 4,000 feet long when it became operational on 1 June 1965, even the nimble A-4 required arresting gear to land and a jet assisted takeoff (JATO) system to get safely airborne. Capabilities were improved with the addition of a catapult system, launching its first aircraft, above, on 11 May 1966.

officers.[98] The decision to replace the heavily-armed, long endurance, and accurate propeller driven CAS aircraft with a jet was controversial. Although the Skyhawk was criticized for carrying fewer bombs than the A-1, and it required longer operating fields, its speed conveyed advantages in responsiveness and survivability. Ultimately, the Marine Corps had to go with the more survivable design because it needed to be ready for any limited war to expand, requiring CAS in the presence of top Soviet and Chinese anti-aircraft systems.[99] The small, swift, and maneuverable Skyhawk promised great increases in survivability, as well as an ability for more rapid follow-on attacks on CAS targets.[100] Marine Corps, Air Force, and Navy testimonials from the time of the battle of Khe Sanh (detailed later in this work) show that the Skyhawk was indeed an excellent CAS aircraft, uniformly describing the A-4 as the preferred aircraft for destroying targets which required precision attacks.

The Marine Corps continued to improve its CAS aircraft as it began its involvement in Vietnam. By 1961, the A-4 had been modified to carry a wider range of ordnance, and had been equipped with instruments which allowed it to navigate to and from target areas at night and in poor weather conditions, even though the actually bombing required visual contact with the target. To ensure that night and poor weather did not deny ground troops the air support they needed, the Marines also participated in another joint project with the Navy: the A-6 Intruder. Although primarily designed around the Navy's need for a heavy tactical attack aircraft, the Intruder was able to provide all-weather support to the Marines from advanced bases by means of a sophisticated radar-beacon targeting system. As long as a FAC on the ground had a radar reflector or beacon, he could get an

An A-6A Intruder from Marine All-Weather Attack Squadron-242 demonstrates its ability to deliver a devastating payload of 500-pound bombs near Chu Lai in July 1967. The Intruder provided the Marine Corps not only with a heavy tactical attack aircraft, but also one that could be counted on for support in poor weather and hours of darkness.

A-6 to drop bombs on the enemy in any weather, day or night, merely by providing the target coordinates to the aircrew.[101] The A-6 was backed up by another all-weather bombing guidance system, the TPQ-10. This ground based radar (discussed in much greater detail later on) could track and direct any aircraft to drop its bombs on a target the aircrew could not see. Developed from the MPQ-14 system the Marines had used successfully in Korea, the TPQ-10 was in operation from the first days of the 1st Marine Air Wing's arrival in Vietnam, and was the only ground-based radar bombing system in the country for over a year.[102]

Some of the Marine policies designed to foster ideal close air-ground cooperation did not survive the stresses of war. As the U.S. commitment in Vietnam increased, ultimately about half of Marine air units were deployed overseas, and all but a few squadrons of these were in Vietnam.[103] The demand for trained aviators became so great that the Marine Corps began to make exceptions to the policy of sending all of its aviators to The Basic School, and it still had trouble filling its combat squadrons with highly trained pilots. Many officers were commissioned, sent immediately to flight training, then given only four months in training in the United Stated to learn the aircraft they would fly in combat, before they were assigned to a combat squadron in Vietnam.[104] In such circumstances, the Marine Corps was further forced to reduce the number of FAC's assigned to each battalion to just two: one to serve as the ALO in the FSCC, and one to control aircraft attacks for maneuver companies.[105]

The pilot shortage created by the war affected the pool of FACs in another way. Since Marine Corps policy was that each Marine would serve a 13-month combat tour in Vietnam before being rotated to a noncombat unit, the Corps was unable to draw upon its pool of combat experienced pilots for FAC duty if it waited until their year in Vietnam was over. As a result, the decision was made to pull the needed pilots from the pool of those already flying in Vietnam once they had completed the first half of their tour. The result was system similar to that under which Air Force FACs served, spending five or six months flying, then the last five or six months (and sometimes as little as three months)[106] of their combat tour as FACs. The new policy for assignment to FAC duty also affected the training of FACs, since the Marine Corps could not afford to send these pilots through the standard five-week FAC training course when they only had 13 months in Vietnam to begin with. By 1967, these officers were sent to shortened courses in the U.S.,[107] or sometimes just a two-day course in Da Nang, which focused only on the most basic duties of FACs, and a familiarization with fixed-wing and helicopter CAS procedures for the aviators who flew the opposite type aircraft.[108] Apparently Marine leaders felt that five or six months' experience delivering CAS support in Vietnam was enough to prepare these officers to coordinate and control such attacks.

The landing gear begins retracting as an F-4B Phantom II of Marine Fighter Attack Squadron-115 takes off from Da Nang in May 1967. The Phantom was a tri-service aircraft, and although Air Force and Navy design requirements prevented it from being an optimal Marine Corps CAS platform, it could carry a large load of bombs and had a fast response time when launched from an alert "hot pad." The Marine Corps was able to achieve superior results from its Phantoms by loading them with "snake-eye" high-drag bombs (shown) and training its pilots to deliver them from low altitudes under the control of Forward Air Controllers.

Reducing the number of FACs assigned to infantry battalions also allowed the Marines to employ more FAC(A)s. As experience was gained in Vietnam, the Marines realized that the heavy vegetation, steep terrain, and elusive nature of the enemy meant that FAC's on the ground with the infantry had limited success in sighting targets far enough away from friendlies to be safely attacked by aircraft. To compensate for this, the Marine Corps created more airborne FACs.[109] The Forward Air Controller (Airborne), or FAC(A), was not a new concept in Vietnam. In World War II, aviators and artillery spotters had gone up in small observation aircraft like the OY Sentinel, which was similar in general appearance to a modern Piper Cub or Cessna 172. These slow-moving aircraft were able to obtain a different perspective of operations on the ground to help the infantry units build their picture of the battlefield, and to coordinate attacks on targets beyond their sight which were nonetheless important to their operational objectives. The capability was maintained in the Korean War, and proved especially critical in the early phases of the conflict.[110] Unlike the Air Force, the Marine Corps maintained this capability between wars and was ready to provide FAC(A) coverage of its forces from the start of its involvement in Vietnam. There, the use of FAC(A)s was increased at the expense of reducing the number of ground FACs because they were often able to observe the enemy and control attacks more effectively. The Marine Corps was very specific, however, in stating that FAC(A)s existed as extensions of the ground tactical air control parties, not to hunt independently.[111]

For FAC(A) operations, the Marine Corps continued to operate relatively low-performance aircraft like the O-1 Bird Dog. Although the Marines were using the same aircraft for the mission as the Air Force, it was not because they shared a similar neglect of the air observation mission. In fact, in the Korean War the Marines expanded their observation and control capabilities with the Kaman OH-43D helicopter designed for reconnaissance,

An OY-1 Sentinel, commonly called a "Grasshopper" after the Army aircraft of the same design and mission, flies over Naha on an artillery air spotting mission during the Okinawa campaign in 1945. The Marine Corps had eight Marine Observation Squadrons by the last year of the war and recognized the continued value of such aircraft for supporting ground operations through the Korean War and into Vietnam.

and artillery and naval gunfire spotting.[112] As the new UH-1 Huey was fielded to replace the OH-43 and O-1 in Vietnam, the Marine Corps continued to recognize the value of a fixed-wing propeller driven aircraft capable of operating from forward airstrips, and began development of the OV-10,[113] which did not see combat deployment until July 1968. The O-1s were retired on the expectation that the new fleet of Huey helicopters, which were more versatile and able to operate without runways at all, could meet the Marines' needs in the meantime. Unfortunately, the enormous increase in U.S. military commitment in Vietnam in 1965 upset this plan when the Hueys were found to be indispensable in escorting heliborne troop movements, and the majority was converted to armed gunships. As a result, the Marines had to recall the O-1's to service to assist the multitasked UH-1 community.[114] At the time of Khe Sanh, the Marines were supported by 14 O-1s conveniently operating out of Quang Tri Airfield, assisted by the 50 UH-1s of VMO-2 and VMO-6 (see Appendix B).

An O-1 Bird Dog flies low over a column of Marines advancing on a sweep and destroy mission south of Hue in February 1967, displaying its ability to get "down in the weeds." O-1 crews were able to gain a solid awareness of the needs of the units they were supporting and used their mobility and vantage to provide reconnaissance and artillery spotting services, as well as air control of high-performance attack aircraft.

The Marines made sure both seats of these two-seat aircraft were put to use, since an additional crew member could dramatically increase FAC(A) capabilities. The first crew member was the pilot. The community was led by senior aviators like Lieutenant Colonel Wayne C. Andersen, a pilot who had flown O-1s in Vietnam before the 1965 buildup, and who was retrained on the Bird Dog specifically to return to Vietnam and command the O-1 detachment at Quang Tri.[115] To meet the needs of the expanding war, however, most O-1 pilots were drawn form the ranks of A-4 and F-4 squadrons. These men had completed half of their tours in Vietnam, just as was done in the Air Force. In the Marine Corps, however, this assignment was a highly sought-after opportunity, and was considered the best of a series of alternatives, including service as a ground FAC, or even a desk job on the wing staff.[116] Considering their solid base of experience as CAS pilots in combat, these O-1 pilots were given several flights to qualify them to fly the aircraft itself, then six more flights to qualify each one as a FAC(A). Despite the extremely complicated duties of a FAC(A) and the Marine Corps' commitment to proper air-ground coordination, the Corps considered this simple transition program sufficient because the pilot was part of a two-man team, and it has been argued that he was in fact the least important of the two members. His counterpart was an Aerial Observer (AO), an infantry or artillery officer who brought just as much experience and expertise in ground tactics to the crew as the pilot brought expertise in aviation matters. The result was "the ability to coordinate air and artillery assets in devastating combination."[117] Ideally, AOs were trained at a three-month school in Quantico, Virginia, before deploying overseas, but just as with FAC assignments, this policy became infeasible in the face of the rapidly growing demands of the expanding war. As a result, most AOs were assigned to fly O-1s only after finishing the first six months of their combat tours in Vietnam with infantry and artillery units. Many of these men had enlisted experience in such units before being commissioned, so that they brought even more expertise to the cockpit than the average officer, and all were trained at a short school established at the division level in Vietnam.[118] These AOs were not assigned to the O-1 squadron, but were instead kept in the Aerial Observation Unit established in the Artillery Regiment, or as part of the division headquarters' intelligence section. The ground units assigned the O-1 crew its daily mission, which was flown over the territory it controlled. This arrangement had several benefits. First, the AO had a detailed knowledge of the terrain he was flying over because he had spent the first half of his combat tour walking and fighting over that same ground.[119] Next, his contact with the ground units supported brought a knowledge of both their current operations and key leaders, which enhanced the ability of the O-1 crew to support them. Finally, after each mission the AO was in much better contact with the ground units supported to facilitate the exchange of information based on airborne observations.

During each mission, the O-1 pilot was responsible for flying the aircraft, as well as for shooting rockets to mark targets for aircraft, and for providing terminal control. The AOs used different radios than the pilots, and were responsible for all coordination with ground units engaged with the enemy, including artillery support. Bringing crew

An O-1, seen from the perspective of an attack aircraft, conducting bomb damage assessment of a target after an air strike.

A TF-9J Cougar from Marine Aircraft Group-11 taxies for takeoff from Da Nang on the aircraft's last combat sortie in Vietnam. The two-seat version of the Cougar, originally developed by the Navy for training, was used for Strike Coordination and Reconnaissance (SCAR) north of the DMZ, where enemy defenses proved too dangerous for the O-1. Known as a Tactical Air Controllers (Airborne), or TAC(A)s, these aircraft also served as FAC(A)s when controlling attacks in support of ground forces. In 1967, the TF-9J was replaced in the TAC(A) role by the two-seat TA-4F Skyhawk, pictured on the left.

members with such great expertise in air and ground operations together in an aircraft which offered such good observation, the Marine Corps established an unparalleled capability for coordinating air support of ground units.[120] Compared to the single-crewed Air Force O-1s, the capability of this truly optimized dual-crewed aircraft is dramatic.

At the time of the 1968 battle of Khe Sanh, O-1 FAC(A)s were augmented by two other sources: helicopters and jets. The O-1s had been brought back into service to alleviate the UH-1Es of the heavy burden of providing both FAC(A) and helicopter gunship support, but the UH-1E squadrons still maintained a FAC(A) capability which was exercised regularly. Most often, UH-1 FAC(A) missions were flown with two pilots, although AOs sometimes joined the helicopter crews.[121] As O-1 FAC(A)s had begun roaming further north away from ground forces, they were also successful in locating ground targets in interdiction operations which had no immediate impact on the operations of ground units. Operating north of the

DMZ, they often were faced with higher concentrations of antiaircraft guns and even surface-to-air missiles. More survivable aircraft were needed to direct attack aircraft in this environment. Initially, the two-seat TF-9J Cougar jet was brought in for this purpose, which was replaced by the TA-4F in late 1967. As can be seen in Appendix B, both types of aircraft were still being flown out of Chu Lai during the siege of Khe Sanh. These high-performance air controllers designed to fight the interdiction battle were known as Tactical Air Controllers (Airborne), or TAC(A)s.[122] They flew missions in the "route package" areas north of the DMZ, where they would search for and locate enemy targets, then call in other attack aircraft to destroy them. Although this Deep Air Support mission was much closer to the Air Force concept of applying air power, Marine TAC(A)s were also trained to work in close proximity to ground forces, and often did so. Both FAC(A)s and TAC(A)s were used at Khe Sanh to control close air support.

Summary

The performance of the two services to provide close air support of ground forces in Vietnam is perhaps best summed up by a special congressional subcommittee formed to look into the matter in 1965:

While we honor the Air Force for its accomplishments in the strategic field, in the field of air superiority, in its interceptor capabilities, and in its improved tactical airlift capabilities, we feel that in its magnificent accomplishments in the wild blue yonder it has tended to ignore the foot soldiers in the dirty brown under. They need and are entitled to better support than they have received…

The Navy/Marine Corps doctrine, organization, and the equipment employed in close tactical air support of ground forces are obviously superior to that of the other armed services. They meet the requirements for limited war operations, such as the current conflict in South Vietnam, and are readily adaptable to an escalating conflict.…

In substance, the Navy and Marine Corps have devoted primary emphasis to the development of close tactical air-support operations for ground units and are properly organized, trained, and equipped to carry out this important function.

The knowledge, the technique, the capability for effective close air support exists. It could well be emulated by the Army-Air Force team."[123]

By the time the battle of Khe Sanh was joined in 1968, then, the Marine air-ground team had been tested and proven in Vietnam, where close air support was a basic and essential part of Marine tactics in fighting the VC and NVA. Although some of the Marines' policies designed to ensure close coordination had to be compromised by wartime exigencies, the foundation laid in peacetime held firm, and the culture of air-ground cooperation was intact. In 1968, Lieutenant General Victor H. Krulak, commanding all Marine forces in the Pacific theater, declared that for a Marine commander, "air support is as inseparable to the combat team as is his artillery, his tanks, or even his infantryman's M16."[124] Another Marine added, "the Marines down to the so-called lowly rifleman are very much attuned to this integral close air support and … they expect it, they don't just anticipate it."[125] This was because the Marine Corps had an institutional commitment to high-quality close air support.

The Air Force lacked such a focus entering into the Vietnam War. While the Marine Corps enjoyed unity of command and a common culture stressing the use of air power to support ground operations, the Air Force's establishment as a separate service led to a heavy concentration on strategic missions at the expense of tactical support for ground forces. Inter-service disputes about the proper use of air power between the Army and the Air Force, and the Air Force's unanticipated demands in Vietnam heightened its interest in expanding it close air support capability, but this effort was a reluctant one. In execution it was further plagued by disunity of command, diverging interests, and lack of communication between air and ground forces. In combat it could not overcome the long-term neglect of such a complicated and essential mission.

KHE SANH BACKGROUND

During the early years of U.S. escalation in Vietnam, Khe Sanh was a remote village located in the northwest corner of the Quang Tri Province of the Republic of Vietnam. As such, it was within the northernmost of South Vietnam's four military areas of responsibility, the I Corps Tactical Zone (ICTZ, or I Corps), located along the Demilitarized Zone (DMZ). After 1965 the U.S. forces in this area fell under the command of the III Marine Expeditionary Force (III MAF). Khe Sanh itself was a village of several thousand Vietnamese clustered in nine hamlets which made up the capital of the Huong Hoa district, a local administrative division of approximately 600 square miles. This mountainous rain-forest district's populace was divided into two groups. Less than half of them were ethnic Vietnamese from the coastal lowlands who had emigrated to the mountain region over several centuries. In contrast with the concrete and wood structures which made up their residences were those of the original inhabitants, the Bru tribesmen. These people, lumped under the broader classification of Montagnards, or "mountain people" by the French colonists, lived a separate existence. The majority of the 12,000 Bru living in the area had been relocated to a half dozen hamlets of grass-roofed huts on bamboo stilts on the periphery of Khe Sanh village. The Bru were despised by the Vietnamese, but it was hoped that the relocation would prevent the Communists from turning them against the

One of the many Bru hamlets that sat on the edge of Khe Sanh village.

South Vietnamese government. Scattered among the Vietnamese and Bru population in the late 1960s were also a small number of Caucasian Christian missionaries and a few French coffee planters who had maintained their plantations in the fertile mountain soil around Khe Sanh after French colonial rule ended in 1954.[126]

The main village of Khe Sanh itself sat astride Route Coloniale Number 9, the single-lane dirt track that the French had built from the coastline at Dong Ha westward through the increasingly mountainous terrain into Laos, terminating at Savannakhet. The road was little more than a wide

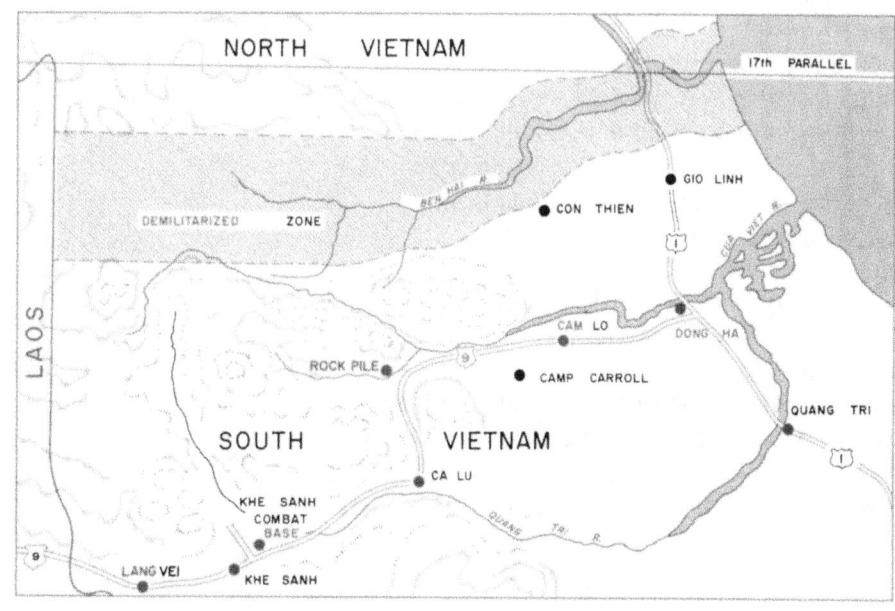
Figure 1. Key locations in Northern Quang Tri Province, in the Northern I Corps Tactical Zone. Illustration by E.L. Wilson for Captain Moyers S. Shore II, The Battle for Khe Sanh *(Washington, 1969), 7.*

A convoy of trucks heads west on the tortuous Route 9 toward Khe Sanh on 28 March 1967. The road had been closed to traffic for several years by a combination of poor development and the constant threat of enemy activity, as it would be again after just four months. This left the forces at Khe Sanh completely dependent on the airfield for supply, reinforcement, and casualty evacuation.

path through the jungle, running 63 kilometers from Dong Ha on the coast to Khe Sanh, across 36 aging bridges, most of which had been built by the French and were not safe to traverse by the 1960s.[127] Even after considerable development by the U.S. military to support operations at Khe Sanh, Route 9 was only one lane wide. The only way it could support two-way traffic was by a scheme under which every 12 hours the one-way flow alternated between westward traffic inland and eastbound traffic seaward.

The region itself protruded westward into Laos so that Khe Sanh was essentially surrounded by enemy territory on three sides. Twenty-two kilometers to the north was the DMZ, separating the Communist Democratic Republic of Vietnam (DRV) from the Republic of Vietnam (RVN). The border with Laos crept southward from the DMZ approximately 16 kilometers to the west of Khe Sanh, then wound back toward the coast, passing just seven kilometers to the southwest of the village. Just on the other side of that border was the Ho Chi Minh Trail, a veritable highway that served as the main supply route for NVA and VC forces in South Vietnam. The trail was so close that veterans of Khe Sanh reported being able to see fires burning along the path at night. As early as 1961, the NVA took advantage of Khe Sanh's remote location to harass the small ARVN forces there.[128] The highlands around the village truly represented the "wild west" of Vietnam, where the law was defined only by the strongest force in the region willing to make its influence known at any given time.

The first U.S. military presence around Khe Sanh began in August 1962, when MACV sent a Special Forces team to lead a Civilian Irregular Defense Group (CIDG), a local militia force formed from the Bru tribesmen, to stabilize the region. For more than two years, the Special Forces and Bru CIDG occupied an old, abandoned French fortification two kilometers east of Khe Sanh village along Route 9, which appropriately became

Figure 2. Khe Sanh and key locations in the immediate vicinity. Based on map in Prados and Stubbe, Valley of Decision, *facing p.1.*

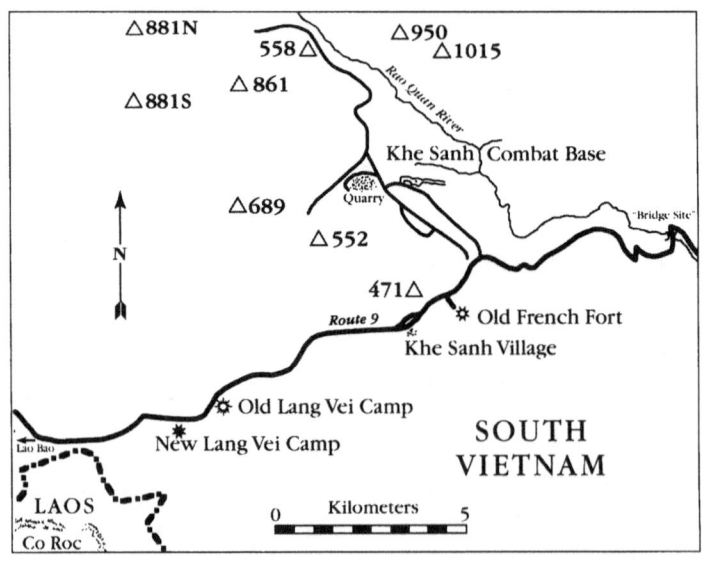

known as "Old French Fort." In November 1964, an increase of enemy activity in the region inspired the Green Berets to seek a more defensible position closer to logistic support, so they moved about three kilometers north of Khe Sanh village to an airfield built on a plateau by French colonial forces in 1949.[129] The airfield was particularly important because Route 9 could not be relied upon for logistical support, and was threatened, if not closed, by NVA activity for much of the 1960s. This location later became the focal point of the 1967 and 1968 battles for Khe Sanh, as it was the site upon which Khe Sanh Combat Base would be built.

As the United States became fully committed to fighting the war, its interest in Khe Sanh increased correspondingly. Early in the war, military efforts like the Special Forces unit had enjoyed some success in pacification, especially among the Bru, who as mountain tribesmen were a distinct cultural element from the Vietnamese. The proximity of Khe Sanh to Laos, however, made it a place of increasing military significance with the adoption of "big unit war" by the NVA in late 1964. As the volume of traffic along the Ho Chi Minh Trail supporting guerrilla operations in South Vietnam increased, the Commander of U.S. Military Assistance Command, Vietnam (COMUSMACV), General William Westmoreland, sought to use the area both to monitor NVA movements southward and as an advance warning post for attacks eastward into the I Corps area. The dirt airstrip was developed into a combat base which included a short aluminum matting runway adjacent to a security compound, and came to be known as the Khe Sanh Combat Base (KSCB). By the end of 1965, the compound consisted of a single perimeter of wire containing 17 buildings and a number of bunkers alongside the 3,300-foot runway. From this base, Special Forces teams regularly patrolled the surrounding area, including Laos. At various times the airstrip was used by the Special Forces, CIA, a MACV Special Operations Group, Marines of signals intelligence units and the 3d Reconnaissance Battalion, and even a U.S. Air Force light air reconnaissance detachment.[130]

In November and December 1965, after one year of the "big unit war," the special operations radiating from Khe Sanh apparently created enough of a thorn in the side of the NVA movements through Laos that the Communists decided to take action against the combat base. Human intelligence gathered by Special Forces personnel confirmed that approximately two regiments of NVA were moving into the area with the intent of conducting operations there, and that the NVA were not merely passing through. Limited attacks on the U.S. and allied forces operating around Khe Sanh soon followed.[131] At this point, General Westmoreland resolved to reinforce the base as a key outpost both for monitoring the operations of the NVA and as an obstacle to any NVA attacks eastward into the coastal plain of the ICTZ. Westmoreland also saw the Khe Sanh Combat Base as a stepping-stone for future large-scale operations into Laos against the NVA.[132] Westmoreland's decision to hold Khe Sanh put him at odds with the Marine in charge of the ICTZ, the Commanding General of III MAF, Lieutenant General Lew Walt.

General Lewis W. Walt shared the belief of most senior Marine leaders, including Commandant of the Marine Corps General Wallace M. Greene Jr., that III MAF should concentrate its forces in the coastal plain, winning the loyalty of the local population in the Combined Action Platoons (CAP) program,[133] a relatively insightful strategy that was enjoying some success. To General Walt, the diversion of combat resources to a remote mountain outpost of no political importance depleted his ability to accomplish his primary mission of pacifying the ICTZ. This became an especially sensitive issue in the spring of 1966 when the NVA presence in the coastal region was increasing. In April, Westmoreland ordered III MAF to send a battalion to Khe Sanh to search for and destroy the NVA forces he suspected were massing there. By 1 May, the Marines had found no indications of a significant NVA presence in the region, so the operation was cut short. Over the course of summer 1966, the Marines concentrated on eliminating an NVA division which had moved into the lowlands, and regular contact in Operations Hastings and Prairie succeeded in driving the enemy from the region.[134]

Walt's success in the lowlands in the summer of 1966 seemed to validate his strategic approach, which would have left only a simple observation post at Khe Sanh merely to provide warning of an NVA attack into the ICTZ, at which time he could withdraw his forces to defend the coastal plain by establishing a line of defense in the foothills. Westmoreland, however, kept his attention focused on Khe Sanh, which he continued to envision as an intelligence gathering base and potential springboard for operations against the NVA sanctuary in Laos. The strategic tension between Westmoreland and Walt would lead to problems later on, but ultimately COMUSMACV would get his way as the senior officer.

Human intelligence and smaller-scale patrols continued to indicate that a growing NVA presence in the area was menacing Khe Sanh, and in September 1966, Westmoreland ordered the Marines to reinforce the combat base, explaining that "every enemy soldier diverted to Khe Sanh is one less to threaten the population."[135] Seabees improved the fortifications in the compound, with the perimeter extended to encompass the runway, and the runway surface itself was improved. When increased enemy activity was detected on an east-west trail network near the combat base, Westmoreland ordered Walt to send a battalion to protect the growing base,[136] apparently with the recent destruction of the A Shau Special Forces camp fresh in his mind.[137] First Battalion, 3d Marines (1/3) was delivered to the base to provide protection for the Special Forces and intelligence units there. As part of Operation Prairie, 1/3 also conducted aggressive patrols around the base for more than four months. Without a joint commander to coordinate the activity of the various units at Khe Sanh, the Marines collided with the patrols of the various other "friendly" agencies in the area as much as they did the NVA, with whom they had relatively little contact. Some evidence of recent activity was found, but it only proved how elusive the enemy could be. Again, Marine leaders interpreted the lack of contact as an absence of any threatening NVA activity in the area.[138]

As more intelligence-gathering units were deployed to Khe Sanh, they became more dispersed and harder to protect. An element of MACV's Studies and Observation Group (SOG) came to region to conduct clandestine operations against the NVA, often into Laos, with the assistance of the Bru. Known as Forward Operating Base-3 (FOB-3), these soldiers began their operations in Khe Sanh village but eventually moved their compound into an annex of KSCB. This left only a small MACV advisory group in the village itself until in February 1967, the Marines sent Combined Action Platoon "O" (CAP Oscar) to the village. With the introduction of CAP Marines, General Walt was attempting to expand the success of his pacification program in the lowlands to this new area of interest. The Special Forces CIDG which originally established the presence at the airfield, meanwhile, became the victim of interservice tensions in the buildup around Khe Sanh, and actually moved further away from the airfield in December 1966.[139] They relocated to a new compound in the village of Lang Vei, which was much closer to the Laotian border than Khe Sanh village.[140] By the first months of 1967, therefore, the U.S. military presence around Khe Sanh had certainly increased, but at the expense of seriously complicating the mission of the Marines sent there to protect these same forces.

It is somewhat surprising therefore, that when 1/3 was rotated out of Khe Sanh after five months in February 1967, that it was replaced by a single company. The arrival of Company B, 1st Battalion, 9th Marines was essentially simultaneous with that of CAP Oscar, further reflecting Walt's desire not to waste combat forces on the defense of Khe Sanh when a pacification effort could capture the hearts and minds of the Vietnamese, and along with it the territory they lived in. B/1/9 continued the aggressive patrols begun by 1/3 but was unable to simultaneously provide a robust perimeter defense for a base that had once required the attentions of an entire battalion. It was fortunate for Khe Sanh, however, that the Marines made patrolling the highest priority, since a major NVA presence was growing just a short distance to the west. In April 1967, Bravo company's patrols kicked over a hornet's nest which would have had disastrous consequences for the combat base if left undisturbed.

THE HILL BATTLES OF 1967

From 25 April to 11 May 1967, major NVA and Marine forces collided in the hills west of Khe Sanh. Over the two-week period, the Marines gradually fed in larger and larger forces in response to the increasingly apparent reality that the NVA were not yielding to the Marines they had already engaged in combat. This ongoing battle later came to be known as the first battle of Khe Sanh, or the "Hill Fights." While a distinct operation from the siege that would follow a year later in the spring of 1968, the first battle of Khe Sanh is important to this study for several reasons. First, the NVA objectives in 1967 foreshadowed their goals for 1968. When the two Marine battalions thwarted their plans to seize Khe Sanh in 1967, the NVA apparently returned in greater force the following year to complete the task. Second, the Marine operations of 1967 were dynamic maneuvers to dislodge the enemy, unlike the static defense of 1968. Therefore, while setting the stage for the events of the following year, the Hill Fights also present an opportunity to examine the extent and manner in which close air support was actually integrated with the fire and movement of Marine forces. The U.S. Marine Corps operational history for 1967 claims that "the heavy fighting at Khe Sanh in late April and early May provided a classic example of integrated employment of modern, fixed-wing aviation in support of ground maneuver elements...The defeat of the enemy in this critical terrain was the product of skillful and closely coordinated air-ground action."[141] Close examination of this battle supports this assertion, demonstrating that Marine doctrine developed for the close integration of air and ground forces was effective practice in 1967.

Prelude to the Hill Fights

Following five months of relatively unrevealing patrols around Khe Sanh, the 1st Battalion, 3d Marines was withdrawn in February 1967 and replaced with a single company. It is unclear why General Westmoreland permitted III MAF to make this change when COMUSMACV placed such clear emphasis on the importance of Khe Sanh, but B Company of the 1st Battalion, 9th Marines was hard pressed to continue patrolling and provide security from the sprawling combat base, a task that had previously consumed the efforts of an entire battalion. Fortunately, the Marines opted to focus on aggressive patrolling instead of perimeter defense.

Approximately seven kilometers northwest of the Khe Sanh Combat Base was a group of three hills, shown in Figure 2. The three peaks form a rough triangle, with the apex pointed southeastward at Khe Sanh. The closest of the peaks, at the apex, is Hill 861. At the two farthest corners are the twin peaks 881 South and 881 North, joined by a saddle. The military significance of these hills was that they were the dominant high ground overlooking Khe Sanh and offered a sanctuary to fire rockets and mortars at the combat base. It was signs of increasing activity by the then-elusive enemy that prompted the dispatch of a routine patrol on 25 February 1967. It was ordered to investigate reports that a number of bunkers and large formations of NVA troops had been seen on Hill 861. Lead by Sergeant Donald Harper, this patrol was ambushed as it approached the hill. Harper was able to contact an airborne FAC, who brought in a section of two F-4 Phantoms with 500-pound bombs. After four passes, the Phantoms had dropped four tons of ordnance on the NVA, destroying the ambushing force.[142] Several days later, on 2 March, the combat base sustained a heavy attack by indirect fire. The fact that the NVA were willing to try and stop patrols from investigating the hills west of Khe Sanh, and had actually fired upon the base itself, was ominous. It gave Marine commanders reluctant to waste combat forces in the region reason to reconsider their strategy, prompting the reinforcement of KSCB with Company E of the 2d Battalion, 9th Marines on 7 March.[142]

It was not long before the new arrivals at Khe Sanh also came in contact with the enemy. On 16 March, a platoon of E/2/9 was ambushed while returning from a patrol of the same area. The Marines called in artillery on the NVA while a relief force was sent from KSCB, but the enemy refused to withdraw. Only after air strikes were coordinated to drive the enemy from the crest of Hill 861 were the Marines able withdraw by helicopter, and even then it was under enemy fire.[144] The confrontation cost the Marines 18 dead and 59 wounded, but it did provide a new indication of enemy strength in the area, now assessed to be at two regiments.[145]

For all the Marines suspected, the NVA 325C division operating in the region was still not ready to reveal itself in force. Even as an American engineer and infantry task force finally managed to reopen Route 9, which had been closed for two years, on 27 March,[146] there was no further contact with the enemy until 30 March. Even then, that brief contact was accidental. A Marine patrol discovered an empty NVA base camp a few kilometers northwest of Hill 861, where the last contact had occurred. While searching the vacant camp, the Marines came under mortar fire from an unknown location. Fortunately, they were able to contact an airborne FAC, who was then able to locate the mortar position, as well as an NVA company approaching the small Marine patrol. The FAC(A) hit the enemy with tactical aircraft, allowing the Marines to withdraw.[147] Similar to the patrol of two weeks before, the NVA responded in strength, but were beaten back by effective close air support and melted away into the highland jungle. The contacts of March 1967 were ominous, but again the enemy chose not to reveal himself in force until provoked by the patrol that would begin the ongoing two-week-long Hill Fights on 24 April, almost a month later. When the confrontation did happen, its intensity and duration were fueled by the fact that the Marines discovered an entire NVA division preparing to attack Khe Sanh in order to repeat the tactical, operational, and strategic success of Dien Bien Phu in 1954.[148]

The Hill Fights Begin

On 24 April, a patrol was again sent to reconnoiter Hill 861, the site of several earlier confrontations. As had happened before, the patrol was ambushed, and a relief force was sent out to rescue them. That relief force was also ambushed as it approached, but this time the lieutenant in command immediately called for air support, which broke the ambush's fire on the Marines.[149] This time the Marines did not merely withdraw after using air support to break contact. Two platoons of B/1/9 were ordered to seize Hill 861 from the enemy. Since they found themselves dramatically outnumbered, they temporarily backed off a short distance to allow aircraft and artillery to soften the NVA defenses. Even after these preparatory fires were delivered, the attack went poorly. Realizing that the determined and sustained NVA resistance represented a significant change in the enemy's behavior, the 3d Battalion, 3d Marines was sent to reinforce Khe Sanh. Committing a company to the attack on the day it arrived, 25 April, 3/3 began a pattern by which the Marines fed increasingly larger sized units into the battle piecemeal as the ones that were engaged were chewed up by the NVA. K/3/3 was virtually destroyed in its attack to support what remained of B/1/9, so III MAF's company-sized reaction force, designed to answer any emergency needs throughout the ICTZ, was moved in.[150] K/3/9 did not enjoy much greater success.

Even as the NVA mauled the Marines in their sustained effort to take Hill 861, the enemy also began to attack the combat base itself with heavy mortar and recoilless rifle fire. Coming from Hill 881S further to the west, these positions were hit with air support and artillery until the NVA ceased to fire on KSCB. Simultaneously, helicopter gunships were suppressing NVA fire from Hill

861 to allow the evacuation of Marines from the battle on Hill 861, a process that took all day.[151] Now estimating that at least an NVA battalion was operating in the triangle formed by the three hills, on April 27th the Marines sent another battalion to reinforce Khe Sanh. What remained of the two companies in contact on Hill 861 for the last few days were withdrawn and replaced to keep the enemy engaged, while the 2d Battalion, 3d Marines prepared to launch a battalion assault on the hill on 28 April.

Because Hill 861 had proven so deadly to the two companies that attacked on 25 and 26 April, 2/3's battalion attack was preceded by a tremendous volume of supporting arms. The preparatory fires of 27 to 28 April included 764,700 pounds of aviation ordnance and more than 1,800 rounds of artillery of various calibers.[152] While two B-52 "ARC LIGHT" strikes were delivered further to the north and west of Hill 861 to discourage the NVA from reinforcing the Marines' objective, the vast majority of the ordnance was delivered by tactical aircraft, especially those of the 1st Marine Air Wing, holding in huge stacks until they could be sequenced in to attack Hill 861 under the

Marines of G Company, 2d Battalion, 3d Marines on the edge of a bomb crater on top of Hill 861. The destruction wrought by the two-day bombardment required to reduce the NVA defenses is apparent.

control of both Marine and Air Force FAC(A)s.[153] The FAC's working over the objective developed a new technique for locating and destroying the enemy bunkers which had sheltered the NVA from the Marines attacking the hills on the previous days. CAS aircraft were directed to deliver 250-pound and 500-pound high-drag "snake eye" bombs in long "rippled" strings from low angle dives, stripping the hillside of trees and heavy foliage to expose the well-camouflaged bunkers. Once the bunkers were located, tactical aircraft delivered heavier ordnance, including 750-, 1000-, and 2000-pound bombs, from more precise high angle dives to destroy the bunkers themselves.[154] The hill was also heavily blanketed with napalm. On the first day of bombardment alone, nearly 75,000 pounds, or approximately 10,000 gallons of the jellied gasoline, was delivered.[155] All of this was concentrated on a piece of terrain of approximately one square kilometer in size. It is little wonder, therefore, that on the 28th, when 2/3 launched its attack up Hill 861, it found the objective, with its 25 bunkers and more than 400 fighting holes, completely unoccupied.[156] Without losing a single Marine, 2/3 captured a hill that had cost 39 Marines their lives just a few days earlier. The victory was an obvious triumph of supporting arms, especially the destructive power of fixed-wing close air support.

The attack was continued in a two-battalion operation the next day to dislodge any NVA that might have remained in the twin hill complex of 881N and 881S further to the west. Unfortunately, the NVA were apparently equally as determined to hold these hills as they had been on Hill 861, and the Marines encountered an interlocking network of defenses. The Marines had prepared for the contingency by preplanning another massive onslaught of supporting arms, but on the first day even the 1,685 artillery rounds fired and 323,750 pounds of ordnance delivered by 118 air sorties could not crack the NVA defenses.[157]

As the Hill Fights continue, Marines of G Company, 2d Battalion, 3d Marines attack up Hill 881N. The battalion withdrew after sustaining heavy casualties, as did the 3d Battalion in its attack on Hill 881S. As happened on Hill 861, the attacks were halted for two days of heavy bombardment, after which 881S was taken with little resistance.

The decision was made to continue the attack the next day, after supporting arms had more time to soften the NVA defenses. The two hills were bombarded by artillery and air throughout the evening and night, ending only when the battalions crossed the line of departure at 0800, with another massive assortment of preplanned support on call. Yet again, the Marines met fierce resistance from a well-entrenched enemy. On the approach to Hill 881N, 2/3 withdrew after sustaining 9 KIA and 43 WIA. Artillery and aircraft were used to work over the enemy, while on Hill 881S, 3/3 enjoyed even less success. After meeting withering fire from NVA soldiers in a network of well-camouflaged bunkers, the attack ground to a halt. Attack aircraft and helicopter gunships delivered suppressive fires as close as 50 meters from friendly positions, but after several hours the attack still failed and the battalion withdrew. The only thing 3/3 had to show for its efforts was 163 NVA bodies and 26 dead Marines.[158]

The Bombardment of Hill 881S

The horrible losses of 30 April were compounded by the fact that the Hill Fights were the first major battle by Marines equipped with the new M16 rifle. The untested weapon proved deadly in combat because of its tendency to jam. This shortcoming that was only rectified after a Congressional inquiry, precipitated by stories of Marine bodies from the Hill Fights being found lying next to rifles with cleaning rods stuck down the barrels. These Marines had been killed not while firing back at the well-entrenched enemy, but while attempting to clear spent casings from the chamber of jammed weapons.[159] Lieutenant Colonel Gary Wilder, the commanding officer of 3/3, was surely disturbed by reports of the new rifles jamming when they were needed most. Whatever the reason, he refused to attack the hill again until it had been subjected to an even heavier program of preparatory fires.[160]

The preparatory fires scheduled and delivered on 1 May were nearly unprecedented in Vietnam for their intensity and duration, and Robert Pisor goes so far as to say that no other target in the

More than four months after the Hill Fights, the sheer destructiveness of the bombardment of 1-2 May is still evident. Although the NVA had abandoned the hilltop as most of its defenses were reduced to rubble, some of the 250 bunkers built there did survive, like this one, just 15 feet away from a large bomb crater.

Vietnam War was so heavily bombed.[161] At the very least, the attack delivered nearly twice as much ordnance as each of the days preceding it. 1445 artillery rounds and 166 Marine air strikes hit the two hills, concentrating on Hill 881N in the morning and 881S in the afternoon. A combination of tactical aircraft and B-52s delivered over 650,000 pounds of ordnance on the hills, including 130 of the heavy 2,000-pound bombs.[162] The senior Marine in the area, Colonel John P. Lanagan, observed the bombardment. Even this veteran, who had been awarded the Silver Star for his performance in combat on Okinawa 23 years earlier, stated that he had never seen more devastating firepower than the hell rained down on 881S.[163] Psychologically, the bombardment became too much for the NVA to endure. At one point in the middle of a series of heavy air strikes, a platoon-sized element abandoned their bunkers and ran out to certain death in the maelstrom of fire and steel.[164] When the Marines finally advanced up 881S on the morning of 2 May, the only resistance they encountered was sporadic sniper fire. Arriving on top of Hill 881S, they found the hill deserted, and approximately 80 percent of the 250 bunkers there caved in by the bombardment.[165] The volume of ordnance employed over the four days of heavy air strikes and artillery bombardment had been staggering. Nine months later, when Marines returned to this same hill to build their own bunker complex, engineers could not harvest what few trees remained in the moon-like landscape because the trunks were too full of steel shrapnel for their chain saws to cut.[166] The body count reported by the pilots who flew the missions on May 1st totaled at only 140 NVA dead,[167] but this dubious measure of combat effectiveness certainly overlooked a number of additional casualties. The following year, as Marines dug their own bunkers on Hill 881S, their entrenching tools periodically struck pockets of putrefied flesh deep in the red clay soil, the remains of NVA soldiers who had been buried while defending the hill from 3/3.[168]

The Cleanup

With the capture of Hill 881S, a major obstacle to the final objective of clearing the NVA from the hills west of Khe Sanh had been achieved. The NVA, however, were not ready to give up. Unknown to the Marines, the 325C division had withdrawn what remained of its 18th Regiment from 881N to base camps in Laos, only to replace it with elements of the 95C Regiment. As Wilder's battalion swept over the abandoned Hill 881S, Lieutenant Colonel Earl R. Delong continued 2/3's attack from an intermediate objective seized east of 881N. Once again the Marines were met by automatic weapons fire and mortars. Supporting arms were used to silence the enemy, but poor weather and stiffening resistance as they attempted to press the attack further convinced the Marines to abandon the effort.[169]

The fresh enemy troops tried to capitalize on the situation by attacking launching a counter attack at night to cover the withdrawal. In the early morning hours of 3 May, the NVA advanced right up to the Marine lines. The attack was halted at 0430 only by a combination of artillery, air support from tactical aircraft, and the arrival of a C-47 gunship. The delivery of flares by the gunship and a supporting flare ship also allowed the Marines to make better use of their own organic small arms, and enabled 3/3 to call in artillery missions from their newly-won vantage point on 881S.[170]

At some point on 3 May the Marines decided to try a new approach, and 2/3 moved south to join 3/3 on 881S. From that position, on 4 May 2/3 attacked northward along the saddle between the two hills, rather than up the steep eastern face. The new attack was quickly repulsed, weakened by poor weather which ruled out the use of fixed-wing CAS.[171] The next day the weather was good enough to allow a through preparation of the objective with artillery, napalm, and 250-pound and 500-pound bombs. As a result, the final attack which seized the entire Hill 881N complex succeeded at a cost of only six wounded Marines.[172]

Even as the Marines were succeeding in driving the 18th Regiment from the hills west of Khe Sanh, the NVA were modifying their plans. The introduction of the 95C regiment to 881N not only brought a night counter attack on 2/3's defensive positions east of the hills, but also an attack by part of the regiment on the Special Forces/CIDG camp in Lang Vei, far to the west. As 2/3 prepared to attack Hill 881N from the south on the night of 3-4 May, the NVA attempted to overrun the Green Berets. The nighttime battle raged in the distant sight of the Marines over the hills seven kilometers northward on 881S, who could not reach the isolated camp. The NVA penetrated deep into the heart of the camp, but ultimately Lang Vei was saved. It is unclear whether the NVA made a planned withdrawal because the attack was merely a diversion for the Hill Fights, or if they were driven back by the combined effects of Marine artillery support, two helicopter gunships, a C-47 "Spooky" gunship, and the arrival of other fixed-wing CAS aircraft as dawn approached.[173] Either way, supporting arms were an important contribution to the defense of the outpost.

As Hill 881N was finally occupied on 5 May and the two battalions began searching the area, the second NVA regiment withdrew. FAC(A)'s remained on station to monitor the likely avenues of retreat for lucrative artillery and air targets, but the enemy slipped away. In the few fleeting glimpses achieved, there were some gunship attacks and artillery missions, but the most notable aviation-related event of the period was the first known surrender of an NVA soldier to an aircraft. A Huey FAC(A) spotted a soldier waving a white flag at him, and swooped down to transport the Vietnamese back to the rear.[174]

The NVA proved almost as elusive to the ground units operating around Khe Sanh after 5 May. During this period large patrols were sent out 10-15 kilometers daily, but the Marines did not encounter any NVA with two exceptions.[175] On 9 May, one patrol was operating in a deep valley when it became surrounded by an NVA force of undetermined size. The artillery forward observer and FAC with the patrol could not establish radio communications with their supporting agencies due to the intervening terrain. Fortunately, the company commander's resourceful radioman managed to contact a passing F-8, probably by hailing the aircraft on guard. Although the aircraft had already delivered its ordnance on another mission, it did make two "dry" runs on the NVA, simulating its attack profile in an effort to intimidate them. As a testament to the psychological impact of close air support after the recent devastation around Hills 861, 881S, and 881N, the trick apparently worked.[176] The second and final contact in the period immediately after the Hill Fights occurred the next day when the much smaller Recon Team Breaker was surrounded. Artillery and airstrikes did manage to keep the enemy at bay (who may have only been using the recon team as bait), but heavy ground fire prevented three rescue attempts. The fourth succeeded only with close fixed-wing and gunship coverage.[177]

Summary of the Hill Fights

In terms of operational objectives, the Hill Fights were a success. From 24 April to 13 May, the Marines cleared the NVA 18 and 95C Regiments from the hills west of Khe Sanh. In the process, they stopped a force which had probably been massing to attack the combat base. Most sources estimate that there were at least 940 NVA killed at a cost of 155 Marines killed and 425 wounded.[178] Of the Hill Fights, the Marine Corps operational history for Vietnam in 1967 states, "Although aggressive infantry assaults finally took the various objectives, much of the credit for overwhelming the enemy force belongs to the supporting arms... Air attacks were particularly affective in uncovering and destroying enemy bunkers and fortifications."[179] The 1st Marine Air Wing provided the bulk of this support, with over 1,100 sorties dropping over 1,900 tons of ordnance. While 23 B-52 strikes did attack deeper interdiction targets in support of the battle, like enemy formations, stores, and lines of communication,[180] they could have accounted for no more than 690 tons of additional ordnance.

During the Hill Fights, close air support was used extensively and decisively by the attacking forces. The Marines repeatedly advanced to make contact with the enemy until resistance became significant, and then used artillery and close air support to destroy the NVA. Sometimes they would withdraw a short distance to allow the more liberal use of heavy ordnance and to minimize the risk to the infantry Marine, but the attack was never resumed until the enemy positions were judged to have been reduced. In this effort, air power was primarily directed at targets identified by friendly maneuver elements in close proximity to the enemy on a fluid battlefield, all in order to accomplish ground force objectives. In other words, true close air support was decisively employed.

In *The End of the Line*, Robert Pisor observed that it was standard Marine practice in Vietnam to seek contact, then pull back to let artillery and air wreak destruction on the enemy.[181] For this study, the Hill Fights provide a dramatic illustration of Marine air-ground tactics and their effectiveness, as well as a framework to understand the even more dramatic application of close air support to the siege of Khe Sanh the following year.

THE SIEGE OF 1968

Following the Hill Fights, as the enemy force seemed to fade away in early May, the Marines took advantage of the opportunity to reduce the size of the force they had a Khe Sanh. 2/3 and 3/3 were replaced by the 1st Battalion, 26th Marines, which began saturation patrols to fully explore the area in Operation Crockett on 14 May 1967. These patrols radiated outwards from the company defensive positions in the hills that had been the bloody scene of the Hill Fights just weeks earlier. The Marines did not want to patrol beyond the range of supporting artillery at Khe Sanh, so the outposts set up on Hills 861 and 881S both prevented the enemy from simply reoccupying the bitterly contested positions, and provided places from which mortars could provide additional cover for the patrols operating out to 4 kilometers from their lines. Events soon proved that the NVA had not actually abandoned the field, but had merely withdrawn to break contact and end the bloody Hill Fights

On 6 June, a small enemy force attacked the radio retransmission station located on Hill 950, one of the three peaks of Dong Tri Mountain, just 3,000 meters north of the Khe Sanh Combat Base perimeter. The NVA overran the position, only to be thrown back by a small group of survivors who rallied from within. The next day a platoon-sized patrol from Company B, 1/26, was attacked west of Hill 881S. In response to the enemy's sudden willingness to reveal himself, and the increasing enemy activity further east at Con Thien, 3/26 was sent to KSCB. This brought Khe Sanh back to two-battalion strength so the hill positions and base defenses could be reinforced, while more forceful and regular patrols were conducted.

The Isolation of Khe Sanh

While a relative lull began in contact between the combat forces around Khe Sanh, the NVA did succeed in isolating the village and combat base by effectively closing Route 9, which after

The defensive position on Hill 861 seen from the air in July 1967. Hill 861 was one of the critical outposts guarding the western approach to Khe Sanh Combat Base.

two years of non-use had only been opened for four months. On 21 July, a convoy of 85 vehicles was proceeding west, bringing heavy U.S. Army 175mm artillery to KSCB that would more than double the range of the artillery at Khe Sanh. The convoy was ambushed and the escorting infantry succeeded in engaging the NVA, but the artillery could not pass further west, and was forced to return to Camp Carroll. While smaller convoys occasionally did make it through for a short while afterward, they were high-risk operations that consumed an inordinate amount of security forces, even as enemy activity was increasing and stressing III MAF's resources throughout the rest of the ICTZ. During the fall, the matter was even more decisively settled when a critical bridge over the Roa Quan River was destroyed,[182] and the movement of heavy equipment to and from Khe Sanh ceased. Six tanks and Ontos tracked recoilless rifle carriers, which had been moved in to reinforce KSCB, were stuck at Khe Sanh, and the 175mm artillery could move no further west than the Rockpile. This effectively denied the defenders of Khe Sanh 18 kilometers of additional range to fire on NVA forces in Laos, and put them at a disadvantage. They could be hit by the NVA 130mm heavy artillery from 27 kilometers away, but could not answer with counterbattery fire further than 14.6 kilometers from the combat base.

There were several changes that occurred at Khe Sanh itself during this period. The first was that Colonel David E. Lownds took over the 26th Marines in a regularly scheduled change of command on 14 August. In assuming this command, Lownds became the senior officer at Khe Sanh and would remain so for the next eight months, through the famous siege of 1968. Lownds was 46 years old, had fought as a young officer on Kwajalein, Saipan, and Iwo Jima, and had just arrived for his first tour in Vietnam one month earlier. Lownds practiced leadership with flair, exemplified by the nonregulation handlebar mustache he grew and refused to shave until the siege was over, but he also brought a very cautious approach to dealing with the NVA. His wise leadership paid off by foiling NVA plans on several occasions, including his supervision of the immediate task of patrolling around Khe Sanh in Operation Ardmore.

An even more dramatic effect on Khe Sanh was created by decisions made by General Westmoreland in the summer of 1967. Khe Sanh had always been a place of special interest to him, as he later wrote of his first visit in early 1964,

> The critical importance of the little plateau was immediately apparent… Khe Sanh could serve as a patrol base for blocking enemy infiltration from Laos; a base for [secret border crossing] operations to harass the enemy in Laos; an airstrip for reconnaissance planes surveying the Ho Chi Minh Trail; a western anchor for defenses south of the DMZ; and an eventual jumping-off point for ground operations to cut the Ho Chi Minh Trail.[183]

By 1967, Khe Sanh had already been used for the first three purposes, and with the beginning of construction of barrier defenses along the DMZ that spring, Khe Sanh was considered a key link in the "McNamara Line." This was a string of manned strongpoints along the northern edge of the ICTZ behind a strip of cleared land which was seeded with seismic and acoustic sensors, supposedly forming an "electronic barrier" against NVA infiltration southward. Westmoreland believed that this barrier guarded Khe Sanh's eastern flank from NVA infiltration. At the same time, Khe Sanh would serve as the westernmost strongpoint, preventing the NVA from going around the barrier to enter I Corps from the west.[184] Westmoreland was also convinced Khe Sanh would soon be prepared for the last use on his list: a base for operations into Laos.

From the start of his assignment as COMUSMACV, Westmoreland harbored ambitions of even-

Seabees of Mobile Construction Battalion-301 set and seal aluminum runway mats into place at Khe Sanh Combat Base.

tually taking the war to Laos to stop the frustrating infiltration that was occurring along the Ho Chi Minh Trail. In 1966 and 1967 he had his staff draft plans to use a corps-sized force of at least three divisions to try and apply this conventional ground strategy to an unconventional war.[185] Westmoreland told his staff that there were two preconditions which had to be satisfied before active combat operation into Laos would begin. The first would be the end of the monsoon season, and the second would be the securing of the operations right flank along the DMZ by completion of the McNamara Line. Even during the Hill Fights, Westmoreland had been arguing for the further reinforcement of the base and an invasion of Laos.[186] After the tactical and operational success of the Hill Fights, which most likely interrupted the NVA in preparations to seize Khe Sanh, Westmoreland resolved to hold the outpost as a base for future operations into Laos. On 4 September, MACV sent a proposal on this plan to Admiral Sharp, CINCPAC.[187] In the meantime, Westmoreland took the liberty of beginning to prepare the base.

Khe Sanh's runway was a strip of the same pierced aluminum matting that had found such wide use in the Second World War. Laid directly on the dirt surface of the plateau, it was only designed for light aircraft. During the high logistic demands of the Hill Fights, the runway was pounded by a continuous stream of heavily loaded

A C-123 Provider becomes the first fixed-wing aircraft to land on the improved airfield at Khe Sanh Combat Base. In the background are several revetted helicopters, and in the foreground is the Precision Approach Radar used to guide aircraft in to land during low visibility conditions.

C-130s. The "Hercs" would touch down and ripple the aluminum matting in front of the aircraft, pushing a wave of metal ahead of the aircraft as it rolled down the strip. In addition to damaging the matting itself, the wave action pumped the water and mud from beneath it, washing away the dirt supporting the runway. On 17 August, after a Navy construction unit arrived, the runway was closed to be completely rebuilt. Over the next three months, the Seabees tore up all the old matting and replaced the undersurface with crushed rock quarried just outside the base perimeter. Once the undersurface was completed, a new runway of solid aluminum planking was laid down. In the meantime, with Route 9 closed, KSCB was completely dependent on helicopter-delivered supplies. Perhaps to reduce this burden, and considering the diminished NVA contact around the base, 3/26 was withdrawn. This left 1/26 as the sole battalion defending Khe Sanh once again, preventing the Marines from conducting aggressive patrols. The base was increasingly isolated, especially as its critical air link to the coastal region was weakened by the arrival of monsoonal winds and foggy, low rain clouds (referred to as crachin by the French) in October and November. As soon as the new runway was opened ahead of schedule on 27 October, Westmoreland began stockpiling supplies for a multi-division strike across the border.[188] His plans, however, were interrupted by the enemy.

The Growing NVA Presence

In December 1967, NVA activity around Khe Sanh increased considerably. Enemy vehicular traffic along the Laotian roads and trails nearby increased from a monthly average of 480 trucks in the fall, to 6,000 by the end of December. Evidence of heavy weapons was found, as well as new bunkers on Hill 881N. Sniper fire on the Marines occupying Hill 881S increased, and the NVA began probing attacks to test the Marine defenses on Hill 861 and the radio relay station on Hill 950.

Ultimately, intelligence assessed that the NVA 304 and 325C Divisions had crossed into South Vietnam in November and were closing in on Khe Sanh from the west, while the 320 Division was further to the east, in the vicinity of the Rockpile. While not an immediate threat, this third division was within a short march of supporting the other two. Also to the east was an additional regiment and another battalion, probably devoted to preventing movement along Route 9.[189] Except for the fact that the runway had been reopened and combat stores had been stockpiled at KSCB for a month, things were looking grim for Khe Sanh.

The increasing enemy activity was monitored by Lieutenant General Robert Cushman, who had taken over as the Commanding General of III MAF in June 1967. On 9 December, he decided that Khe Sanh was a likely target for NVA attack, and that the combat base would have to be reinforced in accordance with Westmoreland's objectives, instead of abandoning it as III MAF had earlier planned. Major General Rathvon M. Tompkins, who had assumed command of the 3d

General William C. Westmoreland visits Marine positions, escorted by the Commanding General of III MAF, Lieutenant General Robert E. Cushman Jr., on the left.

3d Battalion, 26th Marines, just after landing to Khe Sanh Combat Base on 13 December 1967 to reinforce the garrison in response to the growing NVA presence. Most of 3/26 was subsequently sent to occupy outposts on Hill 861 and 881South.

Marine Division just 16 days earlier, diverted 3/26 to Khe Sanh from another mission. With two battalions at Khe Sanh once again, the Marines struggled to regain the initiative. Search and destroy operations recommenced immediately, feeling westward over the same territory where the Hill Fights had been waged. These operations found the traces of large enemy units, but as before, the NVA refused to reveal themselves in force. Looking back on it, one Marine recalled,

> We went several days. We headed out towards Laos... We found some old NVA fighting positions. We sat on ridgelines at night and sent out ambushes. We just made no contact...I look back on it now and try to reflect sort of how crazy it was for just a company to be that far out of Khe Sanh, knowing later that there was just thousands of North Vietnamese just hiding there, just waiting, not wanting to make contact with us. It's...amazing that any of us came back.[190]

In the meantime, the hilltop positions west of Khe Sanh were strengthened. As one staff officer put it, "Both General Thompkins and Colonel Lownds were well aware of what had happened at Dienbienphu when the Viet Minh owned the mountains and the French owned the valley. It was essential that the hills around Khe Sanh remain in the hands of the Marines."[191] Closest was Hill 861, where the newly arrived K/3/26 continued the major mission of that outpost, patrolling the terrain immediately west of KSCB. Further to the west, 881S was considered by many to be the most important of the hill outposts, anchoring a ridgeline reaching all the way eastward from Laos. The hill had excellent observation of the combat base itself, and was the highest

The defensive positions on Hill 881S, the westernmost of the critical hill outposts.

of the surrounding hilltops. Not only had 881S proved immensely costly to capture during the Hill Fights, but it also sat very close to the extended centerline of KSCB's runway. If the NVA were allowed to capture the hill, aircraft taking off to the west, or approaching to land from the west in low and slow flight profiles, would be very vulnerable to antiaircraft fire. This could cause serious problems for a major combat base dependent on supply and reinforcement from the air.[192] I/3/26, commanded by Captain William H. Dabney, took over the defense of Hill 881S to prevent this from happening. At its peak, this critical outpost was reinforced with elements of a second company, 81mm mortars, 106mm recoilless rifles, three 105mm howitzers, a helicopter support team, and even signals intelligence Marines, for a total of more than 400 men.[193] Reconnaissance patrols ventured out further into the mountainous jungles, even searching for elephant feces which would indicate the presence of pack animals carrying heavy NVA equipment down from the North. Searches on the ground were supported by even greater efforts in the air. Beginning in late December, a great variety of sensors were being employed, including aerial photography in the visual and infrared spectrums, side-looking airborne radars, electrochemical sensors capable of detecting trace amounts of sweat and urine in the air, and signals intelligence aircraft.[194] The Marines knew the enemy was out there, but their efforts to locate the NVA were rewarded only with frustration. Until the NVA allowed themselves to be discovered, the Marines had to be content with reinforcing their defenses.

The Decision to Hold Khe Sanh

In the early morning hours of 2 January 1968, a Marine listening post 400 meters west of the main combat base perimeter heard movement in the dark. A reaction force was mustered and sent out to investigate, and surprised six figures walking in the dark nearby. When the intruders did not answer the challenge, the Marines opened fire. Receiving no return fire, but fearing that a major assault was imminent, the Marines withdrew back to the perimeter. No assault ever materialized, but the next morning five bodies were found where they had fallen, and blood trail indicated that a sixth had escaped after stripping the others of their rank insignia and documents. The evidence that remained was sufficient to conclude that the party had been a group of NVA officers, one of them senior enough to be a regimental commander. The fact that at least five NVA officers would approach so close to Khe Sanh did not bode well. It spoke not only of an enemy with great confidence inspired by familiarity with Marine dispositions and NVA numerical superiority, but it also suggested that these officers were conducting a "leaders' reconnaissance" in preparation for an attack.[195] News of the encounter was expedited up the chain of command and reached Westmoreland within hours. He accepted the evidence as final confirmation that a large-scale enemy attack on Khe Sanh was imminent.[196] Now had two choices: hold the base or withdraw. He chose to hold Khe Sanh despite the increasing NVA presence both to preserve the outpost as a future base for operations into Laos, and as part of the larger interlocking barrier defense system along the DMZ. Khe Sanh served to protect the left flank of the McNamara Line, which would in turn protect the right flank of operations from Khe Sanh into Laos.

Westmoreland, unlike the Marines at Khe Sanh, was not alarmed by the enemy activity. The reinforcement of Khe Sanh to defend against an attack would be a win-win situation for his strategy. On the one hand, if the enemy refused to attack, MACV would be one step closer to having the necessary force in Khe Sanh to invade Laos.[197] On the other hand, if the enemy did attack, the NVA would have to commit massive forces if he was to have any hope of taking Khe Sanh, creating a conventional battle in a frustrating unconventional war where U.S. firepower could seldom be brought to bear on an elusive enemy. In many ways, Westmoreland saw an enemy attack at Khe Sanh as simplifying his problem because it would allow him to destroy the primary enemy forces that would oppose his invasion of Laos. The defeat of the NVA in a pitched battle would also have been a well-timed political victory for Westmoreland, whose conventional strategy was facing increasing criticism and crumbling political support from the American public, Congress, Secretary of Defense McNamara, and even President Johnson.[198] With regard to Khe Sanh specifically, in Washington there was great concern that defending Khe Sanh was ceding the initiative to the North Vietnamese, offering them another Dien Bien Phu, and diverting U.S. forces that were needed elsewhere.[199] Westmoreland countered this concern by arguing that fighting the enemy in the wilderness of the highlands would merely preclude having to wage the same battle in the lowlands, where fire support would be hampered by the much denser civil population.[200]

Con Thien and Dien Bien Phu: The Historical Precedents

Westmoreland's decision to wage a battle of annihilation against a numerically superior force at a location so close to their sanctuary in Laos, but so distant from tenuous, weather-dependent U.S. support on the coast, was a daring one.[201] He made this decision, however, with two historical precedents in mind that he believed supported his decision, the battles of Con Thien and Dien Bien Phu.

Con Thien was a small village about 30 miles northeast of Khe Sanh, 2 miles south of the DMZ, and 14 miles inland (see Figure 1). The location was significant for two reasons. First, it was the northwest corner of a region that came to be nicknamed "Leatherneck Square." Roughly 11 kilometers on a side, the area was bounded by Gio Linh to the east, Dong Ha at the southeast corner, and Cam Lo south of Con Thien. Here the Marines of III MAF engaged in some of the bitterest and most sustained fights with the NVA over the course of 1967 and 1968 trying to stop southward infiltration from the DMZ. Con Thien was a small hill 158 meters high in the middle of a flat plain, allowing excellent observation in all directions, but most critically north to the DMZ along the Bien Hoa River, and across Leatherneck Square to Dong Ha, 14 kilometers to the southeast. This made the location the logical choice for one of the strongpoint defensive positions that would overlook the McNamara Line's electronic barrier along the DMZ and protect the ICTZ from enemy thrusts southward through the DMZ. In April 1967, as the Hill Fights were raging at Khe Sanh, engineers were building a road connecting Con Thien to the next outpost 11 kilometers to the east, Gio Linh, the northeast corner of Leatherneck Square. This activity apparently got the attention of the NVA, who began a buildup in the foothills to the west. On 8 May 1967, the 13th anniversary of the victory at Dien Bien Phu, the NVA attempted to overrun the defenses of two companies of 1/4 at Con Thien. An estimated two battalions of NVA armed with flamethrowers, RPGs, and automatic weapons assaulted the hill after an artillery and mortar bombardment. Once the NVA breached the defensive wires with Bangalore torpedoes, a desperate hand-to-hand fight broke out, and the Marines eventually succeeded in restabilizing the lines only after six hours. Having failed to completely capture the hill, the North Vietnamese were forced to withdraw under fire and without cover in the flat plain around it. One hundred ninety-seven NVA bodies were found, and eight of the enemy were captured.[202]

Despite the setback, the NVA were unwilling to give up on Con Thien. They had approximately 35,000 troops massed north of the DMZ to invade northern Quang Tri Province, and feared that the continued construction of the strongpoint barrier system would soon block any southward attack. Con Thien was deemed a keystone of the Marine defense, and remained the focal point of NVA effort. Two more major thrusts were made, but they both collapsed in the face of Marine ground unit maneuvers combined with supporting arms.[203]

The first NVA attack began in the early days of July. The Marines responded aggressively to the new threat with search and destroy operations under the code name Buffalo. This sustained contact from 2 to 7 July ultimately occupied two battalions of the 9th Marines before the second attack by the NVA regiment was defeated, and the enemy retreated northward under continuous air and artillery attack.[204] When Operation Buffalo was officially concluded on 14 July, the Marines counted 1,290 enemy dead for the 159 Marines they had lost. Artillery and naval gunfire were credited for killing more than 500, and while the killed by air (KBA) estimate was unstated, Marine aircraft had dropped 1,066 tons of ordnance in support of the operation.[205]

While air power was a key component in defeating the NVA infantry attacks of May and July 1967, it was less successful against the enemy artillery. Intelligence reported that it had located approximately 130 of these sites exposed during the operations around Con Thien, and MACV decided to capitalize on the opportunity by massing its air power against them in a new plan it optimistically classified as a SLAM (Seek, Locate, Annihilate, and Monitor) operation. This specific plan, Operation Headshed, used the entire joint spectrum of Strategic Air Command B-52s, tactical aircraft of the 7th Air Force, 7th Fleet, 1st MAW, and VNAF, as well as artillery and naval gunfire, in attacks on the enemy fire support positions. By the end of the year, however, less than 40 NVA weapons had been destroyed.[206] While air power helped defeat enemy assault forces massed around Con Thien, concentrating joint air power in SLAM operations was unsuccessful when the enemy targets were dispersed. Westmoreland and his staff were willing to overlook this qualification in favor of a more optimistic precedent for Khe Sanh.

The precedent which Westmoreland and his staff chose to focus on in January 1968 was the second major NVA assault on Con Thien, which occurred in September, concentrating the enemy in such numbers that another SLAM operation could be decisive. General William W. Momyer, the new Commanding General of the 7th Air Force and Westmoreland's Deputy for Air Operations, planned to capitalize on the opportunity by massing air power once again, using Con Thien as bait in Operation Neutralize. 3/26 was brought in from Khe Sanh after the Hill Fights to reinforce Con Thien, and 13,000 villagers were removed from their homes along the Ben Hai River to give his heavy bombers freer reign to attack NVA crossing the DMZ.[207] Three thousand shells were fired at Con Thien in a nine-day period, causing the Marines heavy casualties, but when two NVA battalions massed to attack Con Thien, they were decimated. In September alone, 790 of the 830 total B-52 sorties flown over the entire country were targeted on NVA forces around Con Thien, and the heavy bombers dropped 22,000 tons of ordnance in 49 days.[208] The combined effort of strategic bombers and tactical aircraft attacks from all four services in Operation Neutralize were credited with killing 2,000 of the NVA attackers.[209] Westmoreland voiced an estimate that 7,000 NVA had died in the futile attempt to take Con Thien, and called it a "Dienbienphu in reverse."[210] With the victory at Con Thien, Westmoreland and Momyer felt they had perfected SLAM operations as an excellent tool for turning enemy sieges into battles of annihilation. Westmoreland later stated that "Off and on for forty-nine days SLAM strikes pummeled the enemy around Con Thien and demonstrated that massed firepower was in itself sufficient to force a besieging enemy to desist, a demonstration that was destined to contribute to my confidence at a later occasion [Westmoreland's emphasis]."²¹¹ The situation to which he referred was Khe Sanh.

Of course, there was another historical precedent which was on just about everyone's mind on both sides of the conflict in January 1968: Dien Bien Phu. The specter of Dien Bien Phu haunted many Americans, from the young Marine privates at Khe Sanh all the way up to their commander in chief, who agonized over the subject throughout the three-month siege.²¹² Westmoreland, however, felt he had every reason to assure President Johnson that this siege would be a victory for the defenders. In addition to the recent victory at Con Thien, Westmoreland could also point to the 29 October defeat of an NVA force attacking the Loc Ninh Special Forces Camp. In this battle supporting arms were credited with killing up to 2,000 members of what Westmoreland claimed were four NVA regiments attacking the camp. Incidentally, this battle was also the occasion when MACV announced that a crossover point had finally been reached in the war, since communist forces were finally losing troops faster than they could recruit replacements to fight the Americans in Westmoreland's war of attrition.²¹³

The resemblance between Khe Sanh and Dien Bien Phu was more than superficial. In addition to the fact that one of the divisions attacking Khe Sanh was a veteran of the victory at Dien Bien Phu, the NVA had again achieved an advantage by occupying high ground surrounding their enemy. To make matters worse, in 1968 the North Vietnamese were equipped with even heavier artillery than they had been in 1954. The enemy forces were also still under the command of Vo Nguyen Giap. His leadership in 1954 had resulted in the capture of the 9,600 man French garrison after 56 days of siege, including three major assaults and a total of more than 7,000 killed and 15,000 wounded. Most hauntingly, at Dien Bien Phu the French, like Westmoreland, had been attempting to lure the Viet Minh into a conventional battle where they could be destroyed by superior firepower.

When President Johnson looked at the startling similarities and warned, "I don't want any damn Dinbinfoo,"²¹⁴ Westmoreland was armed with a battery of explanations why the two sieges would have different outcomes. Unlike the remote Dien Bien Phu, Westmoreland insisted that Khe Sanh would benefit from much heavier air support from a whole host of nearby bases that were only a quarter of the distance away. Statistics told him that the Americans were much better equipped than the French had been to use air power to both supply and defend the combat base. To supply a smaller garrison, the Air Force's 834th Air Division had 240 transports in January 1968. Even after the delivery volume of this fleet was cut in half by poor weather, enemy fire, and other factors, this fleet alone could deliver

After enemy activity around Route 9 forced their Khe Sanh-bound convoy to turn back on 21 July, the Army 175mm guns had to set up at Camp J.J. Carroll, more than 30 kilometers to the east. Although the 16 M107 guns of the 2d Battalion, 94th Artillery Regiment fired many missions into the hills around Khe Sanh in support of the defense, from Camp Carroll they could not range the NVA heavy artillery kept along the Laotian border. As a result, the enemy's heavy artillery was untouchable, except when it could be located and attacked with air power.

three times more supplies to Khe Sanh than the French had been able to send to their garrison at Dien Bien Phu, which was more than 50 percent larger.[215] When the 273 helicopters and five C-130s of the 1st Marine Air Wing in Vietnam were added to this number,[216] the Americans could be expected to benefit from a logistics volume that was many times greater per defender than the French had enjoyed at Dien Bien Phu. The Americans also had the benefit of superior fire support for the forces at Khe Sanh. While the French had a total of 200 planes to support their defense, but were weakened by a inadequate air command and control system, and an insufficient number of pilots and maintenance services to keep all these planes in active use. The Americans, on the other hand, benefited from an armada of 2,000 attack aircraft, 3,000 helicopters, and 24 B-52s—in short, more than 50 times the destructive air power. When weather hampered air support, Khe Sanh would also be provided with around-the clock artillery support,[217] including the sixteen 175mm guns at Camp Carroll. With the recent victory at Con Thien in mind, and the conviction that he would succeed at Khe Sanh where the French had failed, Westmoreland ordered the planning for a massive SLAM campaign to begin on 5 January. The next day he personally selected the code name—Operation Niagara[218] —evoking the image of an unstoppable waterfall of bombs which would sweep the enemy aside by its sheer volume.

Preparation for Battle

Planning for Niagara was conducted under the supervision of Westmoreland's Deputy for Air Operations, General William Momyer, U.S. Air Force. The operation was to be conducted in two phases. In the first phase, Niagara I, air and ground reconnaissance assets would locate the enemy. In the second phase, Niagara II, air power would destroy the massed enemy forces through B-52 carpet bombing and precision air strikes by tactical aircraft.[219] Even before III MAF was notified of the general outline for the new plan on 6 January, and before detailed planning occurred at Da Nang from 9 to 15 January,[220] MACV began preparations for the battle. The first major effort was to ensure that every available intelligence asset was being brought to bear to locate the NVA around Khe Sanh and prevent any more surprises. On 8 January, MACV directed that all of the various services' intelligence gathering activities focus on Khe Sanh.[221] Next he began to move forces northward to reinforce I Corps, under the code word Checkers. The end result of this movement was that the ICTZ would have nearly 50 U.S. combat battalions, or half of all U.S. combat troops in Vietnam, for a total of 250,000 allied troops positioned to meet the NVA. The pattern of reinforcements indicate that Westmoreland was looking even further ahead. As the NVA movements met his expectations by massing in an even more imminent threat to Khe Sanh, Westmoreland sent his two premier divisions, the 101st Airborne and 1st Air Cavalry, northward to base camps only 30 minutes from Khe Sanh by helicopter. COMUSMACV was preparing for the follow-through to a victory of air power at Khe Sanh by positioning forces for the invasion of Laos.[222]

The Marines were troubled by some of the changes Westmoreland wanted to make to command relationships. General Momyer had been arguing for some time that the fixed-wing air assets of III MAF should be consolidated under 7th Air Force control for a true joint air effort, and Operation Niagara gave him an urgent situation to get Westmoreland to commit to the change. MACV had already set up a command post in a hanger at Tan Son Nhut Air Base, the home of the 7th Air Force headquarters, outside Saigon. This command post was designed specifically to orchestrate air operations around Khe Sanh, and throughout the entire siege Westmoreland or one of his two primary deputies, General Creighton W. Abrams Jr. and Lieutenant General William B.

Aerial view of Khe Sanh Combat Base, as seen from the east.

Rosson (both of the U.S. Army), manned the post, studying incoming reports and poring over maps and a sand table model of the terrain. Westmoreland decided to personally retain the clearance authority for all B-52 missions in Southeast Asia, ensuring that he would have to personally approve each and every target.[223] With a huge SLAM operation in progress to fight such a pivotal battle for his strategy, Westmoreland also agreed to support Momyer's plan for "single management of air assets." On January 18th he cabled his intent to Admiral U.S. Grant Sharp, CINCPAC. To the Marines' relief, he was swiftly overruled.[224] On January 15th the planning for Niagara was completed, and Momyer briefed MACV on the plan. The only thing that remained was for the enemy to show himself, and the floodgates holding back the deluge of bombs would be opened. The Americans did not have to wait long.

The action most frequently cited for precipitating the series of events which finally brought the siege was the 14 January ambush of a small reconnaissance patrol operating between hills 881S and 881N, the same bloody terrain over which the Hill Fights had been fought.[225] Like almost every one of the other deep reconnaissance teams sent out in January, these Marines required emergency extraction.[226] This indicated that the NVA apparently decided that they either could not or would not continue to evade the Marine patrols as they made their final preparations to attack. The patrol was rescued by a force sent out from Hill 881S, but most significant was that a radio and the code sheets used to encrypt radio transmissions against NVA exploitation were left behind. This meant that even as the enemy began probing Marine defenses on 15 January,[227] I/3/26 on 881S was forced to send out patrols to try and recover the classified gear and prevent a compromise. Those patrols evoked a violent reaction.

Assessing the growing threat, III MAF decided to reinforce Khe Sanh further and sent 2/26 to join the 1st and 3d Battalions at Khe Sanh on 16 January.[228] This event marked the first time since Iwo Jima that the entire regiment was formed for battle as a unit.[229] 2/26 was sent to establish a battalion outpost on Hill 558, holding the western

Figure 3. The positions of Marine units defending the key hill outposts around Khe Sanh Combat Base. KSCB itself was defended by 1/26, a company from 3/26, the 37th ARVN Ranger Battalion, and numerous other small units. Illustration by E.L. Wilson for Captain Moyers S. Shore II, The Battle for Khe Sanh *(Washington, 1969), 50.*

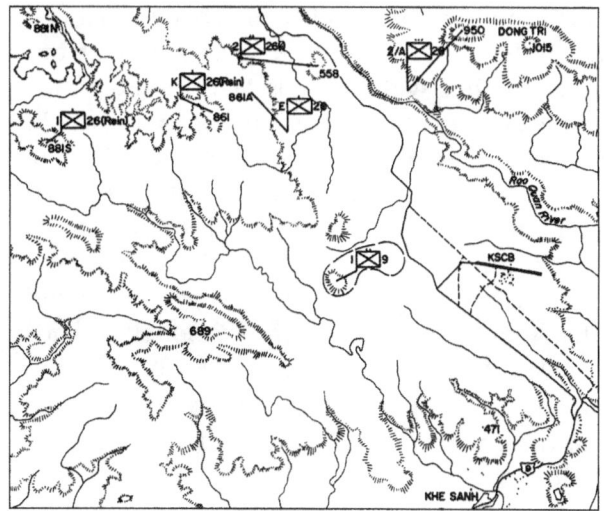

edge of the Khe Sanh plateau and blocking the movement of large enemy forces into the deep ravine that dove down into the Roa Quan River, right at the very edge of the combat base's northern and eastern perimeters. By the end of January, KSCB and the nearby hills were defended by a formidable assortment of units (see Figure 3). Five rifle battalions protected three 105mm artillery batteries and a 155mm battery, in addition to a 4.2 inch mortar battery, within their perimeters. They also harbored a number of tracked vehicles, including six tanks, Ontos 106mm recoilless launchers, and quad 40mm U.S. Army "Dusters."[230] In addition to the huge volume of air power Westmoreland was about to make available, the defenders of Khe Sanh could also depend on 24-hour all-weather support from 16 U.S. Army 175mm guns at Camp Carroll and the Rockpile,[231] and Westmoreland had moved half of his infantry combat power in Vietnam northward into I Corps.

Contact is Made

From Hill 881S, Captain Bill Dabney of I/3/26 had sent out a reinforced platoon to rescue the small patrol ambushed on 14 January, which was located and evacuated to KSCB for medical treatment. He later learned from the 26th Marines that the reconnaissance patrol had left behind a radio and some of their code sheets. Dabney was ordered to recover the gear, and sent out a platoon, but withdrew his Marines after they made contact with an NVA unit. Since he would be unable to send out a larger unit with his company responsible for holding 881S, he requested permission to conduct a reconnaissance in force with his entire company to investigate just how many NVA were out beyond his perimeter, and what they were doing there. Colonel Lownds believed that the MACV and 3d Marine Division intelligence estimates were grossly inflated and that the enemy had no more than a regiment in the area,[232] so he consented to the patrol and sent M/3/26 to hold 881S [233] while India Company was probing for the enemy.[234]

On the morning of 19 January, Dabney's force of approximately 200 men moved out, but was stopped short of Hill 881N by heavy fire, and withdrew to spend the rest of the day calling in artillery, mortars, and air support to clean the enemy from Hill 881N and the saddle between it and 881S. The situation was repeated the next day, and the Marines were preparing for a third attempt when word came over the radio that Lownds had ordered a withdrawal.

Dabney was not told the reason for the withdrawal, only that he had to pull his men back into the defensive perimeter on Hill 881S without delay. It took several hours of fighting for I/3/26 to break contact, and as night approached the company withdrew under the cover of air support and artillery.[235] Meanwhile, the 26th Marines headquarters bunker deep underground seven miles to the east was a flurry of activity. Just hours earlier, as I/3/26 was attacking Hill 881N, Marines on the main combat base's western perimeter had been shocked to see an NVA officer approaching the wire waving a white flag. A group was sent out to take him in, and Lieutenant La Thonh Tonc was turned over to two interrogator/translators. Disillusioned with NVA leadership and the Communist cause, he spoke freely and without duress, shocking the Marines by revealing the plans for an assault on Khe Sanh that was to commence that very night. The defector told the Marines that the 304 and 325C divisions had indeed taken final positions around Khe Sanh to recreate the success of Dien Bien Phu.[236] He claimed that an NVA battalion was preparing to attack Hill 861, after which two NVA regiments would attack the main combat base with heavy artillery, rocket, and mortar support. If the first two regiments failed to take KSCB, they would be reinforced by a third.[237] The incredible detail and candidness of the confession made some of the Marine leaders skeptical, but they decided to take every precaution. As General Tompkins later said, "I decided that we would accept Tonc's information as valid, since we had nothing to lose, but much to gain."[238] Word was immediately sent up the chain of command to MACV, and a helicopter was dispatched to warn the Special Forces camp at Lang Vei. The news of this imminent assault was the reason Lownds recalled Dabney's attack on 881N, fearing that his men were on the verge of being surrounded by an NVA regiment targeted on Hill 881S.[239] Dense clouds closed in around the hills that afternoon, and after nightfall, word came back that Dabney's men had finally reached the safety of his perimeter on Hill 881S, and were keeping the area to their west under constant artillery bombardment. The air at KSCB was thick with ominous anticipation.

The Siege Begins

At half past midnight on 21 January 1968, almost exactly as Lieutenant Tonc had predicted, Hill 861 was subjected to a heavy bombardment. At 0100 approximately 250 NVA soldiers attacked up the hill, rushing through breaches made by sappers despite heavy artillery, mortar, and rifle fire that the Marines poured down upon them. The NVA managed to seize half the position, and were repulsed after four hours only by a combination of indirect fires called on the top of the hill, and a savage counterattack by Marines in desperate hand-to-hand fighting.[240]

At 0530, just 15 minutes after the Marines had finally driven the enemy from Hill 861, a massive bombardment of the main combat base began. This attack, which lasted almost three hours, was a complete surprise despite Tonc's warning because it contained a significant amount of artillery, which was not considered mobile enough to join the man-portable rocket systems known to be in mountains to the west.[241] From the southern slopes of 881N a massive rocket attack was

Bunkers along the trench line that ringed the combat base. The innermost defensive wire barriers can be seen on the right.

launched, which scored a direct hit on the 1,500-ton ammunition dump on the eastern end of the runway, where the main NVA assault was expected. The impact set off a chain reaction of explosions from within the massive ammunition dump Westmoreland had been building for months in preparation for an invasion of Laos, destroying 98 percent of the ammunition available to the 26th Marines. The air was thick with shrapnel, and dangerously hot unexpended ordnance fell from the sky in showers up to 2,000 feet away from the immense crater that was created. In some places the trenches the Marines had dug behind the defensive wire were filled chest deep with unexploded ordnance, debris, and shell casings.

Secondary fires and explosions resulting from the detonation of the ammunition dump continued for 24 hours,[242] but most frustrating for the Marines was that in the heavy fog they could not find any enemy to return fire at. Until the NVA appeared at the wire, all the Marines could do was crouch in the bottoms of their holes and bunkers and pray that they would survive the bombardment.[243] Some of them were convinced that if the NVA had mounted their assault after the ammunition dump had exploded, the enemy could have overrun the combat base.[244]

Marines of the 1st Battalion, 9th Marines at their outpost near the Rock Quarry. The small hill was adjacent to the site that had been used to produce gravel for bedding the new runway. 1/9 was not moved to Khe Sanh until 22 January, the day after the major NVA attacks began. These Marines occupied the closest outpost, overlooking both the final western approach to the combat base and the drop zone that was used for the parachute delivery of supplies.

Remarkably, the enemy infantry assault on the main combat base that night never materialized. In fact there were only two positions in the vicinity of Khe Sanh attacked by infantry on 21 January 1968: Hill 861 as previously discussed, and Khe Sanh village. As the Marine forces in and around Khe Sanh grew in size over the fall and winter of 1967, the village itself had swelled. Entrepreneurial South Vietnamese sought to exploit the increased availability of American cash by providing services that otherwise never would have been profitable in the highlands. With the addition of laundry shops, souvenir stands, restaurants, and brothels, Khe Sanh village now included 1,500 people. Alongside the Hung Hoa district headquarters were a four-man U.S. Army advisory group, and the 915th Regional Forces Company, a Vietnamese unit, as well as the headquarters of the Marines' regional pacification effort, Combined Action Company Oscar, and two of its subordinate units, CAP Oscar-1 and CAP Oscar-2. At 0100, concurrent with the assault on Hill 861, a small NVA force attacked Khe Sanh village, perhaps to further isolate the combat base. The attackers were driven back by the various allied military forces there in the early morning hours, but returned in force in the late afternoon. The defenders were prepared for the second attack, and fixed the NVA in place with machine guns so they presented a stationary target for 1,000 rounds of artillery and air support. The enemy attack was broken, but Colonel Lownds decided that the village would be untenable if the NVA made a committed effort, so he decided to evacuate it.

The Situation Stabilizes

In the initial attacks on Khe Sanh, the Americans were forced to withdraw from the village itself, and had sustained a terrible bombardment, but had succeeded in holding the combat base and all of its outposts. Now that the enemy had apparently committed himself against Khe Sanh as Westmoreland hoped, the Americans reinforced the base in preparation for the siege they believed was just beginning. Khe Sanh was most vulnerable on 21 January, the day after the initial assault, but other than a second vicious bombardment that evening, the NVA did not capitalize on the weakness created by the ammunition dump explosion.[245] That next day, the 1st Battalion, 9th Marines arrived to occupy a hill near the rock quarry west of the perimeter (see Figure 3). Now the closest of the outposts, this position guarded the immediate western approach to the combat base, as well as some flat terrain between the hill and the base which could serve as a drop zone for parachute-delivered supplies. In addition to another artillery battery that was soon moved to the combat base, Colonel Lownds increased the strength of key outposts. Hill 861, the objective of the first NVA assault, was reinforced with a fourth platoon, while 2/26 sent a company to occupy a new defensive position on Hill 861A nearby.[246] By the time the major movements were complete on

23 January, Colonel Lownds was in command of 6,053 men at Khe Sanh, half of whom were distributed to the various outposts in the hills. This number did not include the 400 CIDG troops and soldiers of the U.S. Army FOB-3 occupying their own defensive perimeter on the outside of, but attached to, the Marine lines on the southwest perimeter.[247] When it was realized that the Vietnamese had made no regular military contribution to a battle Westmoreland considered so crucial to their nation's eventual victory, 318 men of the 37th ARVN Ranger Battalion were also sent in on 27 January. As with the CIDG troops, the Americans were suspicious of the Rangers' reliability, and placed them in their own defensive perimeter attached to the outside of the Marine wire.[248]

The Marines also decided to limit their patrolling activity outside these perimeters for two reasons. First, they felt the presence of large enemy forces around Khe Sanh made such patrols unwise, since they could easily be ambushed, requiring larger rescue forces to be sent out to fight a battle of attrition on the NVA's terms. With this in mind, General Tompkins limited patrols to 500 meters distance from the combat base perimeter, where they could be observed and covered by the fire of Marines safe inside the defenses. This restriction on patrolling was supported by General Westmoreland for a second reason as well. By confining the defenders to their static defensive positions, aircraft would have maximum flexibility to attack the NVA around them. The NVA would be forced to come to the Marines if they wanted to attack, and as the enemy massed at these known points the NVA could be defeated by American air power.[249]

The NVA concentrations around Khe Sanh were presenting some suitable targets for American air power, just as Westmoreland had hoped. As early as the 22d, aircraft from all three services were attacking known and suspected enemy positions, so that by the midnight of the 23d, tactical aircraft alone reported that they had created 40 secondary explosions, 28 secondary fires, 39 NVA killed, and 5 bunkers collapsed in the area immediately around the combat base.[250]

The Fall of Lang Vei

In the first 10 days after the siege commenced on 21 January, the NVA bombarded the combat base regularly, but did not launch any other major ground assaults against the Marines. Their second major ground attack began on 4 February and came in two main thrusts: one directed toward the combat base's western outposts, and another toward the Lang Vei Special Forces Camp. The first thrust was defeated by U.S. firepower, the second was an NVA victory.

Beginning on 3 February, electronic sensors began to indicate the presence of several NVA battalions gathering near Hill 881S. At 0230 on 5 February, an artillery concentration was fired at the location where these forces were thought to be massing for attack. Hill 881S was never assaulted, but later that morning the NVA did attack

Two soldiers of the ARVN 37th Ranger Battalion in the defensive positions they established on the southeast perimeter of the combat base.

Once the heavy bombardment of the base began, the Marines who had not already moved their activities to underground bunkers quickly did so. The Marines of B Company, 3d Reconnaissance Battalion demonstrated a sense of humor upon having to abandon their former shelter.

Hill 861A without warning. The Marines on the new outpost were assisted in their defense by artillery fires designed to cut the NVA off from reinforcements, and tactical aircraft controlled by a ground-based Marine radar team. The attack was broken, and a sweep to clear the NVA off the hillside after daylight found more than 100 dead.[251] Lang Vei, the objective of the second thrust, was not so fortunate.

The Special Forces men at Lang Vei had relocated their camp a thousand meters further west to a more defensible position after the first was penetrated by the NVA during the Hill Fights of May 1967. Colonel Lownds's evacuation of Khe Sanh village after the NVA attack on 21 January placed the camp even further from allied support, since the new location was nine kilometers away from KSCB as the crow flew over some densely jungled hills, and more than 14 kilometers away by road.[252]

In the early morning hours of 7 February, an infantry force from the NVA 304th Division, supported by a company of PT-76 tanks hit Lang Vei. Despite a valiant defense fought without the benefit of antitank weapons, the NVA rapidly overran the camp. Some of the Special Forces survivors withdrew to a bunker in the center of the camp. A tank drove up on top of the bunker, and the NVA gathered to throw grenades inside. The survivors held tight, and were able to call for help by radio. Colonel Lownds, however, refused to send a relief force, considering such an attempt suicidal.[253] The decision became the source of much inter-service bitterness, but was a wise one, considering the distance involved and the size of the NVA force that was probably waiting in hopes that just such a relief force would give up the security of the combat base to walk into its ambush. Aircraft were sent to assist, including an Air Force FAC(A) and a flareship, but their effectiveness was limited by their inability to locate the enemy in the darkness. The B-57 bombers sent also did not carry anti-personnel weapons which could be used on the NVA without penetrating the bunker and killing the Americans inside as well.[254]

As daybreak arrived, air support became more effective and the NVA attack subsided. By afternoon the survivors managed to escape the camp by exploiting the suppression created by the strafing runs of fighter aircraft.[255] The survivors fled eastward to join the remnants of a Laotian battalion fleeing along Route 9. A rescue mission was launched, including six A-1Es, four tactical jets, and five or six helicopter gunships under the control of a FAC(A). This force located the survivors at the old Lang Vei camp abandoned earlier in the year, and provided cover for some CH-46s to deliver a relief force and pick them up. The Americans were lucky to escape as the camp was abandoned in the first major NVA success of the campaign.

Westmoreland reacted violently to this first major setback in his crowning campaign.²⁵⁶ Hours after Lang Vei was overrun, he visited the III MAF headquarters in Da Nang for a special meeting. He had sent the Americal Division, the First Air Cavalry Division, a brigade of the 101st Airborne, and a South Korean Marine Corps Division to the ICTZ, but the pandemonium of the Tet Offensive seemed to have overcome the region. With two NVA divisions laying siege to Khe Sanh, another near the Rockpile, another fighting at Hue, and two more loose in the ICTZ, he did not believe the Marines were being active enough. Now that Lang Vei had been lost, he considered a major assault on KSCB imminent, and he took steps to assert greater control over the situation in the ICTZ. Westmoreland resolved to send his Deputy, General Abrams to the ICTZ with his MACV (Forward) headquarters, and decided to push once again for General Momyer's centralized control of all air assets in Vietnam.²⁵⁷

The Nature of the Ongoing Siege

After the fall of Lang Vei, the NVA began to focus on Khe Sanh Combat Base itself.²⁵⁸ KSCB had been subjected to regular bombardment daily since 21 January, but it intensified as Lang Vei was overrun, apparently to suppress American fire support for the Special Forces camp. Next, three companies of the NVA 101D Regi-

A mortar impacts near some of the tents still standing after three weeks of bombardment.

An NVA rocket impacts the combat base during the period of peak bombardment in late February.

ment moved into attack positions near the Rock Quarry outpost of 1/9. Their target was a smaller outpost set up on a knoll in front of the battalion, manned by one reinforced platoon to guard the western approach to 1/9. In the early morning hours, less than a day after Lang Vei had been lost, the NVA assault began. The Marines were caught completely off guard and were quickly pushed back into a small portion of their perimeter, but managed to hold the NVA off from completely overrunning the hill until the next morning allowed a relief force to set out, supported by an air strike. That force found 150 NVA bodies, while the Marines on Hill 64 had suffered 24 killed and only had 30 survivors.²⁵⁹

This event is significant because it is the last time the NVA assaulted one of the Marine outposts with the apparent intent of destroying it.²⁶⁰ From this point on the siege was characterized by repetitive bombardments, concentrated attempts to sever the aerial resupply "bridge" supporting Khe Sanh, and trenching efforts focused on KSCB. Because the next two months lack any other assaults of significance, it is hard to be specific about the events that followed, but some of the general aspects of the siege warrant discussion.

The most immediate concern of the Marines

Two Marines search for indications of NVA mortars firing on the combat base. The NVA indirect fire weapons were a very high priority for the Marines to find and destroy, but they were kept carefully hidden. While mortars had to be set up close to the base, and could sometimes be seen by ground observers, FAC(A)s were critical for finding the long-range artillery that fired from far beyond the normal visual limits of observers on the ground.

was the constant bombardment they were subjected to by the NVA. The North Vietnamese hit the base almost daily with artillery, rocket, and mortar fire, so that the Marines never felt completely secure, and had to live with the constant threat of death. Incoming aircraft trying to deliver supplies and reinforcements, and evacuate casualties from the base, were fired upon on every single attempt. The Marines' problems with the NVA fire were compounded by the fact that the NVA artillery outranged the Marine artillery based at Khe Sanh. The largest American artillery was 155mm, and could reach only 15 kilometers from the combat base, compared to the NVA 130mm artillery which could reach almost twice as far.[261] KSCB was supported by the U.S. Army's heavy 175mm artillery based at the Rockpile and Camp Carrol 15 and 24 kilometers to the east respectively, but these guns could reach no further west than the Marine guns at Khe Sanh. The proximity of the Laotian border, meanwhile, gave the NVA plenty of places to situate their guns near the Ho Chi Minh supply route, and imposed political restrictions on the American efforts to deal with them. The NVA sought to align their artillery positions along the long axis of the combat base to simplify their fire control problem. As a result about two-thirds of the rounds fired at the combat base flew over the westernmost Marine outpost on Hill 881S, from a distance of 12-14 miles from the combat base.[262] This made 881S a key location for providing the combat base with warning. Whenever rounds were fired overhead a Marine would radio back to the 26th Marines command post at KSCB, where a siren was sounded, giving the Marines at the combat base a few seconds warning before the rounds hit. Hill 881S was also important for dealing with the NVA rocket attacks. The range of the 122mm Katushka rocket was almost equal to the distance between KSCB and 881S, which meant any rockets to be fired from a position along the long axis of the base had to be set up near the outpost. Over the course of the siege more than 5,000 rockets were fired from that position,[263] which the NVA referred to as a 122mm rocket

The remains of the original sick bay, built above ground but abandoned at the start of the heavy bombardments in January 1968.

firebase. In a number of cases the men on 881S were able to spot the NVA loading the rockets into launching racks in preparation for a barrage. The Marines would wait until the racks were fully loaded, and then call in artillery or close air support missions to destroy them. In one case they waited just a little to long. When one A-4 rolled in to attack, the NVA fired the rockets fired directly in his face, bracketing the aircraft in its attack dive. By sheer luck the pilot and his aircraft escaped unharmed, and the flight spent the rest of its mission pounding the empty launcher to relieve their frustrations.[264]

The Americans set records with the fire support they devoted to the battle, but they were not the only ones. In the daily bombardments the NVA consumed huge amounts of ammunition, taxing their tortuous overland supply system. One the day of peak bombardment, 23 February, for example, some of the rounds fired did not even have fuses.[65] This did not mean that the bombardment was easy to weather, however, with 1,307 rocket, artillery, and mortar rounds counted impacting on or near the base. Twelve Marines were killed, 51 were wounded, and another ammunition supply point was hit, consuming 1,600 rounds of recoilless rifle and artillery ammunition in a smaller replay of the first ammunition dump's explosion.[266] This was the largest NVA bombardment of the war to date, surpassing the former record of 1,065 rounds fired near Con Thien one day the previous July.[267] By no means did the daily bombardment drop off rapidly after the peak, either. That very same day more heavy artillery was detected moving towards the combat base, and the following day 130mm guns joined the fight for the first time.[268]

The Marines dealt with the bombardment in a number of ways. They kept their flak vests closed, and they always kept their eyes and ears open when moving about, looking for the nearest place to dive for cover while listening for the sound of

Marines stacking empty 105mm artillery casings. The huge pile of empty casings illustrates not only the immense firepower being expended in the hills around Khe Sanh, but also the incredible logistics demands of such efforts, all of which had to be supplied by air. Many Marines used empty casings filled with dirt to create additional protective layers for their bunkers.

One means of dealing with the stress of constant bombardment was a macabre sense of humor, which many Marines expressed on their helmets. Also on the side of this helmet are the Marine's initials and the last four digits of his service number, to aid in identification.

incoming artillery, rockets, or mortars.[269] If aware of incoming rounds, they would adopt a posture that became known as the "Khe Sanh Shuffle," a bent-over crouch while running for cover. They also reinforced their bunkers with anything and everything they could find—empty artillery shell casings filled with the red mud of the plateau, timbers stolen from the Seabees, and even steel and aluminum cargo pallets stolen from the Air Force cargo handling team. When bombardments occurred, however, the Marine artillery men always tried to fire back, even when they knew the enemy was out of range. It was considered vital for the defender's morale for their artillery to be heard firing back, so that every man would not have the feeling he was just sitting still and taking beating, waiting for death to find him.

When enemy positions could be located near the combat base they were frequently engaged with counter-battery fire by the Marine artillerymen, but the preferred weapon for finding and locating the enemy guns was aircraft, which were not subject to the same range limitations. The FSCC was ruthless in targeting known and suspected artillery, rocket, and mortar positions, but very often it was only the eyes of a FAC(A) which could find the enemy guns. When they did, the results were deadly for the NVA, whose guns were not mobile enough to escape, and were very vulnerable to air attack when spotted. When the Marines did enjoy a respite from the bombardments, they gave at least some of the credit to the air support they were receiving. After a remarkable two days without incoming on 20 March, one Marine chalked it up to "A-Number-one air support."[270]

The most vulnerable aspect of the siege was the tenuous air bridge upon which the 26th Marines relied for supplies and reinforcements. After the detonation of the ammunition depot in the early hours of 21 January the combat base's runway was closed for two days as the Marines

Marines constantly improved their defenses during the siege. Extensive portions of the trench line were equipped with overhead cover.

72

Two Marines digging new trench line with picks even as the siege of the combat base was coming to an end. The work of improving the defenses was never considered complete.

rushed to conduct repairs and clean up the hot, unexploded ordnance scattered everywhere. Working from just a tiny fraction of the reserves that had been so carefully stockpiled, the Marines were happy to welcome the first fixed-wing cargo transport which landed on 23 January.²⁷¹ The combat base and its outposts consumed a huge volume of ordnance and supplies on a daily basis, and the daily NVA bombardments were inflict-

The western perimeter of Khe Sanh Combat Base, defended by the 1st Battalion, 26th Marines. Although in this picture visibility has cleared, the persistent clouds that made air operations so difficult around Khe Sanh can be seen in the background.

ing casualties which had to be evacuated and replaced. Unfortunately, the NVA were equally anxious to greet arriving and departing aircraft with rocket and artillery fire. The NVA apparently had forward observers well positioned to observe the airfield, because veterans unanimously state that every single aircraft that landed at Khe Sanh during this period was attacked by artillery or mortars. Before long, none of the arriving aircraft came to an actual halt anywhere within the combat base. While they had formerly taxied clear of the runway to allow forklifts to unload their cargos in a process that would take half an hour or more, now the aircraft landed and turned around on the runway. To dispense their cargo the loadmasters unleashed entire pallets from their restraints so that they simply rolled out of the back of the taxiing aircraft onto the runway. Anyone departing Khe Sanh had to run and board the moving aircraft as it taxied down the runway to begin its takeoff, passengers on board or not. Helicopters followed similar procedures, avoid-

Despite the regular bombardments that drove the defenders underground in elaborate bunkers, essential flight support services were provided continuously. In the foreground is the airfield fire truck used to extinguish fires started by the bombardments, and in the background are the antennas and bunkers of Marine Air Traffic Control Unit-62, responsible for coordinating the many arrivals and departures of aircraft with as much safety as the enemy situation allowed.

Marines watch the burning wreckage of a KC-130 that crash-landed on the airfield on 10 February. Piloted by Chief Warrant Officer-3 Henry Wildfang and Major Robert E. White Jr., the aircraft was hit by NVA heavy machine gun fire on approach to Khe Sanh, igniting the bulk fuel bladders inside. Despite heavy smoke and flames in the aircraft, the pilots managed to land the C-130 and got it off the runway to keep the airfield open. As the aircraft was engulfed in flames, the pilots escaped out the cockpit windows. Three other Marines made it away from the burning wreckage, but ultimately 8 of the 11 men on the plane perished. The wreckage became popular among reporters visiting the base to use as a dramatic backdrop while recording their stories.

ing the artillery and mortar fire by staying constantly in motion. Teams of Marines ran up the boarding ramps to unload boxes of supplies and bring casualties on stretchers aboard, so that the helicopters never had to stop in a running drop-off and pick-up.[272]

In February, the situation grew worse for two reasons. The unseasonably good weather which had graced the Marines during the last days of January was replaced by the low-lying crachin rain clouds, shrouding KSCB in mist. The runway itself had already been considered marginal due to the mountain winds that flowed through the area, but the crachin now made it completely unsafe to operate there.[273] The Marines guided aircraft to landings using a ground-controlled radar approach, but pilots routinely had to violate the safety standards that normally applied to such procedures in order to get to the base.

The second major problem the cargo pilots had to face at Khe Sanh was enemy antiaircraft fire. The NVA sought to sever the air bridge at Khe Sanh, just as they had succeeded in doing at Dien Bien Phu. To do the job, they brought in anti-aircraft artillery of up to 37mm, which was emplaced as close to the combat base and the aircraft approach corridors as possible.[274] During the worst weather, the NVA fired blindly into the clouds at the sounds of landing aircraft being guided in by the Marine radar. During the breaks when cargo aircraft rushed to exploit momentarily good visibility, the NVA were able to accurately target the large aircraft as they came in low and slow to land. By the 10th of February, when a Marine C-130 full of fuel bladders was hit on final approach and burned on the ground after a heroic landing, 10 Air Force C-130s had been hit. When two more were hit on 11 February, General Momyer decided that he had had enough. He issued a prohibition against any more C-130s landing at Khe Sanh beginning 12 February. For the delivery and pickup of personnel and sensitive cargo at Khe Sanh, the Marines were now dependant on the smaller C-123K and C-7A transports, capable of carrying 5 and 3 tons respectively, compared to the 13-ton payload of the C-130.[275]

Concurrent with the increasing risk, Khe Sanh reached its highest logistic demands in February. The Marines could simply not do without the support of the larger C-130s. The Air Force responded by using three other cargo delivery techniques, which ultimately accounted for two-thirds of the cargo it delivered.[276] The first was the Ground Proximity Extraction System (GPES), in which the cargo pallets loaded in the back of the aircraft were attached to a "tail hook" that hung off the back of the cargo ramp. The aircraft would approach the runway as if about to land, and level off just two or three feet above ground level, allowing the hook to catch an arresting cable stretched across the runway. The arresting gear would then pull the cargo out of the back of the plane as it flew down the runway. This method did not prove effective at Khe Sanh because the arresting gear, which the Marines had struggled to install under constant artillery and rocket barrages, had not been sufficiently secured into the ground. When the first GPES delivery was attempted, the load was pulled from the aircraft, but it also pulled the arresting gear out of its mounts, and the entire system went skidding down the runway. As an alternative, the Air Force tried a second system, the Low Altitude Extraction System (LAPES). In this technique the aircraft would fly a similar profile, but deploy a drag chute to pull the cargo out of the aircraft flying a few feet off the ground. The problem with this system was that the drag chute had to be deployed at exactly the right time, and any malfunction could result in the cargo landing somewhere other than was intended. This is exactly what happened on 9 March, when a load was released late. The nine tons of cargo, traveling at more than 100 miles an hour, went skidding off the end of the runway and into the base's defensive perimeter, demolishing a bunker and killing one Marine. Another fatality on 21 February was enough to convince the Air Force to try another technique, parachute drops outside the base perimeter. Because of the success of this third method, LAPES deliveries were reserved for only the most sensitive cargo that could not be risked falling into enemy hands.[277]

The Air Force crews became quite skilled at delivering their cargo by parachute drop, being careful not to repeat the errors of Dien Bien Phu. There, the French had delivered a significant amount of supplies to the NVA rather than their own forces. At Khe Sanh, the drops were made to a level area between the main combat base perimeter and the Rock Quarry outpost to the west held by 1/9. The Marines swept this area for booby traps every morning before any drops began, and kept working parties ready to recover paradropped supplies, usually under NVA harassing fire. In the cases when the supplies could not be recovered by dark, the Marines called in artillery to destroy them, thereby preventing them from falling into enemy hands. By 15 March, the 852 airdrops made in support of Khe Sanh exceeded the total number of all drops made in Vietnam before the siege began.[278]

Resupplying the outposts was another matter. Because they were too small for runways and did not have secure drop zones nearby, the hill outposts had to be supplied by helicopter. Much like at Khe Sanh, these deliveries touched down for only moments to load and unload, but were still subject to constant mortar fire. At the outposts they faced the added danger of heavy machine guns hidden outside the Marine perimeters. In order to reduce the risks of multiple landings under fire, the helicopters stopped carrying supplies from KSCB to its outposts. Instead, the cargo was

Once antiaircraft fire proved too heavy for frequent landings at the airfield and other delivery means were proven impractical, Khe Sanh Combat Base was primarily supplied by airdrops from C-130s. A flat area between the combat base's western perimeter and the outpost manned by 1st Battalion, 9th Marines near the Rock Quarry served as the drop zone.

Although helicopters like this CH-46 Sea Knight, shown here on 23 January, were used to ferry supplies to the main combat base, they were most critical in resupplying the hill outposts, which were too small for the delivery of supplies and reinforcements by any other means.

loaded at one of the coastal bases and carried directly to the hill outposts, bypassing the combat base. The Marines also developed very sophisticated fire support plans to protect the helicopters as they arrived as the hill outposts.

The 26th Marines FSCC gave antiaircraft positions a very high priority in targeting, and once a 37mm position was identified, it was repeatedly attacked until it was destroyed or abandoned.[279] By the end of the siege, the Marines reported that more than 300 had been destroyed, but not without cost. Thirty-three helicopters had been shot down or permanently disabled over the course of the siege. The poor February weather also provided the NVA with concealment to move more AAA into the area immediately around the base. When the weather cleared on 6 March, they managed to shoot down an Air Force C-123.[281] Overall, however, the effort was a success meeting an average daily logistic requirement of 150 tons of supplies. As shown in Figure 4, the bulk of these supplies (72 percent) were delivered by the Air Force, the majority of which was by using new and innovative methods. In this respect, air power was a very critical element of the American victory at Khe Sanh, and air-centric historians like Donald Mrozek and Bernard Nalty are entirely correct to celebrate the importance of Air Force contributions. When it came to contributions of offensive firepower, however, it will be shown that the score was quite different.[282]

The NVA Siege Trenches

Sometime after the final assault on 8 February, the NVA apparently turned to more deliberate means of attacking the combat base. While the Marines waited for a final assault that never came, the NVA used the cover provided by poor weather to dig siege trenches near the combat base's perimeter. NVA trenches had already been located more than a kilometer south of the base on Hill 471, but when the fog cleared on 25 February, the Marines were alarmed to hear from an aerial observer that trenches had been dug as close as 25 meters outside the perimeter. More than 700 meters of trench appeared to have been dug the previous night.[284]

The trenching was ominous because the same technique had proven very successful for the PAVN at Dien Bien Phu. The Marines responded by redoubling their efforts to stop the NVA from

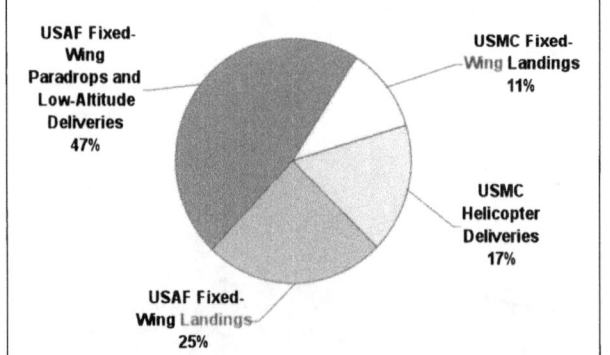

Figure 4. Aerial logistics deliveries to Khe Sanh and its outposts, by service and delivery mode.[283]

digging any closer or putting the siege trenches to good use. Artillery and aircraft were concentrated on the trenches, but they proved frustratingly hard to destroy, despite a number of creative solutions that were tried. To make matters worse, the NVA were digging faster than the trenches could be destroyed. On one occasion they completed more than 1,700 feet of trench in one night, all of which was deep enough for a man to stand up in without being exposed.[285] The most effective solution proved to be abandoning attempts to destroy the trenches, and instead they were covered with fire by Air Force gunships that constantly orbited overhead.

Although the Marines expected a massive attack by the NVA, one never materialized. On the 29 February, electronic sensors detected the approach of what was suspected to be an NVA regiment moving from Lang Vei past Khe Sanh village. Colonel Lownds put his men on full alert, and his FSCC targeted the estimated location of

As the NVA dug trenches within 100 meters of the combat base, Marines kept close watch for enemy movement that could be targeted by artillery, mortars, or aircraft.

the approaching enemy with artillery, mortars, radar-guided tactical aircraft, and even two B-52s diverted to drop within 800 yards of the combat base. Whatever the cause, an attack in force never materialized. Early the next morning of March, 78 NVA attacked the combat base perimeter at the southeast sector manned by the ARVN rangers, but they failed to penetrate the lines.[286]

It was not long after this that the NVA apparently ceased their siege efforts. Robert Pisor concluded that as early as 6 March, even Westmoreland had decided that the NVA had turned their attention elsewhere. If this is true, the evidence is not clear, but it cannot be far off. On 9 March, Westmoreland told President Johnson that there were only 6,000 to 8,000 NVA left at Khe Sanh, and the next day he reported that they had stopped repairing their siege trenches. Six more minor assault attempts did materialize over the course of March, including one on the night of the 13 to 14 (the 14th anniversary of the victory at Dien Bien Phu),[287] but each one seemed concentrated on the ARVN lines on the southwest perimeters (which Lownds regarded as an obvious weak point), and each was destroyed with artillery and air bombardment.[288]

The various air components continued to take advantage of the improved weather. As the month wore on, NVA activity declined and the tone of the propaganda being delivered to the local population changed, now indicating the NVA were no longer interested in wasting their time on only 6,000 Marines.[289] On 21 March, Colonel Lownds decided to investigate what had happened to the enemy, and a platoon from B/1/9 was sent out, supported by more than 1,300 rounds of artillery. Combined with close air support, this provided the company with a continuous shield of destructive fire. The only sign of the enemy was a few mortar rounds that were fired at the patrol, which were quickly silenced by supporting arms.[290]

That same night, there were indications that

the enemy was massing for attack once again, and one of the ammunition supply points on the combat base was again hit during a heavy bombardment. The assault, however, never materialized, and the enemy activity rapidly faded with the arrival of an AC-47 gunship.[291] In a final act of defiance, the NVA delivered an uncharacteristically heavy bombardment the next day—more than 1,000 rounds—but never again gave indications that they were preparing to attack.

Recognizing that they might be able to gain the initiative, the Marines began to plan their first offensive ground operation since the siege began. A company-sized patrol stepped off on the morning of 30 March. Fog and low ceilings prevented the use of aviation support, but more than 2,600 artillery rounds were fired by noon in support of the attack. The enemy was waiting for the Marines to come out, and brought them under heavy fire. The company commander was unable to back off and employ supporting arms to reduce the enemy resistance as was the Marine fashion, because his men were filled with such a blood lust he could not hold them back from close combat with the NVA. For many of the Marines, these were the first enemy they had actually laid eyes on since the siege began. After returning to KSCB, the Marines ultimately claimed a total of 115 dead NVA at a cost of 9 Marines killed, 71 wounded, and 3 missing.[292] As the enemy withdrew in the following days, it became obvious that siege had ended, but the operation would not be declared officially over until the Marines had been "rescued" by the Army.

Was Khe Sanh Ever Really Under Siege?

Typical of the men at Khe Sanh were the experiences of I/3/26 on the important outpost of Hill 881S. Commanded by Captain Bill Dabney, this unit was probed and invested, but never subjected to any serious assault by the NVA. Daily bombardment and harassing sniper fire, on the other hand, inflicted nearly a 100 percent casu-

Gunnery Sergeant R.L. DeArmond of I Company, 3d Battalion, 26th Marines on Hill 881S, at the start of April. The westernmost outpost on Hill 881S was so isolated and hard to resupply by air that the Marines were permitted to stop shaving in order to conserve water.

alty rate from 21 January to 1 April 1968.[293] Air power was a vital component to the defense of Dabney's position, more than 300 CAS missions having been controlled by the Marines on the hill. Despite all of this, Captain Dabney was clear in his conclusion that Khe Sanh and its outposts were never really under siege. Since the Marines were able to reinforce and resupply themselves with regularity, and could have withdrawn at any time they desired, Dabney concluded that they were surrounded, but were not besieged.[294] The notion that Khe Sanh was never under siege was also advanced by Defense Intelligence Agency analysts at the time of the battle,[295] and by some very informed veterans and historians after the battle. Lieutenant General Krulak wrote that although the appearance of a siege had some political advantages for General Vo Nguyen Giap, in an operational sense, "Khe Sanh cannot have meant more to Giap than a convenient mechanism for drawing the Americans away from the populated coastal area."[296] He added, "the North Vietnamese had no intention of undertaking an all-out assault on the base.... Instead, during the Tet period they elected just to hold at Khe Sanh, keeping pressure on its hill outposts and shelling the base proper, while putting their prime offensive effort on the coastal cities."[297] Edward F. Murphy, a historian of Marine operations in the Vietnam War, described the NVA operation at Khe Sanh as a "feint."[298] Elaborating on this idea, Vietnam veteran and historian Lieutenant General Dave R. Palmer went so far as to say General Giap "never had any intention of capturing Khe Sanh. His purpose there all along had been to divert Westmoreland's attention and resources. Khe Sanh was a feint, a diversionary effort."[299] Such revisionist interpretations suggest that the NVA never did commit 20,000 men in a deliberate attack on Khe Sanh, but instead sought only to commit the minimum forces necessary to present the appearance of a siege. The true NVA goal, under this theory, was to draw combat power away from the coastal plains, and distract MACV's attention during the Tet Offensive. If one accepts that this was the North Vietnamese goal, the longer Khe Sanh remained in American hands, the longer it served its purpose for the NVA.

Dabney stated that Khe Sanh was not considered a siege at the time, and the word was not used until after the battle was over.[300] This may have been true on his outpost, but it was certainly not true for the men who fought the battle, and the press that was following it. Both sides were attracted by the analogy between Khe Sanh and Dien Bien Phu, and the word "siege" was a frequent part of their exchange on the subject. The average Marine at Khe Sanh, for example, was not nearly as thoughtful as Dabney on the subject. These Marines knew they were surrounded by an enemy who apparently wanted to get into the combat base, who was trying hard to sever their air logistics bridge, and who was keeping them penned inside.

The issue of NVA intent may never be known with a high degree of accuracy, but most sources suggest that the North Vietnamese would have taken Khe Sanh if significant resistance had not been encountered. The official NVA history of the war as translated by Merle L. Pribbenow discusses the strategic goal of tying down mobile forces at Khe Sanh that would otherwise be used to suppress the general uprising in the Tet Offensive, but pairs it with another goal of annihilating large numbers of U.S. troops in the highlands. It notes that the NVA was very successful in the first mission, but that its preparations were inadequate and U.S. air power too strong to permit the North Vietnamese to engage the defenders of Khe Sanh in a large battle for a decisive victory.[301] This general assessment is corroborated by several other official NVA sources.

It is true that the NVA viewed Khe Sanh as part of a much larger battlefield than the Americans typically described it. In June 1966, they established a new strategic area for their war effort, the Route 9 Front, which stretched along the entire northern portion of the ICTZ. The original strategic objective of this front was to force their enemies to disperse into the mountainous regions where the NVA could attrite them, and in the process relieve some of the pressure being applied against the insurgency in the populated lowlands.[302] The NVA were successful in attracting attention and drawing Marine forces in the ICTZ westward. The increased contact that resulted from Operations Hastings and Prairie in 1966, incidentally, was part of what led Westmoreland to push the Marines to begin using infantry battalions to patrol from the reconnaissance base at Khe Sanh that same year. Pleased with its success in enticing forces westward, in December 1967 the NVA issued new instructions for the front, now under the direction of a new headquarters known as B5-T8, located just west of the border in Laos. In the context of moving the war into a new phase, the Tet Offensive, the specific mission for the command was "to eliminate a large number of American and South Vietnamese personnel, primarily Americans if the conditions presented themselves, destroy a part of the enemy's defensive line on Highway 9, and to continue into other areas around Tri-Thien Hue, to draw in American and South Vietnamese forces from other battlefields."[303] While the relative priorities of these objectives may seem somewhat open to interpretation, the plan also included a quota to eliminate at least 20,000 enemy troops (primarily American), and specified that it should draw in two American divisions and the better part of a South Vietnamese division.[304]

The NVA divided the Highway 9 front into two battlefields, east and west. The western one around Khe Sanh was designated the focus of effort, committing two of the three divisions at the NVA's disposal, the 304 and the 325C Divisions (which had begun operating in the area in 1967). The Joint High Command then ordered attacks to begin approximately one week prior to the first day of Tet with the specific intent of creating a timely diversion of forces from the rest of South Vietnam.[305] The NVA built some flexibility into their plan so that if too much resistance was experienced at Khe Sanh, or the small-scale attacks in the east on targets like Cam Lo produced unexpected success, the priority of effort could be shifted eastward.[306]

While the credibility of these official histories with respect to intent may be suspect, the deployment of forces to execute such a plan is confirmed by NVA logistics documents. These show that there were indeed two divisions committed to the region around Khe Sanh, and that there was at least one more division providing support from Laos. These documents also show that the NVA presence peaked in mid-February, and began a steady decline in early March,[307] just as U.S. intelligence sources perceived at the time. Approximately half of the NVA combat power on the Route 9 front was invested in the attack on Khe Sanh, totaling as many as 29,000 soldiers in February (not including rear service personnel). They were supported by almost 300 heavy mortars, artillery pieces, and rocket launchers, and almost 200 antiaircraft artillery pieces.[308]

The operational plan for B5-T8 at Khe Sanh was to eliminate the outlying positions around the combat base, and then surround KSCB itself and cut off its source of supply. This would either lure in a relief force which could be ambushed in its counterattack, or force the 26th Marines to attempt a break-out, where they could then be destroyed outside their fortifications.[309]

According to NVA histories on the battle, the North Vietnamese never intended to launch a protracted siege of Khe Sanh Combat Base, gradually reducing the defenses until KSCB was forced to capitulate. They instead describe that "Attacking the enemy outside their fortification was primary, attacking the enemy when within their fortifications when necessary and victory was certain."[310] This reveals that a protracted and costly siege was clearly something the NVA wanted to avoid. These sources further stress that "it was imperative to stop supplies [from reaching Khe Sanh] in order to draw the enemy in; if conditions were favorable, then liberate Khe Sanh,"[311] clearly showing that capture of the combat base itself was not a primary operational objective, although it might be a positive by-product within reach if the rest of the plan allowed them to destroy the preponderance of

U.S. forces sent to protect or relieve and Khe Sanh.

The histories indicate that the seizure of the actual combat base was only a secondary objective, but this distinction was lost to the NVA troops. The NVA histories admit that their soldiers, like many Americans, began comparing Khe Sanh to Dien Bien Phu, which is no surprise since participation in that victory was probably the proudest moment in the 304 Division's history. While the NVA command examined the historical analogy more critically, recognized the American advantages, and determined that even an encirclement without a deliberate siege would be a difficult mission to accomplish,[312] the point is moot. Whether or not the NVA intended to conduct a sustained deliberate siege or merely a diversion for Tet, there is no doubt that the NVA intended to destroy large numbers of American troops, they invested an immense amount of manpower and firepower for that objective, and would have accomplished their goal, potentially including the capture of Khe Sanh, if the Americans had not resisted so fiercely. Such a strategic victory with the echoes of Dien Bien Phu could have had a decisive effect on the war, especially if it occurred simultaneous with the Tet Offensive.

Some revisionist North Vietnamese accounts attempt to obscure the matter, since no such victory was obtained. The NVA history on the campaign written in 1987 states,

> the Highway 9 Khe Sanh Offensive ended in victory, completing the mission the High Command had assigned: eliminating and capturing many of the enemy forces (primarily the Americans), destroying much war material; destroying a large section of the enemy's defensive line to the west of Highway 9; and in particular drawing in and tying down an important force and a large quantity of aircraft ordnance of the Americans into the Highway 9 Khe Sanh area over a protracted period of time, creating conditions that were favorable for the entire battlefield in south Vietnam first of all for (support of) the attack against the enemy in Tri-Thien-Hue.[313]

This assessment is far from accurate. While the capture of Lang Vei and the approximately 3,000 casualties inflicted at KSCB and its outposts may have been significant compared to other NVA victories in the war against the Americans, the losses were a small portion of the American force committed and fell far short of the quota to eliminate 20,000 of the enemy. While the defense of KSCB did occupy a reinforced regiment of Marines and a substantial amount of combat power in logistics, artillery, and attack aviation, none of these assets would have been decisive in other parts of South Vietnam, where the Tet Offensive failed in its operational objectives anyway. To say that this campaign was especially beneficial for the attacks in the eastern portion of the Route 9 Front also involves some questionable logic; these were considered smaller, secondary attacks, and were quickly defeated except for the stubborn resistance at Hue. The NVA certainly did not succeed in drawing in almost three American and South Vietnamese divisions, as they planned. The force sent to relieve Khe Sanh, built around the 1st Air Cavalry Division, was not sent until April, when any danger of Tet was well over and the preponderance of NVA forces had already been withdrawn from the area around Khe Sanh.

The question remains, then, why did the NVA retire in mid-March without accomplishing their objectives—because they had been beaten back in a severe pounding by American air power, or because the Americans held out and did not expose a large mobile relief force, making the NVA encirclement pointless? Only 1,288 NVA bodies were reported as visually confirmed killed by air (KBA) over the course of the operation, but this does not mean that many more were not killed.

Considering the range from the static Marine defenses at which many air attacks occurred, and the awesome destructive potential of the B-52, there was no definite way to observe and quantify the effectiveness of Operation Niagara. In order to measure the effectiveness of air power, the Americans unfortunately resorted to the questionable assumption that ordnance expended and secondary explosions observed was proportional to the damage inflicted upon the enemy. MACV's evaluation section applied three different mathematical models to ordnance expenditure reports, secondary explosion observations, and estimated enemy concentrations to deduce the number of NVA killed. The final tally estimated that 28,900 NVA soldiers had been killed or sustained injuries serious enough to make them combat ineffective. The report admitted that this was nearly twice the number of NVA believed to be in the region in the first place, but explained that the NVA had been able to partially replace their losses.[314] Since these calculations told them that many NVA had been destroyed, it was logical for Westmoreland and many others to conclude that the air power they had massed for the battle had been decisive. This conclusion led to numerous triumphalist claims in the years after the battle that two divisions of the NVA had obligingly presented themselves for destruction by air power at Khe Sanh, just as the Americans designed.

Regardless of what the Americans believed had happened, the NVA unit histories show that even if capture of the combat base in a siege was not the primary goal, American air power had a large impact on their decision making. The first phase of the battle was designed to eliminate the western outposts and open Route 9 to larger forces, which could then move in and surround KSCB, to both isolate the base and lay in wait to ambush any counterattacks. This phase began with the assaults on the night of 20-21 January, but by noon of that next day, the assault elements of the 304 Division were withdrawn after suffering heavy casualties in air strikes.[315] When after three days the Americans proved unwilling to expose themselves in a counterattack, the NVA leadership decided to capture Lang Vei, more completely surrounding Khe Sanh and hopefully provoking a response. This task was completed on 7 February,[316] but in the process of concentrating their forces for this effort the NVA again suffered heavy casualties. One battalion of the 304 Division was devastated by B-52 strikes on 6 February. Even the triumphalist NVA account admits inflicted nearly 200 casualties and caused such severe morale problems (manifest in desertion and self-inflicted wounds to avoid combat) that the parent command doubted the battalion could be used again.[317]

With Route 9 open, the NVA were able to move on to Phase II, the close encirclement of the combat base. This phase began on 10 February, with the NVA committing the bulk of its forces to the main effort of isolating KSCB and cutting its vital air bridge, while smaller units were deployed around the American outposts on Hill 881S and Hill 861. It was during this phase that the battle most resembled a siege for the NVA. They settled into more static positions and dug trenches toward KSCB, and organized several assaults that were unsuccessful.[318] As they suffered severe losses to American supporting arms, many frustrated NVA soldiers came to forget that their true objective was not the capitulation of the combat base. The 304 Division's official history stated,

"The morale of the cadre and troops of the Division during this period of time began to exhibit condition [sic] that were based on practical situations created on the battlefield. The troops felt that we had the ability to liberate Khe Sanh so why did the higher command not order an attack? Why continue an encirclement day after day and permit the enemy artillery and airstrikes to cause mounting casualties? …we were in control of the battlefield, and if the higher command ordered an attack to overrun Khe Sanh, we could do it. There were those who asked the question:"Who knows how much longer the higher headquarters will wait before giving as a gift to Johnson a Dien Bien Phu in Khe Sanh?"[319]

Even as the political cadre reminded their men that their mission was actually to draw in as many Americans as possible, NVA leaders had already come to the realization that they could not sustain the same level of combat effort, and had ordered the withdrawal of the 325C Division to be refit and redeployed to the central highlands.[320]

The casualty statistics in the NVA histories support the analysis that the NVA were suffering too heavily for the payoff they were receiving. They show that by the time the 325 Division left the area on 7 March, it had sustained 15.27 percent casualties. The 304 Division, which remained at Khe Sanh for the duration, suffered more than 38 percent casualties.[321] NVA casualty reports confirm this, showing that the collective forces near Khe Sanh sustained 33 percent casualties during this period.[322] Of note, according to the NVA the majority of these casualties were inflicted by air power. In the 304 Division, 59 percent of combat casualties came from bombs. One of its regiments, which sustained only 37.8 percent casualties from air strikes during mobile operations, saw that percentage rise to 62.3 percent during the encirclement.[323] Interrogations and captured NVA documents from the battle showed that they feared American air power above all else.[324]

The NVA were ready to call Phase II complete by March 31st. Although their official history suggests a high degree of satisfaction with "Phase III—Attacking the Enemy Relieving the Siege (1 April to 7 May 1968),"[325] it should be noted that the relief effort was begun by the Americans only when NVA movements indicated that they had lost interest in the siege. When that relief effort began, the NVA no longer had sufficient forces in the area to destroy an American counterattack, as they originally planned.

While it may never be known with certainty if the NVA intended to conduct a sustained, deliberate siege with the intent of forcing Khe Sanh to capitulate, and were therefore defeated by air power, at the time the Americans had every reason to believe that another Dien Bien Phu was being attempted. The political stakes for both sides were just as high, and the intensity of the bombardments and antiaircraft fire attempting to sever the air bridge left little room to underestimate the enemy effort. Even Lieutenant General Krulak, who warned Westmoreland that nothing would be gained by holding the base, and who afterwards described the NVA attack as a diversion, admits to calling it a siege at the time.[326] The defenders of Khe Sanh fought the battle as a siege, preparing for an imminent assault, and seeking only to survive inside the base, while aviators and artillerymen searched for and attacked the enemy. The NVA were foiled in many, if not all, of their objectives because the American plan did not play to NVA strengths as the enemy had hoped. The NVA plan, meanwhile, did play to American strengths, just as Westmoreland had hoped, and as a result large numbers of NVA died, and the defenders of Khe Sanh were safe. Even if conservatism requires that the terms "siege" and "victory" be avoided when describing the outcome of this battle for the Americans, despite revisionist claims, the NVA were indeed defeated. NVA plans were foiled by the Marines' ability to remain in a sanctuary and suspend mobile operations until enemy forces in the area had been significantly reduced. Air power was the key element in destroying enemy forces and convincing them to withdraw before they had obtained their objectives.

OPERATION PEGASUS AND THE RELIEF OF KHE SANH

Preparations for the relief of Khe Sanh had begun only days after the siege was finally initiated, on 25 January 1968. Westmoreland had sought the battle as a means of introducing more combat troops to the area, and must have been relieved that the NVA had decided to take the bait and present themselves for destruction by air power. The relief operation, code-named Pegasus, was designed to capitalize on the imminent destruction of the main NVA combat divisions around Khe Sanh by sweeping through the area with mobile forces to destroy what NVA remained. The planning for this operation, however, had to be put on hold when the Tet Offensive erupted just a few days later on 30 January. The MACV staff was soon consumed with fighting that battle, and forces which had been moved north to establish new firebases for offensive operations in the northern ICTZ were diverted to the more immediate task at hand. By 16 February, with Tet under control, planning resumed for the follow-through at Khe Sanh.[327]

As has already been shown, by the second week in March Westmoreland decided that the enemy had "given up, his attempted repeat of Dienbienphu an abject failure."[328] On 10 March, COMUSMACV convened a conference in Phu Bai where he made a number of fundamental changes to facilitate not only an operation to clean up the NVA around Khe Sanh, but also to set the stage for his planned follow-through into Laos. The first thing he did was to reorganize the major combat units in I Corps to increase the Army's supervisory role in this key area of operations. Where the 3d Marine Division had formerly run the war along the DMZ, answering directly to III MAF, Westmoreland now took the MACV(FWD) headquarters he had sent earlier in the battle and converted it to a new organization to run the war in Quang Tri province and most of Thua Thien for III MAF. This headquarters, known as Provisional Corps Vietnam (PCV), was to be commanded by Lieutenant General William B. Rosson and had three major ground combat units: the 3d Marine Division, and the Army's 1st Air Cavalry and 101st Airborne Divisions.

Westmoreland explained the move by stating merely, "In essence, PCV was established to provide closer supervision over the growing U.S. forces and combination with the Vietnamese forces in the northern area."[329] In view of his dissatisfaction with General Cushman before the siege began, and his continued frustration with 1st MAW in the single management controversy, however, it is not surprising that MACV inserted an Army general as the immediate commander of the northern war effort. Despite this, Cushman kept his hands in the pie, for the operation contained more Marines than soldiers, and depended on the Marines more heavily than the air cavalry, for whom Operation Pegasus was named.[331] Cushman and Westmoreland immediately agreed that opening Route 9 should be the priority for this new unit so that Khe Sanh was no longer dependent on air logistics, and Westmoreland set a target date of April 1st for the operation to begin.[331] To call Pegasus a relief operation, then, is incorrect, because planning was not even completed and the operation was not scheduled to start until after Westmoreland and his staff had decided that the battle had been won.

Westmoreland made two other key decisions on 10 March. He decided to overrule the objections of the Marines and implement Momyer's plan for the centralization of air control by designating the 7th Air Force as the single management authority for air operations.[332] It will be shown that this decision had little effect on the battle because it was not fully implemented for several more weeks (by which time the NVA effort had declined even further), because the Marines figured out ways to circumvent direct Air Force control, and because the system that was implemented contained key compromises. The other decisive action Westmoreland took that day

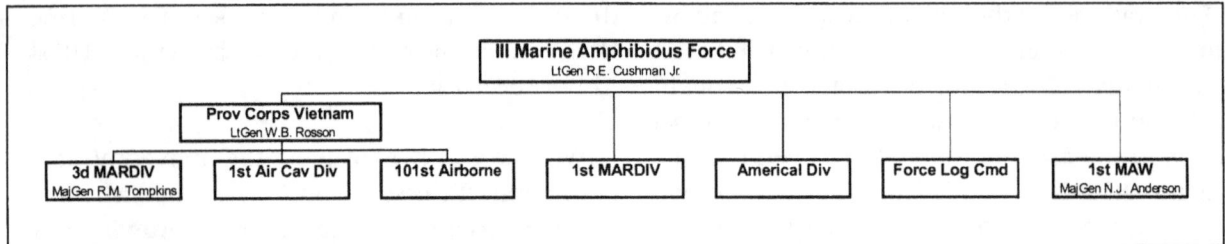

Figure 5. Command relationships between major units and headquarters of the I Corps Tactical Zone during (and after) Operation Pegasus

was to request 206,000 more troops from President Johnson to win the war. Putting this request in the context of the other decisions indicates even more clearly MACV's viewpoint that victory at Khe Sanh had allowed him to "turn a corner" in the war. Unfortunately for Westmoreland, the request was perceived somewhat differently by President Johnson, who eight days later finally announced that Westmoreland would finally be coming home to the United States.[333]

Operation Pegasus was initiated on 1 April, as Westmoreland had directed. The westward attack to reopen Route 9 and clear the NVA from the region around Khe Sanh began from forward bases set up near Camp Carroll, the Rockpile, and Ca Lu, where the 1st Air Cavalry could rapidly spring westward in heliborne assaults. For six days before the attack began, one squadron of the Air Cavalry roamed up and down Route 9 by air, looking for any signs of NVA activity that could be located and hit with artillery, tactical aircraft, or one of the 10 B-52 strikes that had been set aside for daily support.[334] On 1 April, the main ground force, the 1st Marine Regiment, advanced westward along Route 9, supported by elements of the 1st ARVN Division. The 2d Squadron of the 7th Air Cavalry Regiment (2/7 Cav) conducted supporting heliborne attacks into numerous landing zones paralleling the Marines' westward advance in what was the largest combined U.S.-South Vietnamese offensive of the northern provinces during the entire war.[335] From the start, poor weather restricted the effectiveness of tactical aviation, since on most days the weather did not even improve to the basic helicopter flight requirements of 500-foot ceilings and 1-1/2 miles visibility until the afternoon.[336] Fortunately, enemy resistance was light, since only the 304th Division remained in the area, covering the withdrawal of the other NVA units. The NVA force now consisted of approximately 12 battalions, but they either could not, or chose not to coordinate anything larger than company-sized operations.[337] As the 2/7 Cav approached Khe Sanh, it used its air mobility to spearhead the final attack, reaching the perimeter on 7 April, but by then the enemy was essentially gone. If there had been a siege, it had been long over. As Captain Dick Camp, a Khe Sanh veteran who had the added perspective of serving as the division commander's aide during Pegasus, put it, "the Army's 1st Cavalry Division claims it broke the siege by throwing numerous aggressive airmobile assaults into the hills overlooking the combat base. In reality, the enemy broke the siege by leaving."[338]

The NVA departure was expedited by the activity of the 26th Marines, which had technically also been transferred into Operation Pegasus by the operation order. The Marines were anxious most of all to seize the initiative and settle some scores. They also wanted to avoid the appearance that they would be rescued by the Army, a misconception that is reinforced even today not only by Army veterans, but also by Marines who insist on calling the NVA effort at Khe Sanh a siege. General Cushman ordered the Marines to take the offense, later explaining, "The situation warranted it, in that the enemy was defeated and had begun to pull out. I therefore wanted no implication of a rescue force or breaking of the siege by outside forces."[339]

On 4 April, three days before the arrival of the 2/7 Air Cav, 1/9 attacked southward to seize Hill 471, which turned out to hold one of the last pockets of enemy resistance. The attack was halted until after an air and artillery bombardment softened the defenses. G/2/26 attacked toward Hill 558 on 6 and 7 April, and met similar results. The artillery and air preparation took two full days to achieve the desired effects due the limited availability of aircraft and constant check fires for helicopters interfering with artillery missions. Both of these problems were likely the result of the final approach of the 2/7 Air Cav, whose high density air operations must have wrought havoc with the already saturated airspace and fire support coordination system at Khe Sanh. After two days of air and artillery preparation, the Marines' outward attack was resumed on 10 April. The NVA that remained rapidly withdrew.[340]

As the "relief" forces of Operation Pegasus advanced westward and reached Khe Sanh with little resistance, General Rosson apparently decided that there was little reason to waste any more time there. Even though Route 9 was not to be successfully opened until 12 April, air support was rapidly reduced, as shown in Figure 6. Only 45 Arc Light strikes and a total of 1,625 tactical aircraft sorties were devoted to support the operation because Rosson saw additional effort as a waste and wanted to open a new offensive to seek out any NVA that might be hiding in the A Shau valley to the south.[341] General Cushman supported this idea, wanting to keep the enemy off balance,[342] and Westmoreland was won over on 10 April. As a result, when Operation Pegasus came to an end on 15 April, the 26th Marines were continuing to find pockets of NVA in the region around Khe Sanh, and control of the region was never entirely regained from the enemy.[343]

Khe Sanh After Operation Pegasus

When Operation Pegasus ended, the final tally was 1,304 NVA killed at the expense of 125 U.S. and ARVN killed, 853 wounded, and 5 missing.[344] With such numbers Westmoreland could claim that his victory had been complete, but the question remained about what activity the U.S. would pursue in the region. Westmoreland clearly saw opportunities to use the base for future operations against the NVA sanctuary in Laos, as he had originally planned long before the siege ever began. President Johnson's 23 March announcement that Westmoreland's time as COMUSMACV would soon be over, however, doomed this vision, as his subordinates began to take more active roles in planning. General Cushman, for example, saw

Figure 6. Daily attack sorties devoted to operations around Khe Sanh, by service and type.

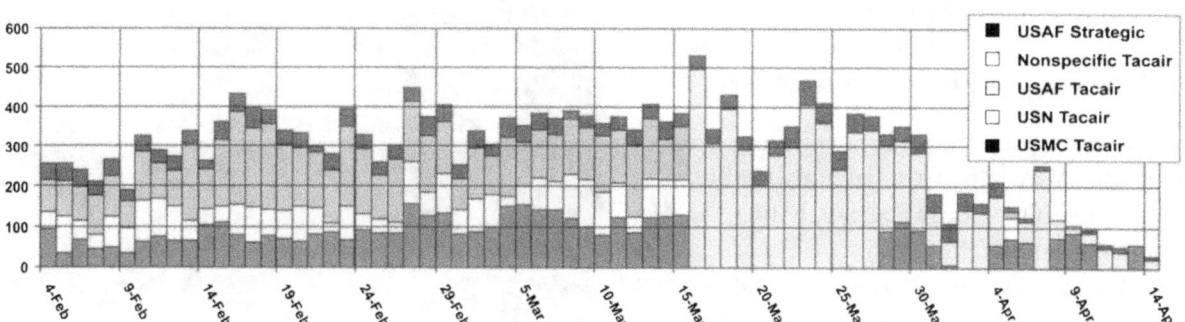

this as an opportunity to withdraw his Marines from the vulnerable outpost, the same course of action he had argued for before the battle ever took place. At Cushman's urging, Ca Lu became the main base of operations in northwest Quang Tri province, which was more suitable because it was out of range of the NVA artillery in Laos, was closer to the coast bases, and was not subject to the horrible crachin weather which had limited air support so much at Khe Sanh. Although Khe Sanh was no longer the main outpost, however, Westmoreland refused to completely close the combat base while he was in charge of MACV.[345] Among other things, Westmoreland did not want the American citizens wondering exactly why so many lives had been lost to hold Khe Sanh, only to surrender the outpost at the end of the battle anyway. As a result, approximately 1,000 Marines continued to operate out of Khe Sanh as their main base of operations in the highland region for the next several months, until Westmorland finally turned over command of MACV to his deputy, General Creighton Abrams, on 11 June. The very next day, Abrams ordered the combat base to be abandoned and destroyed to prevent its use by the enemy. His motivation may have been his desire to switch to a more mobile defense of the region that retained the initiative, a move that was now possible because of the increased numbers of army troops in the ICTZ to assist the Marines. He may also, however, been influenced by a March visit to Washington, D.C.[346] Coincident with Westmoreland's exasperating request to President Johnson for more troops, and Johnson's negotiations with the North Vietnamese at Paris, the visit must have made it clear that an expansion of the war into Laos was very unlikely.[347]

In the meantime, the task of finding and attacking the NVA left in the region by the early conclusion of Operation Pegasus fell to the Marines. Even in the final days of Pegasus, they were engaging in some hard-fought battles, but the waning COMUSMACV interest in the region was causing some problems. As Figure 6 shows, Westmoreland's conclusion that the enemy had been beaten at Khe Sanh meant that the Marines suffered from a considerable decrease in air support. 7th Air Force, the new centralized air management agency, was looking for other decisive points to concentrate air power, and the Marines would now have to depend solely on the support of the 1st Marine Air Wing. The attack they launched on Hill 881N on April 14th was a test of the Marine air-ground team under the new limitations of the new single management plan.

Hill 881 North had been an enemy stronghold for a long time. It was the place where the Marines met the fiercest resistance during the Hill Fights on 1967, it was the place where the Marines of I/3/26 were engaged in a bitter battle on 20 January 1968, only to be recalled to 881S as the siege began, and it was the place from which the NVA had launched so many rockets and assaults on the other outposts over the course of the siege. On 10 April, the rest of 3/26 moved to Hill 881S to reinforce India Company, which had held the hill for the duration of the siege. The battalion began patrolling, and discovered a huge network of abandoned NVA trenches that came as close as 300 meters to the Marine perimeter.[348] Khe Sanh could never be secured until 881N had been cleared of the enemy, so the Marines

A convoy heading to Khe Sanh after Route 9 was finally opened on 12 April. The road had been closed for more than eight months.

of 3/26 set out with the goal of killing as many NVA as they could to discourage any continued presence. Expecting that the enemy would seek close engagements to deny the Americans the standoff needed to employ their heavy firepower, the battalion planned for the Marines to avoid entangling engagements, and withdraw once contact was established so that air and artillery could be brought to bear.[349]

As another test of the Marine air-ground team under the limitations of single air management, the attack was a great success. After two hours of air and artillery preparation, enemy resistance was relatively weak, and as the Marines attacked, the NVA abandoned their primary fighting positions. An NVA force estimated to be a company-sized element attempted to make a stand at its secondary defensive positions, but it was again hit by a combination of air support, artillery, and recoilless rifle fire. The enemy retreated, but was subjected to a pursuit by fire, under constant harassment of artillery and air attacks that prevented any possibility of counterattack. Ultimately the Marines recorded 106 NVA dead at a cost of 6 Marines killed and 32 wounded. The following day, Pegasus was officially terminated and the 26th Marines was replaced at Khe Sanh by the 1st Marines. 3/26 abandoned Hill 881N, having accomplished its mission of driving the enemy from that area.[350]

With the official end of Operation Pegasus on 15 April, the Marines still had plenty of work to do. To begin with, the NVA had withdrawn from contact, but maintained some interest in Khe Sanh. That very day, for example, the base was bombarded by 306 NVA rounds.[351] The 1st Marines, who had marched westward to open Route 9 before taking responsibility for KSCB, now held operational control of six infantry battalions, two of which were veterans of the recent siege (1/9 and 2/26). The operation was named Scotland II, emphasizing that the goal was merely to continue the destruction of NVA around Khe Sanh, which had brought the 26th Marines to Khe Sanh in the first place under Operation Scotland. In the sequel offensive, the Marines mopped up enemy forces with mobile and flexible forces using a maximum of artillery, air, and other supporting fires.[352]

In this effort, Khe Sanh ceased to serve as a true combat base. On 5 May, the logistic pipeline which ended at Khe Sanh was closed down. As a result, all support came from Ca Lu either by helicopter delivery directly to the supported unit, or overland along Route 9. The NVA force quickly recognized this vulnerability and began to increase its activity along the tortuous overland road, with company-sized ambushes and larger attacks beginning 14 May. Many of these were broken only with the heavy mobile fire support of Marine CAS.[353]

At the end of May, III MAF intelligence confirmed what was becoming apparent to the Marines around Khe Sanh: two regiments of the fresh 308th Division had infiltrated into the region to fill the vacuum created by departing American units. The NVA leaders were so interested in large-scale operations that they even ordered a new road built, entering Quang Tri province from Laos. Fifteen kilometers south of Route 9, it ran a parallel track from the west to allow the NVA to feed forces into the region, even as the Marines advanced from the east.[354] Under Scotland II, the Marines were having a hard time keeping the enemy at bay, but close air support was an important part of what success they enjoyed.

The 4th Marines arrived to join the 1st Marines in Operation Robin, countering the enemy buildup in a drive to clear the NVA from the jungles south of Khe Sanh. Air support remained an important part of this strategy. When Robin was initiated on 2 June, it had been preceded by 219 tactical air sorties and 30 B-52 sorties targeted on the NVA control nodes, dumps, and troop concentrations. Air support was also critical in stopping at least one battalion counterattack.[355]

The end came rapidly once Westmoreland was finally relieved as COMUSMACV to assume duties in Washington as the Chief of Staff, U.S. Army on 11 June. The next day, III MAF headquarters published a new concept of operations which included Abrams' and Cushman's plan for abandoning Khe Sanh in favor of mobile operations.[356] One week after assuming command of MACV, General Abrams ordered Operation Charlie to finally evacuate and destroy the combat base.[357] Ideally, the Americans sought to depart without revealing their intent to the NVA, and without leaving the American people wondering why they had fought such a bitter battle to hold a combat base which was abandoned a short while later. Once planning began, however, the word soon got out, and the press, already hypersensitive about any issue relating to Khe Sanh, was quick to publish the information. The story broke in the *Baltimore Sun* on 1 July. Fortunately for the Marines, as 1/3/4 began dismantling the combat base, artillery and tactical jets were able to prevent the NVA from succeeding in an attempt to block the withdrawal. The last Marine unit withdrew from Khe Sanh by helicopter on 11 July.[358]

The operations conducted around Khe Sanh from 1 April to 11 July 1968 are important not only because they reveal much about the thinking of top leaders on both sides of the battle, but also because they demonstrated the continued value of close air support. In the dynamic situation of maneuvering ground forces, the Marines were supported primarily by Marine aviators, and there were no failed attacks due to air support. Even when the 7th Air Force substantially reduced its commitment and held unprecedented control over Marine aircraft as a result of the single management decision, the Marine air-ground team continued to operate under its

A Marine of the 3d Battalion, 4th Marines looks out at the empty runway after the combat base was dismantled. Since there was no longer a need to make repairs to the runway surface at the deserted base, the effects of NVA bombardment can still be seen.

doctrine of close cooperation, and continued to enjoy excellent results.

Control of Air Support Operations at Khe Sanh

Before taking a more detailed look at the contributions the various services made to the battle of Khe Sanh, it is important to understand the means by which air support was targeted at the enemy, and controlled in its attacks. The two institutional approaches to air warfare each produced different command and control arrangements, and created an enormous amount of interservice conflict, which reached its culminating point even as the 1968 battle of Khe Sanh was being fought. Because this conflict revolved around the 7th Air Force's attempt to unify both Air Force and Marine fixed-wing aviation assets in Vietnam under one command and control system, it became known as the single management controversy.

The Single Management Controversy

For all operations in the ICTZ in 1967, the primary air control system was the Marine Air Com-

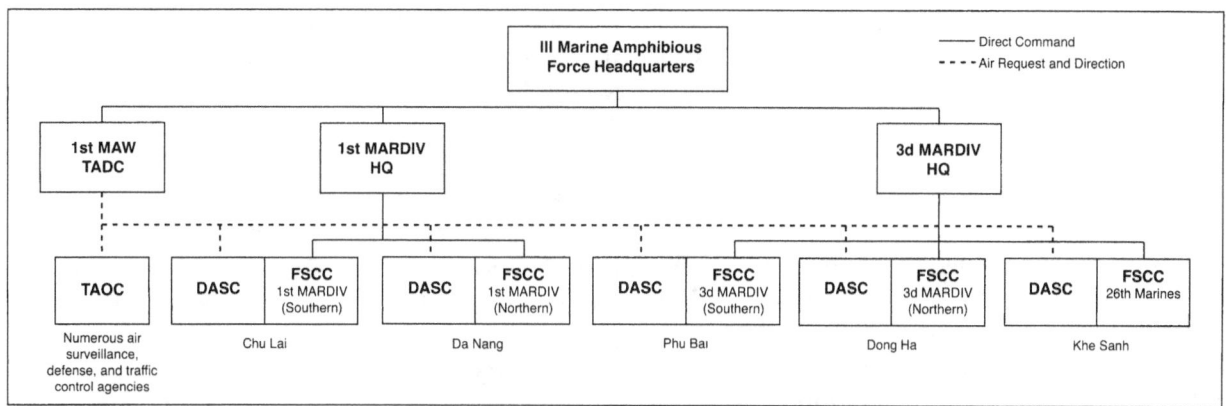

Figure 7. Interface between the Marine Air Command and Control System agencies of the 1st Marine Air Wing and its supported units (1st and 3d Marine Divisions).

mand and Control System (MACCS) provided by the 1st MAW. The highest echelon of this system was the Tactical Air Direction Center (TADC), located at the Wing Headquarters in Da Nang. This organization was responsible for forming and writing the plans for future operations, as well as the production of the daily air tasking order (ATO) and supervision of its execution. In charge of various command and control detachments to provide air defense, radar surveillance, and air traffic control was the Tactical Air Operations Center (TAOC). Of more direct relevance to the support of ground forces were the five Direct Air Support Centers (DASCs) of 1st MAW. These organizations served as the primary links between the ground units and the aircraft which supported them. Generally, they were collocated with the Fire Support Coordination Centers (FSCCs), the ground units' nerve centers for artillery, mortar, and air support. The DASCs processed requests for air support from the various ground units, and passed them up the MACCS system, ensuring that they were prioritized by the FSCCs. When these requests finally reached the TADC, they were "fragged" to the various supporting aircraft units. This was first done informally in a warning order, called a "frag" order because it was based on partial, or fragmentary, information. The frag order was disseminated the night before the mission was to be flown, to give the various squadrons time to anticipate their tasking for the next day. Overnight, the "frag" was formalized in an Air Tasking Order (ATO), which would include all of the details of the mission, including call signs, numbers and types of aircraft, on-station times, ordnance to be carried, and ground unit to be supported. The ATO was published daily, taking effect each morning, and incorporating requests for air support made just 11 hours earlier. More immediate requests for support were serviced by sorties kept in reserve for that purpose, known as alerts. Unlike the Air Force system, which

The interior of a Marine Direct Air Support Center in Vietnam. Each board on the wall was used to track the sorties devoted to a particular mission area. The mission numbers, call signs, aircraft types, and mission times were noted with grease pen to allow the seated controllers to monitor and direct each mission. The fixed-wing CAS flights were recorded on the two boards to the right.

managed only fixed-wing flights, the Marine ATO included all Marine fixed-wing and rotary-wing flights for each day.

Once the TADC published the ATO, each squadron was responsible for making sure its aircraft got airborne with the specified ordnance on time. After departing the airfield and being routed to his tactical operating area by the air traffic control units of the TAOC, the mission commander established radio contact with the DASC of the unit he was tasked to support. The DASC then provided both updated mission information, and deconflicted the flight path of that aircraft from the other aircraft, artillery fires, and mortar missions in that area. Finally, the DASC put the aircraft in contact with a forward air controller, either on the ground or in an observation aircraft, who assisted the attacking aircraft with delivering its ordnance at the time and place most critical to the supported ground unit's operations.

All the airspace above III MAF's ground area of operations was controlled by a DASC, facilitating

Two Marines maintain the communications cables at a DASC work station. As the primary interface between the Marine Corps' air and ground forces, the DASC required an extensive communications capability.

the delivery of air support anywhere within the ICTZ. In southern I Corps, there was a DASC collocated with both the 1st MAW headquarters and 1st Marine Division Headquarters at Da Nang. The southern half of the 1st MARDIV's area of operations was controlled by another DASC at Chu Lai. For the general support of the 3rd Marine Division there were two additional DASCs: one at the division headquarters in Phu Bai, and a second at the division's forward headquarters at Dong Ha.[359] In order to meet the increased demands of the growing battle at Khe Sanh, on 23 January, a third DASC was established at the Khe Sanh Combat Base, collocated with the 26th Marines FSCC.[360]

The existence of a separate Marine air command and control system within the ICTZ had been a point of dissatisfaction within the Air Force in Vietnam for some time before Khe Sanh. The 7th Air Force was the primary subordinate command responsible for MACV's air operations. Since the commanding general of this organization was charged with the supervision of all MACV air operations, it is easy to understand that Air Force leaders did not appreciate the fact that III MAF was essentially operating its own air force to fight its own distinct war in the ICTZ. This was considered in contradiction to the principle that an air commander should have the ability to mass his forces at the decisive time and place on the battlefield, just like a ground commander. The Air Force, therefore, saw the arrangement as inefficient at best, but the Marines saw no such contradiction because they enjoyed unity of command throughout the ICTZ and believed air power was always subordinate to ground warfare.

The Marine Corps defended the existence of a separate air force in ICTZ through its doctrinal establishment as a combined arms team, with a ground combat element dependent on an integral air combat element. A comparison of the Army and Marine structures in Vietnam (Table

1) reveals much behind this argument. In short, the Marine Corps, with approximately one-third more men per infantry battalion, 20 percent less artillery support, and 75 percent less integral helicopter support, needed 50 percent more fixed-wing air support.[361] By Marine Corps doctrine, there should have been one Marine Air Wing deployed to Vietnam to support each Marine Division. With just one reinforced Marine Air Wing actually there they were getting by, but they were not about to voluntarily surrender control of their assets to a joint air management system.

The Marines were anxious to preserve the integrity of their air-ground team not only because their doctrine called for it, but also because they had a right to benefit from an air wing that was squeezing more support from the aircraft it had. The Marine divisions were getting more support out of fewer aircraft because the 1st MAW flew each aircraft two times per day, while the 7th Air Force sortie rate was maintained at only 1.1, saving aircraft readiness for surge operations at the commanding general's discretion.[362] In effect, the Marines were getting 50 percent more air support with only half the aircraft. It would seem that if the Air Force argument for single management was based on efficiency, the Marine Corps had a lot more to offer under its own system. To the Marines, designation of Operation Niagara as a critical joint air effort should have elicited an increased sortie rate out of the 7th Air Force, rather than a renewed effort to impose a less efficient joint air management system.

Unfortunately, General William "Spike" Momyer, the Commanding General of the 7th Air Force, focused on the latter course of action. Momyer had assumed command of the 7th Air Force in July 1966, and there are indications that one of the reasons he was appointed to the job was because he had a tenacious and abrasive personality which could win interservice disputes in Vietnam.[363] To Momyer, MACV's identification of Khe Sanh as an opportunity to annihilate the NVA with air power also represented an opportunity to put new urgency behind the Air Force push for single management. Before Niagara began, Momyer declared to an Air Forces Pacific survey team, "If the battle of Khe Sanh develops, it may be the event to get the air responsibilities straightened out like we had them in Korea and World War II."[364] As soon as planning for the campaign began, he renewed his demands for adopting the unified system. His initial attempts succeeded in convincing Westmoreland that the step was necessary for the proper execution of Operation Niagara, but Westmoreland would not make such a politically contentious step without the approval of his own boss, CINCPAC, Admiral U.S. Grant Sharp. Westmoreland submitted a letter of intent to adopt to the new system to Sharp just a week before Niagara was to begin. Influenced by Marine Lieutenant General Victor "Brute" Krulak, the Commanding General of Fleet Marine Forces Pacific who had been kept well informed of the debate by Generals Cushman and Anderson, Admiral Sharp immediately put a halt to Momyer's scheme. In the two months it took to resurrect the plan, the Marines and Air Force found a way to reconcile their differences enough to begin the application of air power in Operation NIAGARA. As an interim solution, they implemented a more detailed version of the geographic separation that had already existed in the ICTZ, as is detailed later in this chapter.

When single management was imposed, some of the Marines' fears were realized. In his debrief on the battle, Colonel Lownds said,

> The time of request for an on-call mission just about doubled. We got an echelon of command imposed between us. We had to increase our hours from 12 to 16 hours and also pull guys off radios and let guys double up on radios just to take care of the paperwork involved.... If you wanted a pre-planned strike

you could have it the next night following the night you put it in as a TPQ strike—in other words, 48 hours afterwards.... Air should be more responsive than 48 hours! At Khe Sanh the enemy didn't stand still and wait for you to hit him.[365]

Lownds also felt that single management was the primary causal factor for what turned out to be a near-catastrophe. On 5 April, as the Marine units began to advance out of their perimeter, radar controlled aircraft were directed to drop ordnance on a hill that had recently been occupied by 1/9. Lownds explained that the target had been submitted 48 hours prior to the attack, but when 1/9 moved onto the hill the next day, the target request was cancelled. Unfortunately, the cancellation was dropped by one of the many echelons that now had to process it, and the attack was allowed to continue. Miraculously, not one of the 24 bombs dropped on the Marines was properly armed, so they escaped harm for the most part.[366] Lownds, the commander of the supported unit in this campaign, was clearly unimpressed with single management. He had to devote greater effort to a system that was considerably less responsive than the old one, and with it came the potential for disasters he had not had to worry about before.

General William W. "Spike" Momyer, U.S. Air Force (pictured here as a lieutenant general in 1964), was the commander of the 7th Air Force and General Westmoreland's deputy commander for air operations. Momyer had long advocated centralized control of air forces, and was an opponent of the Marine Corps' independent operational control of its own air assets. Momyer saw Operation Niagara as an opportunity to finally achieve his plan.

Table 1. Comparative strengths of U.S. Marine and Army infantry divisions in Vietnam, and the air support they could expect to receive based on assigned air assets, from Shulimson, The Defining Year, *508.*

	Army Division	**Marine Division**
Authorized Strength	17,116 men	20,736 men
Transport Helicopters	479	138**
Observation/Attack Helicopters	184	30**
Fixed-Wing Aircraft	132*	80**
Sorties of fixed-wing air support per battalion per day	4	6

*Equivalent number of aircraft that would be maintained for the support of each Army division by the 7th Air Force at a 1.1 daily sortie rate to meet their joint service agreement.
**Half the aircraft maintained by the 1st MAW to support the two Marine Divisions in Vietnam. These aircraft were able to generate more sorties per battalion than the Air Force because they were flown at a 2.0 daily sortie rate.

Admiral U.S. Grant Sharp Jr. served as CINCPAC from 1964 through the battle for Khe Sanh. General Westmoreland answered to Admiral Sharp, who was in command of all U.S. forces in the Pacific theater, so Westmoreland could not implement Momyer's plan for single management without Sharp's concurrence. Sharp had resisted such centralized plans that would have detached Marine air forces from the operational control of III MAF since the Marines first arrived in Vietnam and delayed the imposition of single management several months. This forced the Air Force and Marine Corps to find another way to cooperate against the enemy at Khe Sanh.

Fortunately, the negative impact of single management on the support of Marines at Khe Sanh was mitigated by several factors. First, although single management was officially adopted on March 10th, the new system was not implemented until 31 March, just 15 days before Operation Niagara and the siege of Khe Sanh gave way to Operation Pegasus and the evacuation effort. Next, since III MAF and the 1st Marine Air Wing owned the bulk of the forces occupying the airfields in the ICTZ, they were the air support providers closest to Khe Sanh. Geographically, this made Marine squadrons the most efficient units for the 7th Air Force to task with close air support missions near Khe Sanh. Finally, even when the watered-down version of single management went into effect, the 1st MAW and individual Marine aviators found ways to circumvent the system to provide the Marines at Khe Sanh with the support they needed. On an institutional level, 1st MAW frequently diverted aircraft or added new missions that were never listed on the 7th Air Force ATO. This was in addition to the 12 attack aircraft kept in an alert status 24 hours a day, ready to take off within 10 minutes of being called, so they could immediately fill any needs not being met by aircraft that were currently airborne.[367] Once airborne, some Marine aviators also took it upon themselves to ignore the new air control procedures. Rather than working through a more convoluted system that might or might not ultimately put them in contact with Marines in need of support, these aviators simply checked in with the Marine air controllers at Khe Sanh who they knew needed their support. By devoting assets to an air support reserve and instituting other "work-arounds," the Marines retained some of the flexibility of the MACCS to make up for the Air Force system's inability to incorporate ground requests made less than the 50 hours before the ATO was published.

In summary, the single management controversy and its effect on the battle of Khe Sanh is often overstated. Although the single management of aviation assets within Vietnam was the subject of heated debate which resulted in a fundamental change of air command and control during the battle for Khe Sanh, Operation Niagara largely became an excuse to put a new twist in an ongoing interservice dispute, and the adoption of single management had a limited effect on the Marines at Khe Sanh. This was largely true due to Marine efforts to preserve the air-ground team by countering the imposition of the system and mitigating its effects, something they would not be so successful at later in the war. A study of air support at Khe Sanh, however, should focus on a more detailed analysis of the two systems that coexisted during most of the siege.

Management of Air Assets Under Dual Command and Control Systems

For the vast majority of the battle of Khe Sanh, the Marines were not subject even to the diluted version of single management, but rather to the pre-existing system. Two distinct air command and control systems had been in effect in the ICTZ for some time. This condition had been considered tolerable, if not ideal by the Air Force, for several reasons. To begin with, the systems provided control for aircraft coming from two command structures, serving as conduits to successfully get both types of aircraft to the same battle area. Once in the area, conflicts were minimized to a large degree because the two different DASCs (the USAF DASC-Victor and USMC DASC-Horn) each supported different ground units which usually operated in distinct subdivisions of the ICTZ.[368] As long as there were Army units within the ICTZ, therefore, DASC-Victor provided interface and control of aircraft (usually Air Force) supporting those units in their specific operating areas, while DASC-Horn provided the same functions for the Marine divisions. Another move that helped minimize conflict was that each of the services assigned a full colonel, an officer with maturity and perspective of the larger battle, to supervise the activities of its DASC on an equal footing with the partner/competitor agency.[369] Over time, as additional units were moved into the ICTZ, the complexity of the MACCS increased, as illustrated in Figure 7. By January 1968, there were two subordinate DASCs supporting the 1st Marine Division in the southern part of the ICTZ, with two other DASCs supporting the 3d Marine Division in the North. Even with four Marine DASCs, as long as the different divisions continued to occupy different areas of operation, as was natural for units of that size, the overlapping coverage of the two air command and control systems was minimized, as was the potential for conflicts. In effect, the systems remained geographically separated within the ICTZ, which facilitated functional separation. Operation Niagara changed all of this.

The problem with Niagara was that it sought a decisive concentration of air power from all of the services in the relatively small airspace around Khe Sanh. If each of the services was attempting to provide support for the same battle, it seemed that there would have to be a central

The crew of an F-4B Phantom of Marine Fighter Attack Squadron-115 scramble to get airborne. Each of the three Marine fixed-wing air groups in Vietnam constantly kept four aircraft in an alert posture on the group's "hot pad." With the aircraft readied for takeoff and the crew dressed and waiting nearby in an air-conditioned trailer, a section of two aircraft could get airborne in 10 minutes to answer any immediate needs for close air support. Once the first two aircraft launched, the next two would increase their readiness to assume the 10-minute alert.

air control authority for two reasons. First, support would have to be deconflicted to ensure that there was not a redundant application of air power. Of more immediate concern, a single system could prevent two aircraft from attempting to occupy the same airspace at the same time, causing a collision. These concerns were exactly what brought such immediacy to the single management argument that General Momyer had been advocating for months. In the meantime, however, airspace conflicts on the first day of the battle made it clear that an interim arrangement would have to be reached, so 7th Air Force representatives met with the Marines in Da Nang on 22 January and developed a compromise solution.[370] The result was a miniature version of the geographical deconfliction that had served the ICTZ so well up to that time. In effect, the airspace around Khe Sanh was divided into a series of zones, each controlled by a different DASC responsible for coordinating the attack of targets identified within its zone.

The ground and airspace around Khe Sanh was divided into several different regions, as illustrated in Figure 8. The three zones closest to Khe Sanh (indicated by areas A and B on the figure) included the immediate battle space around the combat base and its outposts. These were the areas where the fire support integral to those defenses, including mortars and 105mm howitzers, could be used to influence the close battle and defeat attacks by the NVA. This was also the area where all of the Marines were deployed in outlying defensive positions, or were likely to be deployed in patrols at one time or another. As such, the 26th Marines were quite properly unwilling to turn over control of this airspace to another agency. To do so would have meant that the Marines would not have had final clearance authority on any air drops or artillery missions fired in close proximity to their own troops. It would also have meant that they would have had to seek permission from another agency before they could fire emergency missions essential for the defense of their own perimeters. By owning the air and ground space in areas A and B, the 26th Marines could exercise unrestricted control of all maneuver units fighting in this area, as well as all air strikes and indirect fire missions executed in support of those units. The agency responsible for this coordination was the 26th Marines Fire Support Coordination Center. The FSCC exercised control of aircraft in that zone through a fifth DASC added to the ICTZ, which was collocated at Khe Sanh Combat Base. The FSCC could also request the support of long-range Army 175mm artillery batteries stationed further east at the Rockpile, as well as Air Force, Navy, and VNAF sorties, but any additional support provided within areas A and B, came strictly under the control of the 26th Marines.

Immediately to the east was another zone (region C in the figure), left under the control of the 26th Marines' higher headquarters, the 3d Marine Division. The 26th Marines did not require control of this zone because there was a decreased likelihood of NVA forces operating in this area, and the Marines had no outposts in this area. Leaving this zone to higher headquarters meant that the 3d Marine Division could conduct ground operations, artillery missions, and air attacks there without bothering the FSCC at Khe Sanh, which was already task-saturated and had little interest in this area. The 3d Marine Division exercised fire support coordination over this region, like the rest of northern ICTZ, through its own FSCC at the division headquarters in Dong Ha. Air control was provided by DASC-Bravo, also at Dong Ha.[371]

The final divisions of airspace around Khe Sanh were controlled by the Air Force, indicated by regions D and E on the figure. This control also extended to the airspace over Laos. This region lay beyond the reach of most artillery in the ICTZ, and only very rarely contained friendly forces, in the form of small reconnaissance patrols. Since this region was beyond the reach of Marine supporting arms and there was no danger of inadvertently attacking Marine maneuver units, it was divided into a set of free fire zones, and relinquished to the Air Force to fight its deep battle of attrition at its own discretion, and without the need for coordinating or deconflicting with the 26th Marines. Air missions were coordinated by an Airborne Battlefield Command and Control Center (ABCCC, or "A-B-Triple-C"). This was a C-130 configured with a command and communications suite which would orbit over Laos, and essentially functioned as an airborne DASC. ABCCC was in contact with the 7th Air Force headquarters near Saigon, and also with a small detachment of Air Force personnel on the ground in Khe Sanh. During periods when the ABCCC retired, control of missions in the Air Force zones was relinquished to the USAF's DASC-Victor, so that there was always some extension of the Air Force command and control system to supervise its zones, 24 hours a day.

Even though there was a geographic separation of air control responsibilities in the airspace around Khe Sanh, the services were attempting to win the same battle, and they shared information and assets. The 7th Air Force operations center was the central collection point for target information in the region, and targeted most of the strikes in the outer zones, but the 26th Marines FSCC often submitted requests for air strikes on targets it identified in the Air Force's free-fire zones, which were then controlled by ABCCC. If the 26th Marines obtained information on imminent threats to the combat base or its outposts which proved beyond the immediate capabilities of Marine aircraft, they could also request the diversion of 7th Air Force sorties from less important targets in the Air Force zone. If any particular zone lacked a concentration of worthy targets and had extra sorties available, the control agency could contact the controller of an adjacent zone, and send the extra aircraft to that

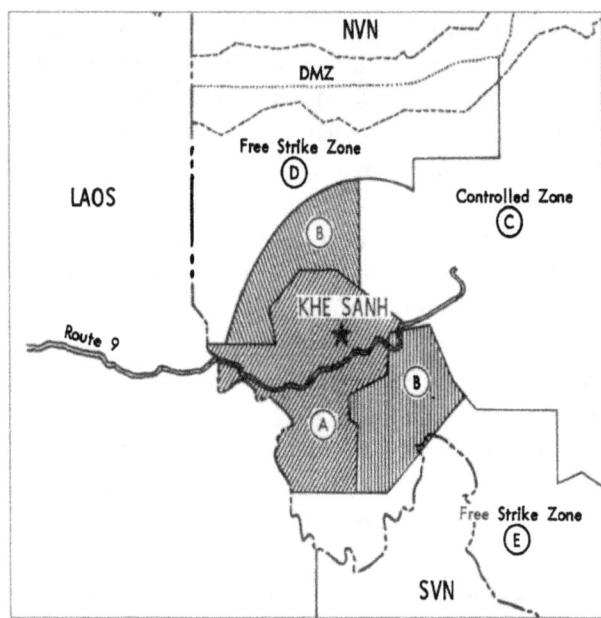

Figure 8. Airspace divisions in the vicinity of Khe Sanh for Operation Niagara, January 1968. Illustration from Bernard Nalty, Air Power and The Fight For Khe Sanh *(Washington, 1973), 75.*

region to be directed against more promising targets. As a result, Air Force aircraft frequently found themselves attacking targets in the Marine zones under Marine control, and Marine aircraft often found themselves directed to work in the outer free-fire zones by ABCCC. Navy aircraft were technically under the domain of the 7th Air Force, but found themselves working for either control agency.

Despite their success at circumventing interservice disputes, there were also problems with these command and control arrangements, and with the geographic division of responsibilities. The 26th Marines, for example, complained that feedback on the conduct of missions controlled by ABCCC was nonexistent, making it difficult for the defenders of Khe Sanh to figure out if threats they identified had been destroyed, which was vital for an accurate picture of enemy capabilities and intentions.[372] The FSCC bunker at Khe Sanh was also too small to allow the Marine

DASC detachment to be truly co-located. With the control of aircraft around Khe Sanh placed in the hands of air wing Marines located in a bunker 75 meters away, communication often broke down when KSCB came under heavy attack, since telephone wires were sometimes broken and messengers could not travel back and forth under heavy bombardment. Unfortunately, this was just the time when the DASC needed an accurate battle picture the most. Fortunately, space was made for the Marine DASC in an Air Force bunker. There the DASC Marines benefited from a host of special amenities rarely seen by other Marines at Khe Sanh, but they fostered a better common air picture for the two services in their attack and support operations.[373] This controller-level interservice communication and understanding was especially critical because the Air Force rotated the majority of its personnel out of Khe Sanh after one week of duty at the combat base.[374] The experience of the Marines who were there for the duration of the siege provided continuity which increased the situational awareness of the Air Force controllers.

Targeting of Air Support Assets at Khe Sanh

Targeting is the process by which the enemy is detected, located, identified, and prioritized for attack. The NVA hit by air strikes around Khe Sanh were subjected to the same targeting process that was used for all of the other supporting arms, centralized in the 26th Marines FSCC. Once targets were located, the FSCC decided which of the supporting arms was best suited to attack each target. For example, an extensive enemy position which had to be destroyed composed a better target for a B-52 raid than a mortar attack, but a hilltop about to be assaulted by a company of Marines required more discriminating weapons. When all other factors were equal, often geographic considerations dictated which supporting arms would be used. The NVA deliberately placed most of their artillery just beyond the range of the Marine artillery, which meant that only air power could be targeted against them. The heavy 175mm Marine artillery based at the Rockpile and Camp Carrol was most frequently targeted to the north, northeast, and east of Khe Sanh, in the heart of their range capability. The 105mm artillery based at Khe Sanh was used to engage targets closer to the combat base, as long as the maximum ordinate (peak of their trajectory) was below the 14,000 altitude at which many of the air support aircraft were controlled.[375]

Air power was an especially critical weapon at Khe Sanh for several reasons. Artillery was not very well suited for the destruction of large enemy targets close to the combat base or its outposts, or for heavily reinforced defensive positions. Every artillery round fired from Khe Sanh also had to be delivered to the combat base by the tenuous air logistic chain, putting more aircraft and Marines at risk. Additionally, a single aircraft could attack with more ordnance in a more concentrated punch. A single 500-pound bomb, for example, delivered only slightly less high explosive mass than a whole battery of six 155mm howitzers. A single aircraft carrying several dozen of these bombs, therefore, had more destructive firepower than several battalions of artillery.

The targeting effort at Khe Sanh was run by Captain Mirza M. Baig, the regimental Target Intelligence Officer, whose job it was to mix art and science to find the enemy. The science in the process started with an incomplete picture generated by electronic intercepts, visual sightings, and other information, to generate a picture of where the enemy was known to be. Then, a thorough knowledge of enemy doctrine and tactics was used to fill in as many of the gaps as possible, and create a more complete picture of what the enemy was doing. In essence, Baig was responsible for connecting the dots to reveal the big picture. Here the art of targeting became increasingly important, as the targeteers had to use their intuition to try and divine what the enemy intended to do, how he would do it, and when he would do it.

To start building the picture, targets were identified in several ways. The most accurate was for a forward observer or forward air controller to visually spot the enemy. The thick vegetation and elusive nature of the enemy at Khe Sanh made the detection of significant targets by ground observers in the fixed defensive positions at Khe Sanh a rarity, so aerial sightings by reconnaissance and observation aircraft became particularly important. Although still limited by the vegetation and NVA camouflage and deception techniques, the movement of large combat units into the region around Khe Sanh was accompanied by unavoidable concentrations of people and equipment which often betrayed their own presence. Visual searches for the enemy were also more productive when the NVA began firing artillery at KSCB. Although the NVA went to great lengths to conceal the locations of their artillery, they had to expose them at the time of firing.

Less reliable than visual spottings were electronic intercepts, which could give away enemy dispositions in one of two ways. First, the actual intercept of radio transmissions by two or more locations could be triangulated to determine the location from which they emanated. Second, the analysis of the content of transmissions could reveal information, such as unit identification, location, and intent. Even when not decipherable, the volume of traffic could be used to estimate the size and activity of enemy units. Electronic intercepts were less reliable than visual spottings because the location techniques were not as precise, and transmissions could be easily manipulated for deception, but they helped complete the picture when combined with other sources of intelligence.

There were other, more creative solutions that attempted to make use of the Americans' technological advantage over the NVA. One of these was the Anti-Personnel Detector (APD), which began to contribute to Niagara at the start of the operation in January.[376] This system was mounted in a UH-1E helicopter and flown over the jungle, where it could detect very minute concentrations of urea in the atmosphere. The urea was theoretically generated by human sweat or urine, and it was believed that the APD could reveal the presence of large concentrations of NVA soldiers that would otherwise have remained hidden in the jungle. Unfortunately, the validity of the concept was never proven in combat around Khe Sanh, and the lack of other evidence led the Marines to conclude that the APD was just as likely to be set off by troops of monkeys and other natural sources as it was by battalions of enemy soldiers.

Early in the battle, before the NVA took actions that revealed their presence in force, the 26th Marines had little idea where the enemy actually was. During this stage, Captain Baig had to depend heavily on the few visual sightings and electronic intercepts he had and was forced to rely on his intuition more than science. During this stage many air strikes and indirect fire missions were targeted on likely and suspected enemy locations—place where the enemy could be— rather than known enemy positions. These missions were known as harassment and interdiction (H&I) fires, because the destruction of enemy assets was too much to be hoped for.

The targeting situation was improved to a large degree after the enemy was discovered in force between 20 and 23 January. In order to accomplish the objectives of Operation Niagara, however, the Americans could not merely wait for NVA units to reveal themselves in their final assaults where heavy U.S. firepower would be useless in close combat. The destruction of enemy combat power around Khe Sanh required the Americans to locate the elusive enemy formations and depots dispersed in the jungles around Khe Sanh. A Niagara intelligence center was set up as an adjunct to the 7th Air Force headquarters at Tan Son Nhut Air Base near Saigon. There, a special team of photo interpreters and analysts was assembled, including specialists brought in from the United States. Despite the huge volume of information processed, however, visual and electronic intelligence proved frustratingly unproductive.[377] On 18 January, General Westmoreland decided to take a significant step toward locating the enemy so that Niagara could be successful.

Up until that time, Westmoreland had kept the electronic barrier component of the McNamara Line as one of his most closely held secrets. The barrier system, code-named Muscle Shoals, consisted of a network of acoustic and seismic sensors which could be dropped by aircraft to monitor the enemy. The Air Force had used the sensors to monitor movement along the Ho Chi Minh Trail since October, but the project had still remained highly classified. While the increasing volume of traffic southward along the trail in November and December were part of the intelligence that led Westmoreland to chose Khe Sanh as his conventional battle ground, very few people knew the actual source of that intelligence. Within the five thousand men assigned to the 26th Marines, for example, only one officer had ever even heard of the program. Now that Westmoreland had chosen his decisive battleground, he made the decision to change all that and risk compromising Muscle Shoals so that he could bring air power to bear against the enemy.[378]

In the few days after Westmoreland made his decision on 18 January, 250 sensors were dropped in various locations around Khe Sanh. The Air Force used the infrastructure that had already been developed for monitoring the McNamara Line and the Ho Chi Minh Trail by adding another aircraft to the daily mix that orbited above Khe Sanh. Its purpose was to collect the data from the sensors and instantly relay it to a surveillance center in Nakhom Phanom, Thailand. There, the emissions were compared to a signal library to determine exactly what the sensors were detecting. From there, the intelligence was relayed both to the 7th Air Force targeting cell, and back to the 26th Marines FSCC in Khe Sanh, where the data was used for targeting supporting arms. It did not take the Marines very long at all to abandon their program of shot-in-the-dark harassment and interdiction fires when this new intelligence began to identify NVA troop concentrations.[379]

The system had its shortcomings. By the end of January, 316 sensors had been deployed, yielding 99 targets, but the exact locations of the airdropped sensors were typically 200 to 1,000 meters from where they were thought to have been dropped. This problem was discovered when repeated attempts to use sensor reports to attack up to 150 point targets a day yielded few positive results.[380] The Marine's division commander was well aware of their lackluster performance, stating, "The results were better than H&I fires, but that is saying very little."[381] Instead, the sensors came to be regarded as trend indicators to predict attacks and put defensive fire plans into action.[382] Like other intelligence sources, Muscle Shoals was sometimes used as the sole source of targeting data when there was a complete absence of other indicators, but the sensors were ultimately only trusted when their reports could be confirmed by other, independent sources.[383]

Even so, the sensors were credited with being the predictors of major attacks on 5 February, the night of 29 February through 1 March, and 21 through 23 March. In each of these cases, the FSCC was able to divert air strikes and other supporting arms to sensor-located targets, and the end result was that no significant attack ever reached the Marine perimeters.[384] For this reason, Colonel Lownds considered the sensors to be well worth the $1 billion-dollar price tag.[385]

The use to which this targeting intelligence was put was another matter all together. It is one thing to detect, identify, and locate your enemy, but it is another entirely to destroy him. To accomplish this, the 26th Marines sought to bring the maximum firepower to bear in the form of supporting arms. Defensively, fire plans were not used to try and prevent the enemy force from reaching the Marines' perimeter wire, but instead to prevent him from escaping or being reinforced once he had committed to an assault—in effect trapping the NVA between a rock and a hard place. To fragment and isolate the enemy, a three-sided box of fire and steel was set up, which was open on the side closest to the Marine defenses. Three artillery batteries fired continuously to form the first three sides of the box, trapping the enemy against the Marine defenses. Then a fourth battery began firing to close the open end, and as the first three batteries kept up continuous fire, the final battery would sweep its fire up and down the inside of the box like a piston within a cylinder, so that there was no way for the enemy to escape the destruction. This box became known as the primary box, because another was soon added. Heavy 175mm artillery was sometimes assigned to fire linear patterns parallel to the two sides of the box at a distance of approximately 500 meters. To close the end of the secondary box furthest from the Marine defenses, aircraft under radar control would drop their bombs in linear patterns. The secondary box was designed to destroy any NVA units which might attempt to reinforce or assist the unit caught in the primary box. To accomplish this, the three sides of the secondary box would be shifted inwards and outwards, like an accordion.[386]

The use of primary and secondary boxes in defensive fires represented the most ideal combination of supporting arms—the massing of many different types of firepower with decisive, synergistic effects. In most cases, however, firepower could not be massed to that degree, or the targets located were judged not to warrant such an expenditure. It is in these cases, where the effects of the various supporting arms could be individually observed, that close air support can best be evaluated.

THE DEEP AIR BATTLE AND THE B-52

Captain Mirza M. "Harry" Baig, the Target Information Officer assigned to the 26th Marines at Khe Sanh, was perhaps the single most important individual when it came to directing the massive fires support available to the Marines for use against the enemy. He classified the battle into three phases of combat. The first was the attrition of enemy forces by a nightly schedule of artillery, radar-controlled aircraft, and B-52 missions. In daylight hours, those enemies that survived and exposed themselves became targets of opportunity in the second phase: attack by artillery and aircraft under the control of forward observers and forward air controllers. Only those enemies that escaped the saturation bombings and detection by forward observers made it to the third phase of combat, face-to-face confrontations with the Marines at or near the perimeter of the combat base. Of the three phases, Captain Baig declared the first to be by far the most important and effective, and he gave the lion's share of the credit to the massive firepower delivered by the B-52s.[387]

The vast majority of personnel involved in the defense of Khe Sanh during the 77 days of siege who remarked on the support of the B-52 shared Baig's opinion, describing them as the single most decisive factor in the successful outcome of the battle. The most significant feature of B-52 support was the sheer mass of firepower that these huge aircraft could deliver, operating around the clock to apply constant pressure on the NVA forces around Khe Sanh, annihilating those that could be located and targeted in sufficient time. B-52s, delivering their bombs under the code name Arc Light, were responsible for 60.3 percent of the total bomb tonnage dropped at Khe Sanh.[388] The wide acclaim for the B-52, combined with this data, is somewhat problematic to the thesis that the Marine doctrine of close air support was a critical element of the battle, and has also lead to the conclusion of Bernard Nalty and others that the unspecific application of air power was critical without further comparative analysis. A closer look at the facts, however, reveals that these observers may have been overawed by the destructive power of the B-52. If Khe Sanh was a victory of air power, the B-52 was certainly a very visible champion, but the Stratofortress' effectiveness was also subject to significant limitations.

Air Support Provided by B-52s

The B-52 was an enormously destructive weapon. Designed for strategic bombing, each aircraft carried a payload of 60,000 pounds of bombs. The typical Arc Light sortie delivered this ordnance on one square kilometer of terrain, achieving full dispersion with a mix of 250-, 500-, and 750- pound bombs, although destructive firepower could be further concentrated by using a smaller number of heavier bombs.[389] Although designed as a strategic weapon, the B-52 was used on an operational and tactical level in the Vietnam War and in subsequent conflicts. In the region around Khe Sanh, for example, as early as the fall of 1966, B-52 raids had been conducted on NVA targets detected by O-1 birddogs during Operation Tigerhound.[390] The use of strategic bombers in these roles was somewhat problematic. To begin with, all of South Vietnam was considered within the bomb line, today known as the fire support coordination line. This meant that any bombing

A B-52D dropping its payload, which could include as many as 30 tons of bombs.

operations conducted within this area had to be coordinated with friendly units responsible for those areas, as well as the government of South Vietnam, to ensure that they would not endanger friendly forces or the civilian populace.[391] The clearance for such missions was therefore subject to the approval of ground forces under procedures much more similar to close air support missions than strategic bombing missions in enemy territory, which needed little more than the approval of the U.S. national command authority. The additional clearance requirements were met with great resistance by the U.S. Air Force's Strategic Air Command, the agency responsible for the employment of B-52s in all strategic missions, from nuclear deterrence of the Soviet Union to helping win the war in Vietnam. Even before the B-52s were used on targets in South Vietnam, SAC had refused to turn control of its strategic assets over to MACV or CINCPAC to facilitate bombings of targets in Laos and North Vietnam. Instead, targeting was controlled by SAC and its leadership in Washington, D.C., which maintained operational control over all B-52s, even those deployed to Thailand and Guam which regularly flew missions in support of the war effort in Vietnam.[392] SAC considered this arrangement beneficial in two ways. It kept the bombing of North Vietnam under the tight control of the President and the rest of the national command authority, which chose to modulate such bombing in response to the changing international political conditions under which the war was fought. It also allowed SAC to keep all of its bombers ready for the defense of the U.S. if needed, while spare sorties could still be made available to service targets selected by CINCPAC and COMUSMACV to help win the war in Vietnam.

Upon assuming command of the 7th Air Force in July 1966 and becoming Westmoreland's Deputy for Air Operations, General Momyer was responsible for advising COMUSMACV on the most effective employment of all assets at his disposal. Momyer was opposed to the use of B-52s in tactical support roles. He considered this a waste of their massive firepower, which he thought would be more effectively used on North Vietnam's war-making capability. Momyer thought the B-52s should only be used to achieve tactical objectives in emergency situations, or in other special circumstances which deserved their attention.[393] As he developed the plans for Operation Niagara, Momyer saw just such a situation developing. Envisioning the upcoming battle of Khe Sanh as an opportunity to draw the NVA into easily targeted concentrations, Momyer saw Niagara as a way of using the B-52's to achieve tactical and strategic objectives simultaneously. By using the firepower of the B-52 to destroy large NVA units massed around Khe Sanh, Momyer would both protect the Marines, and attrite the enemy combat power which usually proved so elusive for airpower in this guerrilla war.

The desire to employ B-52s within the ICTZ brought some complications since the Air Force now had to cooperate with III MAF, which not only had a better awareness of the enemy within the ICTZ, but also had veto authority over any bombing mission conducted within its that area which could endanger its ground troops. For this reason, the target selection and clearance procedures for Arc Light strikes around Khe Sanh were very similar to the procedures for close air support missions. The 26th Marines Fire Support Coordination Center would select most targets, sometimes based on targets of opportunity detected by the subordinate battalions, but more often based on a variety of larger-picture intelligence sources, such as radio transmission intercepts and Muscle Shoals sensor reports. The 26th Marines provided 90 to 95 percent of all targeting for the B-52 strikes,[394] but the requests for B-52 support were still submitted up the chain through the 3d Marine Division FSCC, III MAF headquarters, and ultimately to MACV. At Ton Son Nhut Air Base, near Saigon, Westmoreland directed that a special operations center be set up in an empty hanger adjacent to the 7th Air Force headquarters. There a special "red watch" was established and manned 24 hours a day, always under the supervision of either Westmoreland, General Creighton Abrams (his deputy), or Lieutenant General William Rosson (his Chief of Staff). This watch center for monitoring Operation Niagara passed each B-52 support request to Westmoreland, who personally approved every mission.[395]

This request process took some time to complete. The 26th Marines had to submit their initial request at least 15 hours prior to the desired time on target (TOT) for the attack, and most often had to adjust the TOT to fit a preset schedule of TOTs that the Air Force had established for that particular day. Once a flight of bombers was assigned to the mission, the process could be abbreviated if the target needed to be changed, but the expedited procedures still required at least three hours' notice before the attack was to be made.[396] The Air Force, however, was reluctant to short-cut its 15-hour procedure, and on at least one occasion General Westmoreland himself had to intervene to divert B-52s to help destroy an NVA concentration poised to attack Khe Sanh Combat Base.[397] Ultimately, the time required to process and approve targets for attack by B-52s was one of this weapon's main limitations in the battle for Khe Sanh. The B-52 could only be effective if targeted against an enemy which remained in place for at least three hours, or whose position three hours in the future could be predicted with some degree of accuracy.

Of course, the need for accuracy should not be overstressed with a strategic bomber capable of destroying virtually everything within a square kilometer. The B-52s at Khe Sanh were normally scheduled in flights of three. They would fly in an echelon formation, laying a continuous stream of bombs in a target box one kilometer wide and three kilometers long. To facilitate this, the terrain around Khe Sanh was divided into a grid of one-kilometer square boxes, each with an identification number. With this rather blunt weapon, the targeteers merely had to predict which grid square the enemy would be in during the time on target, and pass a series of four-digit numbers to the attacking aircrew via the fire support coordination process.[398] The terminal guidance to the aircraft in the delivery of its ordnance was usually accomplished through a ground-based radar system, although aircraft could also drop using their sophisticated onboard navigation systems.

To support Operation Niagara, Momyer had about 24 B-52s available on a daily basis. Once he notified III MAF that he was making these sorties available to meet the impending threat to Khe Sanh beginning on 16 January, the Marines were quick to take advantage of them. Although III MAF technically maintained the authority to direct attacks on any targets within the ICTZ, General Cushman's staff immediately gave priority for these missions to the 26th Marines so they would be used around Khe Sanh, just as Momyer intended.[399] The Air Force General must have been disappointed, however, with some of the first targets against which his bombers were used. In the first few days, while Operation Niagara was still in the "seek" phase that would precede the "destroy" phase, and before the enemy had yet revealed himself in strength, the Marines sent bombers on 12 large raids. These raids were against targets based on human intelligence collected by Bru scouts, aerial photographs, or radio intercepts, but lacked any strong proof of NVA presence.[400] The Marines were apparently not as efficiency-minded as Momyer when it came to air power, and were willing to send the newly-available assets against any target that might present a future threat to KSCB if better targets could not be found.

Once the enemy began to reveal his presence in force around 20 January 1968, the targets against which the B-52s were targeted were probably much more to Momyer's liking. Just one such strategic target was identified shortly afterward, on the eve of the Tet Offensive. Radio intelligence revealed the presence of what Westmoreland was convinced was "the north Vietnamese headquarters controlling forces around Khe Sanh, if not the entire region." Located just across the border in Laos, Westmoreland suspected and hoped that Giap himself would be among the NVA leadership assembled there. Deviating from the normal practice of having the 26th Marines select a target for one of the regularly scheduled B-52 strikes, Westmoreland ordered that the Stratofortresses be concentrated to deliver a paralyzing blow to the NVA command system. Thirty-six B-52s were sent out in the single largest air strike of the war to date, dropping 1,000 tons of ordnance on the suspected headquarters location. That same evening, the strike was followed by another composed of nine more aircraft, designed to catch NVA troops and medical personnel, as well as any survivors of the first raid. The radio signals emanating from that location did cease as a result of the raid,[401] and an official NVA operational history on the battle, while notably silent on the matter of casualties, noted that the Campaign Command Headquarters was hit and forced to move, leading to a problematic gap in command and control.[402] Unfortunately for Westmoreland's hopes, Giap apparently escaped harm, far off to the north in Hanoi monitoring the final preparations for the Tet Offensive.

As noted before, such high-level attempts to influence the battle and the war were not the norm. The vast majority of the B-52 missions were requested by the 26th Marines to attack targets they had selected. In order to meet these needs, the Air Force drew upon two SAC bases in the theater. B-52s were provided by the 4133rd Bomb Wing at Anderson Air Force Base in Guam, and the 4258th Strategic Wing, located closer to Vietnam at U Tapao Air Base in Thailand. To provide relatively continuous coverage, these aircraft were scheduled to arrive on a three-plane cell once every three hours, although the actual times on target were varied in order to avoid a predictable pattern that the NVA could better defend against. After the first week of February, 26 additional B-52s were deployed to Kadena Air Force Base in Okinawa. Although this deployment was in response to the capture of the U.S. Navy signals intelligence ship *Pueblo* by the North Koreans, by 25 February it allowed SAC to increase its support of Khe Sanh to one three-plane cell every 90 minutes. Actual times on target continued to vary between one and two hours to minimize their predictability for the NVA.[403] Another change was made in the last week of February from a three-aircraft cell arriving every 90 minutes to a six-aircraft cell every three hours. While the overall sortie contribution remained relatively constant, this created a more devastating concentration of firepower on a more irregular schedule which was harder for the enemy to predict. The increased interval in B-52 support also forced the Marines to save the Arc Light strikes for only the most appropriate targets.[404] This last point is important because under the more frequent schedule of support there had been wasted effort noted. Rather than send the bombers home without dropping bombs in instances when the Marines had not found any known or suspected enemy concentrations, they had resorted to targeting Arc Light's on very minor enemy positions, like single machine gun nests, or even positions where the enemy was merely likely to be, like intersections of trails and streams.[405] An infantryman would have no complaint about sending a B-52 to attack any enemy squad he might have to face, but this was exactly the kind of wasted effort and overkill that Momyer feared was sapping the Air Force's power to win the war on a strategic level. While the increased concentration of sorties apparently reduced this waste, it also had an adverse effect on Arc Light responsiveness, providing support on a less flexible schedule and essentially adding three more hours to the minimum response time. On 2 March, Westmoreland reacted by directing the 7th Air Force to develop a procedure for handling requests that would allow a more rapid diversion of Arc Light strikes, which was accomplished.[406]

At the beginning of the Khe Sanh campaign, the delivery of bombs by B-52 was restricted to targets more than 3,000 meters from friendly troops. The reason for this is that the huge volume of bombs delivered from high altitudes created a great danger to U.S. and allied troops near the Arc Light targets. Other forms of air attacks were not subject to the same restrictions. Radar controlled attacks by tactical aircraft, for example, were allowed to attack targets as close as 2,000 meters from friendlies, and visual attacks by tactical aircraft under the control of forward air controllers were permitted to attack as close as the actual destructive radii of the weapons they were dropping.

While the Americans learned some valuable lessons about the potential of B-52s in tactical operations at the battle of Con Thien, just four months before Khe Sanh, the NVA had arrived at some equally valuable conclusions. The NVA had already adopted the tactic of getting as close as possible to U.S. positions to try and deny the Americans the advantage conveyed by supporting arms. At Con Thien, the NVA determined that once they got within 3,000 meters of U.S. troops, they were rarely attacked by B-52s.[407] At Khe Sanh, therefore, they were quick to try and exploit this vulnerability, moving close to U.S. positions to avoid the devastation caused by a B-52 attack.[408] This tactic was observed by the Marines defending the hills around Khe Sanh,[409] and apparently became known to COMUSMACV.

Westmoreland decided to try and deny the enemy any sanctuary that unnecessary safety restrictions created. On 13 February he wrote to CINCPAC asking for a wavier to the 3,000 meter restriction, emboldened by the knowledge that during Con Thien a B-52 had mistakenly dropped its payload 1,400 meters from friendlies without any adverse effects. In order to validate the technique, permission was granted for a test strike on a target box known as Khe Sanh Red 207, the closest edge of which was just 1,200 meters from the Marine defenses on Hill 881S. The test was successful, although even precautions, which included having the Marines take cover during the attack, could not prevent some of them from getting nosebleeds from the concussions of the bomb detonations.[410] After the test, Admiral Sharp agreed that a wavier was a worthwhile risk, and on 18 February he reduced the minimum safe distance for B-52 missions to just 1,000 meters.[411] The use of B-52s on "close-in" targets became an accepted tactic, although it was generally reserved only for emergency situations. For the rest of the campaign, there were a number of occasions when targeteers took advantage of that reduction, ordering Arc Light strikes close to the new minimum safe distance. There is even one case when B-52s delivered ordnance just 900 meters from friendlies, although it is not clear whether this was entirely intentional.

The reduction in standoff was important for several reasons. First, it reduced the sanctuary that the NVA had been given from this fearsome weapon and increased the utility of the B-52 for fighting the NVA at a more critical stage of the battle. With the reduced standoff the B-52s could now be targeted at NVA who had actually been observed as specific locations by human eyes on the combat base and its outposts, not just on radio emissions or sensor reports. In addition, it allowed the B-52s to attack the NVA as they were concentrating for attacks on the Marine positions. Finally, it placed these attacks within the observation of human eyes, so that their effects could be more accurately judged. The testimonials on these missions are impressive. Captain Bill

Dabney, commanding the key defensive position on Hill 881S, stated,

> we had the B-52s and they were awesome when they turned them on. You know, we figured we could handle anything that came in close if they could break up the attack. And they damned sure could break up the attack if you could give them a target. And in terms of responsiveness, they were fairly fast. I mean to the point where I remember one time we reported some movement and noise and apparently lights on a ridge directly south about 1100 to 1200 meters away. And it was less than—now this is a hazy recollection—but I bet it was less than two hours before we had an Arc Light. And if you've ever been within a click of two of an Arc Light, it's pretty awesome in terms of what it can do to an enemy formation that's massed for attack.[412]

The B-52 had admirers at all levels. A lance corporal defending the perimeter of KSCB itself remarked,

> The air power displayed was incredible. There were constant bombing runs by all kinds of fixed-wing aircraft. By far the most impressive were the B-52 bombing runs. The ground would actually rumble under our bodies as we lay in a bunker while the bombs erupted around our perimeter. I often wondered how the NVA withstood the constant pounding.[413]

The enemy seldom attacked KSCB itself in force, so it was rare that B-52s were targeted close to the combat base. On exception was on 29 February, when a possible enemy buildup was suspected near the garbage dump and French plantation house to the south. Since sensors detected movement on two axes toward the base, the 26th Marines requested the emergency divert of a B-52 strike to these relatively close targets, and got approval.[414] Colonel Lownds reported, "This was the only time that the kids on the lines told me…that they actually saw bodies being thrown into the air." Colonel Lownds concluded that the strike broke up an attack by what was probably an NVA regiment,[415] and NVA sources confirm that an assault (probably by the 9th Regiment of the 304 Division) was launched and defeated that night.[416] The paradox of gauging B-52 effectiveness, however, was that the destructive firepower of these bombers seldom left much definitive evidence to quantify what they had actually accomplished.

Even more important than the American observations, therefore, are the NVA reactions to Arc Light strikes. All evidence indicates that the B-52 was a particularly feared weapon. Westmoreland was quoted as saying, "We know, from talking to prisoners and defectors, that the enemy troops fear B-52s, tactical air, artillery, and armor…in that order,"[417] and stated that captured documents indicated that NVA units had suffered a 20 to 25 percent desertion rate due to the soldiers' fear of

An aerial photograph of the area around Khe Sanh Combat Base, located in the lower right and circled in pen on the original photo. The linear patterns of light spots are the result of B-52 strikes. The landscape around the combat was heavily scarred by the heavy bombardment.

A B-52 strike was impressive, not only for the sheer destruction it created when it seemed to obliterate an entire valley or ridgeline at a time, but also for its suddenness. In the foreground, two Marines can be seen watching the strike from inside a sandbagged trench.

U.S. air power.[418] The diary of one soldier killed in the battle reflected that while moving southward under the pressure of American air power to replace casualties in the 304th Division, three hundred men had deserted rather than face the feared B-52.[419] The 304 Division's official history acknowledges that one of its battalions was so devastated by a B-52 strike that subsequent desertions and self-inflicted wounds to avoid combat caused the NVA leadership to doubt that the battalion would be of any further use at Khe Sanh.[420] In March, an NCO assigned to the same division wrote, "Here the war is fiercer than in all other places...All of us stay in underground trenches...We are in the sixtieth day and B-52s continue to pour bombs...this is an area where it rains bombs and cartridges. Vegetation and animals, even those who live in deep caves or underground, have been destroyed."[421]

One reason why the B-52 was so feared was not only the unbelievable destruction it caused, but also the fact that the obliteration of several square kilometers of terrain was seldom accompanied by any warning. As one private first class at KSCB observed,

> A B-52 strike was truly awesome. There would be no hint of a strike arriving until the bombs exploded. The bombs fell in a staggered pattern. First one bomb, then another to the right and front of the first explosion, then another to the left and front of the second explosion, and so forth. The bombs created a long pattern of craters, churned up earth, and blasted trees. After the bombs had exploded, I would be able to hear the planes. They produced a weird, low moaning that lasted until they were out of range. I never saw the planes, since they bombed from a great height.[422]

A first lieutenant related an occasion when the Marines were warned of a strike about to be delivered outside their lines:

> It was still overcast at the appointed time, 1700, and we all looked up into the sky. Nothing. But three or four minutes later,

we heard this eerie sound—a bubba-bubba-bubba sound…Suddenly, the whole ridgeline exploded from one end to the other… It was a sight to behold, a mountain blowing up right in front of us.[423]

Also describing an Arc Light strike, General Rathvon Tompkins, the commanding general of the 3d Marine Division, added, "It was as if a little part of the world suddenly blew up from no apparent cause."[424]

When the enemy could be detected at sufficient distances from friendly lines, and obliged the American by staying in the same positions for a long enough time, the B-52 could certainly be a fearsome weapon. It is unlikely, however, that the enemy was in fact frequently so cooperative in the battle of Khe Sanh.

Limitations of the B-52s

The effectiveness of B-52s in supporting the ground battle of Khe Sanh (which was never surpassed throughout the war) was bound by three fundamental limitations: the predictability of their attacks, their three-hour response time, and the inability to attack targets closer than 1,000 meters from friendly troops. With regard to the first, Robert Pisor offers several pieces of evidence gathered from NVA sources indicating that the enemy may have used communications intercepts or sources inside the U.S. air command and control system to help them anticipate and avoid B-52 strikes. Even if that ultimately proves to be untrue, it is clear that they managed to exploit the predictability of the B-52 attacks to reduce their losses,[425] and that U.S. air planners had to take active steps to reduce this predictability.

The last two limitations, responsiveness and stand-off from friendly troops, have already been explained, including the measures taken to mitigate each one. Despite such measures these limitations remained fundamental obstacles to use of B-52s in close air support, since by definition this involved the delivery of weapons in close proximity to friendly forces, requiring detailed integration with the fire and movement of those forces. The B-52 was not a weapon for the resolution of dynamic pitched battles fought by the ground commander, although it did reach its peak utility by attacking known and suspected enemy concentrations around the uniquely static defensive positions of Khe Sanh. The only deconfliction with "maneuver elements" required at Khe Sanh was in the opening stages of the battle when the 26th Marines FSCC deconflicted proposed strikes with the positions of long-range Special Forces patrols tracked by an Army captain attached to its staff.[426] In any situation more dynamic than Khe Sanh, the B-52 could not have been as effective a weapon. This conclusion is not only supported by prominent historians of the battle like Ray Stubbe,[427] and by NVA sources which indicate a 40 percent reduction in the percentage of casualties inflicted by air strikes in the mobile stages of this battle,[428] but also by the campaigns which followed. Captain William Dabney, the commander of the defenses on Hill 881S and an ardent fan of the B-52 as a "close air support" weapon at Khe Sanh, had the benefit of serving as an advisor to an ARVN operation in the same region three years later. During Operation Lam Son 719, MACV attempted to use B-52s in a similar role with maneuver forces, but found that the increased number of firebases made clearance of these missions prohibitive. As a result, the B-52s were forced to bomb more than eight kilometers from the key battles in an effort to avoid hitting friendly troops.[429]

The fact that B-52s were not true close air support aircraft does not negate the popular claim that the Stratofortress was the decisive weapon of the battle. There are also, however, no concrete facts to support this claim. The testimonials of Marines awed by the destructive firepower of B-52s in the hills around Khe Sanh reflect observations on a minority of missions. Only 23.1 percent of the B-52 sorties flown in support of Operation Niagara were classified as close-in missions, where their effects could be readily observed.[430] Even so, as noted in Colonel Lownds' testimony, the Marines were awed by the destructiveness of the Stratofortress on terrain, not because of the effects observed on enemy weapons and equipment. While the procedures developed at Khe Sanh for the close-in tactical employment of B-52s undoubtedly contributed to the American success at Khe Sanh, and improved the utility of the Stratofortress later in the war, especially the critical conventional battles of 1972,[431] there was no quantification of their effectiveness even in the most highly observed of their missions, which were a distinct minority.

Even today, there is only one quantitative measure of B-52 effectiveness in the battle for Khe Sanh based directly on known casualties inflicted. The official NVA campaign history reports that the 325 Division sustained 4 percent of its casualties due to B-52 strikes while in bivouac or movement, 18.8 percent of its casualties due to air (assumed to be tactical air strikes) or artillery while in bivouac or movement, and 63.1 percent of its casualties "wounded in action" (a statistic which likely includes the effects of some B-52 and some strikes by tactical aircraft). More impressive for the B-52, the 304 Division reported that its suffered 20 percent of its casualties to B-52 strikes while in movement, and 77.4 percent wounded in action. Most other casualty samples suggest that about 60 percent of those casualties classified as wounded in action were inflicted by air strikes of one form or another.[432] If these sources are to be trusted, they do suggest that in some cases the B-52 could inflict an impressive amount of damage in the deep battle, but they do not prove that the B-52 was the decisive weapon of this campaign.

Even this information was unavailable to the Americans at the time, so it remains to be shown why numerous senior officers, especially within the 7th Air Force and MACV staff which planned Operation Niagara, endorsed the contribution of the B-52 as an unqualified success. They had several reasons to arrive at this conclusion, but unfortunately none of them are grounded in solid facts. More than half of the Arc Light sorties delivered at Khe Sanh were not only outside the range of ground observers, but were also delivered at night and during periods of heavy cloud cover, making aerial bomb damage assessment impossible. This was part of a larger trend in the Vietnam War. As one Air Force historian has determined, aerial photographic analysis could only accurately interpret the results of about 7 percent of the Arc Light missions. For the Khe Sanh campaign specifically, Air Force BDA officers reported that the total confirmed B-52 destruction for Niagara was only approximately 270 defensive positions and another 17 weapons positions.[433] The official assessment for Operation Niagara (shown in Table 2), however, does not give the B-52s credit for the confirmed destruction of a single enemy soldier, vehicle, or structure. The difference may be the result of a questionable BDA technique: the counting of "secondaries."

A "secondary" is the sympathetic detonation of highly explosive materials in a target area caused by the "primary" detonation of the actual bombs themselves. A secondary explosion is generally accepted as proof positive of a very successful bombing attack because it cannot occur unless the bombs are properly targeted and dropped on enemy materials. Unfortunately, the counting of secondaries as a measure of bombing effectiveness was flawed. To begin with, the reporting of secondaries in air combat was roughly analogous to the "body count" which became so infamous during the Vietnam War. For a Stratofortress crew flying more than 20,000 feet above their target, there was no way to measure the effectiveness of their attack other than to look for secondaries. Every combat mission debrief solicited some measure as to the success of the mission, leaving the aircrew with nothing but the reporting of secondaries to personally justify their efforts and quantify their success. Even more vexing was the fact that even well-intentioned B-52 aircrew could not be entirely accurate in their observations. Ray Stubbe points out for example, that these crews were not informed about artillery missions being fired into their target grids at the same time they were conducting bombing attacks. Aircrew observing the detonations of artillery rounds could easily mistake them for secondaries generated by their own bombs, and often did.[434] The result is that aviators would report secondary explosions as proof that they had destroyed enemy war materials, when in fact there was no evidence of any such success.

There were very clear cases when accurate secondary reports clearly proved the destruction of enemy war making potential. In late February, for example, B-52s were diverted to attack two NVA ammunition dumps which had been located. Explosions were seen in the target area for 40 minutes after the bombing ended—very clear evidence that an ammunition stockpile had been accurately located and destroyed.[435] Other than that, however, there is no report on how much ammunition was destroyed, what personnel may have been killed at the same time, or exactly what impact this had on the enemy's ability to attack Khe Sanh. When the 7th Air Force, therefore, reported that B-52 crewman had observed 1,382 secondary explosions and 108 secondary fires during Operation Niagara,[436] this statistic, which represents only 25.2 percent of the total obtained by all air attacks, should be regarded with suspicion in terms of both quantity and quality of observation.

The next problem with evaluating the effectiveness of the B-52 was the lack of positive bomb damage assessments. While there were a number of instances when the Muscle Shoals acoustic sensors listened to target areas when bombs and artillery were delivered, and heard NVA screaming as a result, this was neither a frequent occurrence, nor a necessarily accurate means of assessing damage. Since there were no reconnaissance patrols sent out from the combat base for the vast majority of the siege, there were few opportunities to actually observe the results of bombing missions. The sheer destructiveness of the massive bombings made what few opportunities existed nearly as futile, since the evi-

Table 2. MACV Cumulative Bomb Damage Assessment for Operation Niagara, from MACV Evaluations Memorandum, "An Analysis of the Khe Sanh Battle," 5 April 1968, TAB A.

	7th Air Force	B-52	Navy/Marines	Total
Secondary Explosions	2215	1362	1128	4705
Secondary Fires	1173	108	651	1932
PersonnelKBA	650		638	1288
Trucks (Destroyed/Damage)	204/37		49/15	253/52
Gun Positions (Destroyed/Damaged)	135/18		165/25	300/43
Bunkers (Destroyed/Damaged)	216/19		675/80	891/99
Structures (Destroyed/Damaged)	564/52		497/106	1061/158
Tanks (Destroyed/Damaged)	4/0		5/4	9/4

dence was annihilated or buried, as was several square kilometers of jungle and earth around it. This, therefore, is the paradox of measuring B-52 effectiveness at Khe Sanh: in cases where it was effective, it left no positive proof.

The most common reason that B-52s were given so much credit for the victory at Khe Sanh, therefore, was that expected enemy attacks never materialized. There are several cases where Muscle Shoals sensors gave clear warning of impending attacks, which failed to develop after Arc Light and artillery missions were used to interdict them. On a macroscopic scale, however, this logic is flawed. To say that the interdiction of B-52s was the decisive factor in winning the battle because it prevented an attack by more than two NVA divisions which had massed to strike Khe Sanh is flawed. Most fundamentally, this conclusion is voided by the fact that there is no definitive evidence that the NVA ever meant to seize Khe Sanh in the first place. Throughout the battle, the Marines waited for a major combat assault on the combat base which never came, and the enemy eventually faded away into the jungle. There are a number of historians and officers who were present at the time who believe that this was purely a matter of Giap's choosing, and that Khe Sanh was merely a cleverly executed deception designed to draw U.S. forces and attention away from the coastline in order to increase the success of the Tet Offensive. It has already been shown that the truth is probably somewhere in between, and until more trustworthy North Vietnamese records about the battle become available and prove otherwise, it would be best to assume that the NVA were only willing to sustain limited casualties in their encirclement of the combat base.

In summary, although a large number of witnesses were clearly impressed with the firepower delivered by the B-52 at Khe Sanh, there is no definitive proof that this was the decisive weapon of the battle. Perhaps the most credible participant of the battle with respect to this matter is Captain Baig, the officer responsible to targeting the enemy. Unfortunately, he obviously fell guilty to some dangerous assumptions when he stated that the reason why the 26th Marine's supporting arms were so effective was that

> Tonc's revelation of the concept of operations, prior and detailed knowledge of the NVA methodology, the requirements of siege warfare, and the lessons of Dienbienphu and Con Thien, gave the intelligence and target team all the information we needed to plan the nature of the supporting-arms countermeasures. Though on occasion I had cause to question the accuracy of my assumptions, nevertheless events tended to prove that we were correct.... But some of the credit must go to General Giap and the NVA. They gave us a good fight, and in the process they destroyed themselves. A man and a force, both known as past masters of guerrilla warfare, infiltration techniques, and siege tactics, were finally revealed as stolid, rigid, inflexible, and unbelievably foolish opponents.[437]

With the benefit of considerable hindsight, what is now revealed as a rather triumphalist assessment suggests that Baig's endorsement of the B-52 as the most significant weapon of the battle should be balanced by the viewpoints of other, well-qualified, participants. None other than his fellow targeteer, Major James Stanton, the 26th Marines Assistant Fire Support Coordinator, held a more balanced point of view which shows a little more respect for Giap as the talented strategist history has shown him to be. Stanton stated,

> One school of thought has it that the NVA opened the siege in order to fix a reinforced regiment of Marines in an unimportant corner of the country and oblige us to divert thousands of sorties away form the real Tet objectives, such as Hue City and Saigon. That

is a legitimate observation from a strategic point of view. Another school of thought has it that we wanted to be there because Khe Sanh lay astride their major infiltration route from North Vietnam. In fact, they were going around us, but if we had been able to patrol actively out of the combat base, we would have been able to wreak havoc on the infiltration routes. So this school of thought feels that the NVA pinned us inside Khe Sanh to relieve pressure on the infiltration routes.[438]

While Stanton proposed some pretty big questions about the conventional celebratory conclusions at Khe Sanh, one thing is clear. It is by no means certain that the application of massive airpower, especially by the battle's conspicuous and favored champion—the B-52—won the day. Just as important, the unique conditions that allowed the B-52 to be employed in the first place, like a static defensive position under a large scale conventional NVA assault, would seldom, if ever, be replicated.

Even if it is assumed that the destructive potential of the B-52 was fully realized at Khe Sanh, it is not the whole story. At the time of the battle, the tactical air attacks which are so often overlooked by historians were actually a well-known complement to the B-52. As noted earlier, Westmoreland pointed out that the statements of NVA prisoners and defectors revealed that "enemy troops fear B-52's, tactical air, artillery, and armor…in that order [emphasis added]."[439] showing that the enemy had a great respect for this dimension of air power. Perhaps a greater compliment was indirectly paid by the great advocate of the B-52 at Khe Sanh himself, General Momyer, who declared in his analysis of the battle, "In addition to the fighter strikes, B-52s also made a significant impact on the enemy's efforts [emphasis added]."[440]

RADAR CONTROLLED TACTICAL AIR SUPPORT

For purposes of analysis, it would be convenient to categorize the air support provided at Khe Sanh into two groups: deep air support (DAS) provided by the strategic bombers of the Air Force, and close air support (CAS) provided by tactical aircraft of the Marine Corps. Reality, of course, defies such academic simplification. Both services, for example, "crossed the line" between DAS and CAS when it came to their contributions. Another matter which significantly obscures a comparison of the contributions of the two services was their use of ground-based radars to provide terminal guidance to both deep and close air support sorties. In fact, approximately two-thirds of all bombing missions over Khe Sanh, DAS and CAS, were controlled by these radars.[441] Both the Air Force and the Marine Corps provided such systems to support the battle, increasing the capability of the United States to apply air power in the defense of the outpost. The Marine TPQ-10 system, however, was a more accurate and responsive system developed in anticipation of such battles, while the Air Force MSQ-77 Skyspot was a reaction to unforeseen shortcomings which could not match the performance of the TPQ-10 and the Marine Air Support Radar Teams (ASRT's) that ran it.

The Marine Air Support Radar Team and TPQ-10

The Marine Corps developed its air support radar in response to a critical vulnerability identified during the conduct of close air support in previous wars. Close air support, primarily executed through the visual acquisition of targets or reference marks, was dependent on favorable weather conditions to be effective. Low visibility or low cloud ceilings often made targets difficult or impossible to observe from the air, rendering them safe from air attacks with any degree of accuracy. For an organization as dependent on the heavy firepower of air support as the Marine Corps was, this meant that poor weather conditions could bring an entire operation to a halt, and make the Marines vulnerable to enemy attacks. With the improvement of radar technology, the Marine Corps experimented with several techniques to solve this problem. One idea was facilitated by the development of the A-6A Intruder, an all-weather attack aircraft. This heavy tactical bomber carried an onboard radar for navigation and the attack of fixed targets during adverse weather conditions and nighttime. In order to adapt this system for attacks on fleeting targets in dynamic battles where CAS was needed, friendly forces were equipped with radar reflectors. Since these reflectors could be easily spotted by the A-6 radar, a forward air controller could give the aircrew a direction and distance to offset their attack from the radar reflection in order to hit the enemy. This technique was attempted at Khe Sanh in November 1967, when a reflector was installed on Hill 881S. Unfortunately, that particular reflector proved incompatible with the A-6 radar,[442] rendering this particular technique ineffective at Khe Sanh. The system was later improved by providing the ground FAC with a radar beacon which transmitted on a frequency visible to the A-6 radar. RABFAC (Radar Beacon Forward Air Control) missions were successfully executed later in the siege and the rest of Vietnam War, as well as during the Persian Gulf War of 1991, but the system only allowed A-6s, providing only a small minority of the air support sorties available, to deliver CAS in poor weather. Another system was required to harness radar technology and allow any aircraft to be directed in a "blind" attack with a high degree of accuracy.

That technology was manifest in the TPQ-10 air support control radar. The story of its development was a feat of enough significance that in his seminal work *First to Fight*, Lieutenant General Victor Krulak classified it as one of the great examples of the Marine Corps' innovative nature, along with the development of landing craft and amphibious tractors for World War II. The idea

A static display of the AN/TPQ-10 system at Point Mugu, California, in 1962. In the foreground is the precision tracking radar and in the background on the right is the control van. The van was originally nicknamed a "heli-hut" to emphasize that the entire system could be moved around the battlefield by helicopter. Inside the open door of the control van, two Marines of an Air Support Radar Team can be seen seated at the monitors, as they would be when guiding an aircraft to a computed release point to put its bombs on target. The static display also includes an A-4 in the background on the left, which is significant because the A-4 was designed only for bombing in daylight and permissive weather conditions. The TPQ-10, however, could be used to put a Skyhawk's bombs on target day or night, and in any kind of weather.

of such a ground-based air support radar evolved from a brief Marine experiment in guided missile technology in 1950, when officers assigned to the test unit saw potential not for guiding missiles to a target, but for guiding aircraft to the proper positions in the sky to release their bombs on targets they could not see. Since such a capability would allow continued air support of ground battles during nighttime and poor weather conditions, the potential advantages were immediately apparent. The first version of this system was the MPQ-14. After achieving hits with errors of less than 50 yards in tests, the system was deployed to Korea in July 1951, where it provided Marine CAS aircraft the capability to deliver weapons from higher, safer altitudes with great accuracy, regardless of darkness or poor weather.[443] The capability was the result of both individual and institutional commitments to exploring all opportunities for improving the quality and dependability of air support for Marine operations on the ground.

The TPQ-10 was the replacement for the Korean War's MPQ-14. This radar was capable of tracking most aircraft up to 35 miles away, although aircraft equipped with radar beacons could be tracked up to 50 miles away. The radar was designed to provide steering information to any attack aircraft to guide it to targets identified by the FSCC. The radar's computer tracked the aircraft, then used its speed and altitude to calculate a proper release point to hit the desired targets with the specific ordnance being employed. The radar operator then passed steering commands to the pilot by voice over the radio to get the aircraft to the proper release point, and told the pilot when to drop his bombs. With certain types of aircraft (such as the A-4, A-6, and F-4B) the TPQ-10 could actually be electronically linked to the aircraft autopilot, so that once the pilot gave his consent, the ground crew could steer the aircraft and drop its ordnance without talking to the pilot.[444] In essence, the TPQ-10 extended the TACP's positive control of aircraft, which usually required the aircraft to be in sight, to non-visual conditions. With this system, even at night and in poor weather the TACP could be sure not only that ordnance would be delivered on target, but also that it would not be accidentally dropped on friendly troops.

The TPQ-10 and its ground crew, known as an Air Support Radar Team (ASRT), were part of a Marine Air Support Squadron (MASS). The ASRT was designed to work in close conjunction with both a DASC and its supported FSCC, where it could have timely situational awareness to sorties available, as well as the ground scheme of maneuver and ground commander's needs. At the start of 1968, there were two MASSs in Vietnam, which maintained a total of five ASRTs. Two ASRTs supported the 3d Marine Division at its Dong Ha headquarters, while a third supported from Phu Bai. For the 1st Marine Division one ASRT was located at Da Nang, while a second was based at Chu Lai. It was this last team, ASRT-B (pronounced "as-rat bravo"), which was moved to Khe Sanh on 16 January 1968 with its associated TPQ-10, just as the NVA attack on the combat base appeared imminent. The electronics van which housed the radar operators and the bulk of their equipment was converted into a reinforced sand bag bunker, and was operational by 20 January, the very eve of the siege.[445] The TPQ-10 remained in operation throughout the entire siege, even after a direct hit on the roof of the van by an NVA rocket. In the first month alone it guided more than 4,200 sorties, delivering 20,000 tons of ordnance on 2,880 targets.[446]

From first day of operations, the TPQ-10 was able to direct aircraft in attacks closer to friendly lines than the B-52. While Arc Lights were initially restricted to attack outside 3,000 meters, the TPQ-10 was certified to guide attacking aircraft as close as 1,000 meters from friendly troops. From the start, the Marines made every effort to reduce this limitation. As early as 29 January, the 3d Marine Division had begun arranging for the delivery of a more accurate X-band radar to its most critical outpost, the combat base at Khe Sanh.[447] Once installed, the improved TPQ was able to control aircraft in to significantly closer distances. Under the standard operating procedures, 500-pound bombs could be dropped as close as 500 meters from friendlies, while 250-pound bombs could be brought as close as 250 meters. These decreased restrictions reflected the fact that the accuracy of the radar was no longer considered a limitation, only the destructive radius of the bomb detonation itself. Strikes as close as 500 meters became routine, and under extreme circumstances the ASRT even controlled attacks on targets just 35 meters from friendly lines.[448]

The support of the TPQ-10 proved critical at Khe Sanh, especially during the crachin of February, which brought thick, low-lying clouds that blanketed the ground like fog for days on end. In one 24-hour period alone, 18 February, ASRT-B controlled Marine Corps, Navy, and Air Force aircraft to deliver 480 tons of ordnance on 105 targets. By the end of the campaign, ASRT-B controlled nearly 5,000 missions.[449] As stated by the Assistant Fire Support Coordinator of the 26th Marines, "integration of the ASRT (ground support radar team) [sic] and Marine Corps fire support coordination apparatus was a brilliant but overlooked accomplishment which saved our bacon many times during low visibility…when other close air support couldn't be used."[450]

The TPQ-10 was instrumental in controlling attacks in a number of ways besides replacing the visual close air support techniques that were possible only in daytime and clear weather conditions. The TPQ, designed to guide attacks on targets which could not be seen because of darkness or heavy weather, could also be used in attacks on targets that could not be seen because they were hidden by jungle, or because they were too far from Khe Sanh. In this way, the TPQ-10 was used to guide aircraft to attack targets identified by spotter aircraft and sensors. The ASRT was frequently employed in controlling such deep air support missions, and the Khe Sanh FSCC was innovative in maximizing its effectiveness in such efforts. One technique used when B-52s were not available or when there was insufficient time to get approval for a new Arc Light target all the way through Saigon, became known as the "Mini-Arclight." The idea was to combine the other fire support assets and mass their attacks in a single devastating strike to mimic the destructiveness of the B-52. Under this technique, ASRT-B guided attack aircraft (usually A-6s) against area targets

1,000 meters long and 500 meters wide, while artillery was fired to deliver its rounds (with trajectories deconflicted with aircraft flight paths) simultaneously at a single TOT. Although the ordnance massed was lighter than that of an Arc Light, and the target box attacked was smaller, the result was a more flexible and responsive attack which could be delivered closer to friendly lines.[451] A mini-Arc Light could be coordinated in about one hour's time, and was considered so successful that the 26th Marines FSCC took it one step further. To attack an even smaller target area of just 500 meters by 500 meters, a "Micro-Arc Light" would be coordinated and executes just 10 to 15 minutes after the target was identified.[452] It can be seen therefore, that the ASRT was responsible for increasing the responsiveness, and therefore the effectiveness, of the deeper air battle.

Mini- and Micro-Arc Lights were not restricted to deep targets, like the "major NVA headquarters" obliterated in the second week of February with 152 five hundred-pound bombs dropped by six Marine jets and 350 artillery rounds. During the height of the enemy attack, a nightly average of 3-4 mini-Arclights and 6-8 micro-Arclights[453]

Two A-6 Intruders flying low and level in a tight tactical formation near Khe Sanh. Such formations would be used when under TPQ-10 control to mass the bombs of both aircraft on the target coordinates put into the radar's computer, as when conducting a "micro-Arclight" mission.

were directed against enemy siege works being dug only 500 to 1,500 meters from the combat base perimeter.[454]

The TPQ-10 was also used to guide aircraft in other creative fire support plans. The primary and secondary boxes, for example, were both means of systematically covering pieces of terrain with destructive fires to support offensive and defensive operations. Since the objective was to isolate, entrap, and destroy enemy that were within those boxes, the pilots had to deliver their ordnance at precise locations and on pieces of terrain without the benefit of visually distinct targets or aiming points. The easiest way to do this, regardless of the weather conditions, was to have the ordnance delivered under TPQ-10 control, which could do so reliably without the benefit of visual reference points. This technique was credited with preventing a reserve battalion from joining to support the assault battalion in the attack on Hill 861 on the night of 5 February. As a result, the hill was successfully defended, despite the enemy battalions wasted in the effort.[455]

The innovation practiced by the 26th Marines FSCC in its fire support planning spread to the men of ASRT-B. No ballistic tables had been developed for the delivery of napalm under TPQ-10 control, so ARST-B and the FSCC worked to obtain permission to develop their own tables. Tests were conducted against more distant targets where safe deliveries could be confirmed by a FAC's visual observations. Once the ASRT developed its own tables for the accurate delivery of napalm by low-flying aircraft, the defenders of Khe Sanh were able to tactically employ it at night, and in other circumstances when visual control was impossible, adding to the arsenal available for their defense.[456] As the Air Officer for the 26th Marines summarized, "I cannot imagine what would have happened at Khe Sanh if we had not had ASRT-B. They were always 'up,' always on target and always innovative."[457]

Such endorsements of the TPQ-10 were not uncommon once its value was proven at Khe Sanh. Colonel Lownds himself was more impressed with the contributions of the ASRT missions than he was with the less flexible and discriminate firepower of the B-52, stating,[458] "Anything but the highest praise would not be enough."[459] General Krulak also considered it a "major factor in meeting the needs for round-the-clock fire support of the base,"[460] and agreed with the assessment that TPQ-10 guided support was of greater importance than B-52 missions.[461]

The Air Force MSQ-77 Combat Skyspot System

Ground radar control of attack aircraft was not a capability unique to the Marine Corps, since the Air Force had a similar system in Vietnam about a year and a half prior to the siege of Khe Sanh. In his memoir, General Momyer claimed that this system was modified from a gun-laying radar used by the Army Air Corps in Italy during the Second World War. He asserted that the technique was in regular use during night and poor-weather missions for the remainder of World War II and the Korean War,[462] suggesting that the Air Force valued and preserved this capability. If this was true, however, it is hard to explain why the Air Force lacked such a system in the humid, rainy climate of Vietnam until late in 1966. Most Air Force historians, including Bernard C. Nalty, John Schlight, and John J. Sbrega, point to the loss of the A Shau Special Forces Camp in March 1966 as a "wake-up call" for the Air Force in Southeast Asia when it came to the requirement for an all-weather capability. During this incident ceilings of 300 to 500 feet severely constrained the ability of the few O-1 FACs and fighter bombers that could get below the weather to support the defense of the isolated outpost.[463] The swift fall of the camp was on Westmoreland's mind when he later contemplated the air defense of Khe Sanh.[464] It likewise motivated the Air Force to find new ways to ensure that its tactical air power would not be rendered useless by poor weather.[465]

Sometime before the fall of A Shau, Momyer's predecessor as the head of the 7th Air Force, Lieutenant General Joseph H. Moore, visited 1st MAW and saw the effectiveness of the TPQ-10. He urged the Air Force to develop a similar capability, which it did by adapting a training system known as the MSQ-77 Skyspot. This system was designed to track aircraft during training sorties and score simulated bomb drops on U.S. cities by predicting the point of impact of their bombs. This system was reconfigured to control aircraft in attacks prior to March 1966, but the disaster which occurred at A Shau gave new urgency on the program. Once converted to a system known as Combat Skyspot, it was less mobile than the TPQ-10, but had longer range and provided a similar capability.[466] The MSQ-77 could track beacon equipped aircraft up to 150 miles away, and by 1967, five sites in Southeast Asia provided coverage for all of South Vietnam, Route Package I just north of the DMZ, and most of the Laotian panhandle. Later additions in Laos allowed coverage of Route Package VI, north of Hanoi.[467] The Air Force was quick to make use of the new capabilities provided by this system, whose benefits were obvious in the poor Indochinese weather. By the end of the war one quarter of all strike missions had been controlled by the MSQ-77. By the end of 1966 Combat Skyspot became the primary means for directing Arc Light strikes, since there were few targets large and radar-reflective enough to be detected by the B-52s onboard systems.[468]

Combat Skyspot was not as accurate as the Marine TPQ-10, yielding only a 72-meter circular error probability (CEP) in testing. For this reason, MACV prohibited the use of the MSQ-77 to control missions closer than 1,000 meters from friendly troops without the explicit authorization of the ground commander. Requested deviations from this standard sometimes brought attacks within 500 meters of friendlies.[469] This was still a far cry from the TPQ-10, however, whose miss distances were typically less than 50 meters, especially when one considers that the main cause for such errors was imprecise target location fed into the targeting system, rather than limitations within the radar equipment itself.[470] The first historian to document the battle stated that at Khe Sanh the TPQ was always within 40 meters of the target on the first drop, and that there was virtually no error after adjustment. To ensure that the system was able to consistently deliver this high degree of accuracy it was shut down for one hour of daily maintenance, and calibrated twice weekly.[471] As has already been shown, this precision allowed the TPQ-10 to control attacks on targets as close as 35 meters from friendly positions. The accuracy deficiencies of the MSQ-77 are perhaps best summed up by an Air Force major who was one of the few from his service to spend any time at all at Khe Sahn, as a liaison officer. His conclusion was that close-in air strikes would have been impossible in bad weather (which persisted for much of February) without the TPQ-10.[472]

The use of the MSQ-77 in it specific application at Khe Sanh was subject to additional limitations which further decreased its effectiveness compared to the TPQ-10. Both systems tracked aircraft with radial coordinate systems, the accuracy of which declined as range from the radar increased. The closest MSQ-77 site was 27 miles away from Khe Sanh, at Dong Ha, while the Marines moved their TPQ-10 to KSCB itself to maximize its accuracy and responsiveness. In terms of the latter aspect, this also gave the TPQ-10 significant advantages. The TPQ-10 was located adjacent to the FSCC bunker at Khe Sanh, allowing targets to be rapidly changed in reaction to changing defensive priorities. Requests and direction passed to the Dong Ha Skyspot, however, had to negotiate the interface between two command and control systems (Marine and Air Force).

Since most of the Arc Light missions were also MSQ-77 controlled, the limited responsiveness of the B-52, whose targets could not be changed less than three hours before the attack even with rapid approval from Saigon, further reduced the Skyspot's responsiveness.

During the defense of Khe Sanh, the Skyspot was troubled by other problems. Its remote location made it difficult to rapidly manage unforeseen airspace conflicts. The Combat Skyspot was only capable of handling one flight at a time, which meant that the operator was unable to monitor other aircraft which might be flying near the aircraft under control. With such a tenous link to the other control agencies at Khe Sanh, MSQ-77 operators were also denied the instantaneous face-to-face communications that co-location at Khe Sanh would have enabled. These shortcomings resulted in conflicts between tactical aircraft and B-52s.[473] For a system which had so many limitations, the Combat Skyspot operators at Dong Ha apparently had their hands in too many pies, controlling attack aircraft, multi-role fighters, and B-52s. At times they had so many more aircraft waiting for direction than the system could handle that some aircraft ran low on fuel and had to jettison their bombs without ever attacking the enemy.[474] In the high intensity battle of Khe Sanh, perhaps it would have been better if the less accurate and less responsive MSQ-77 was paired solely with the less responsive and less discriminating firepower of the B-52.

Conclusions

Ground-based air support radar systems provided the Marines of Khe Sanh with an all-weather, day or night, and long-range capability for directing air attacks on almost any target detected. This capability was instrumental in improving the flexibility of employing forces both in the deep and close air battles at Khe Sanh. The TPQ-10, however, was a more accurate and more responsive system which had been developed and proven well in advance of the battle of Khe Sanh. This system was a product of the close alliance between air and ground power in Marine doctrine and practice, and a proactive effort to maximize CAS effectiveness before the war in Vietnam. The Air Force MSQ-77 Combat Skyspot, in contrast, was a reaction to unforeseen shortcomings in Southeast Asia which was inspired by the Marine system, but which still lacked the accuracy and responsiveness of a Marine ASRT equipped with the TPQ-10.

CLOSE AIR SUPPORT

While the tactical jet aircraft that provided the true close air support for Khe Sanh could not match the bulk firepower of the B-52s, they were decisive contributors to the defense. For every B-52 that arrived over Khe Sanh, 10 tactical aircraft were also on hand to provide support.[475] The cumulative effect of the ordnance they delivered was less than that of Arc Light missions, but these 22,000 sorties filled a significant gap left by the air support of the B-52 because the tactical aircraft engaged in CAS were more responsive, flexible, and precise. They could be used not only to attack NVA at very close ranges to friendly troops, but also to conduct attacks on fleeting targets and in other dynamic situations that supported the Marines' ground campaign for the defense of Khe Sanh.

Visual CAS

While some of the bombing missions flown by B-52s and radar-guided tactical aircraft were in relatively close proximity to friendlies, and were integrated into the defensive "scheme of maneuver" at Khe Sanh, they seldom qualified as CAS in its traditional, and most effective form. This was the delivery of ordnance on targets which have been visually acquired by the attack aircraft, or visually marked for the attack aircraft by a forward air controller (FAC). The common characteristic of these attacks, regardless of what the pilot could or could not see, was that they were conducted under the control of a FAC. The advantages of this technique are numerous. First of all, under visual CAS, the pilot of the attacking aircraft was in direct communication with the ground unit he was supporting. Unlike the other systems of air support, which relied on the passage of target information through extensive command and control systems, visual CAS allowed final coordination based on battlefield events as they occurred. Even a moving target could be attacked if it could be identified to the pilot. There was no more responsive way to direct aircraft attacks, since the fire support was coordinated and directed at the lowest level—between the aircrew and the actual maneuver unit being supported. The B-52, even when described as a CAS weapon, was on the opposite end of the spectrum, primarily due to its extensive targeting bureaucracy. While under exceptional circumstances, like the detection of a large enemy unit by theater-level intelligence assets, the B-52 could be retargeted in just a few hours, this was indeed the exception. The units which directly engaged the enemy did not enjoy this level of responsiveness. The FAC on Hill 881S, for example, was permitted to submit up to eight targets each day for destruction by B-52s. He received no response from the fire support coordination system or air control system indicating whether or not he would receive the requested support, and simply had to wait for the next day, when the entire region around the target would either erupt in a wall of explosions without warning, or remain completely untouched.[476] When this FAC had a target of any importance, he could not afford to wait for the next day to see if it would be hit or not, so he had to depend either on radar-directed CAS attacks, or if the target was fleeting, upon visual CAS missions under his own control.

In addition to the obvious benefits conveyed by the immediate responsiveness of visual CAS missions, in combination with the larger volume of tactical aircraft sorties providing more complete coverage, this characteristic made it impossible for the NVA to predict and avoid tactical air attacks, as they did with the B-52. The accessibility and responsiveness of tactical CAS aircraft were not the only reasons they were preferred by maneuver units. A final advantage of conducting final coordination at the lowest level was that this mode of support was the most accurate. It could be tainted by no other errors than the skill of the aircrew and FAC, the aircraft's bombing accuracy, and the tactical manner in which they were employed. Significantly, each service's approach to close air support had an impact on each of these factors, producing a wide variation in results.

The tactical aircraft that supported the 26th Marines in visual CAS missions came from all three services. While this complicates a comparative study by making it difficult to assess their individual contributions, it does provide an opportunity to examine the relative performances of the various services engaged in the same task, side by side. Before going on to a qualitative comparison, however, the quantitative data should be addressed. Unfortunately, no comprehensive summary of solely visual CAS missions has been found, and the manner in which aircraft of the various services were put to use in the mixed missions around Khe Sanh makes it unlikely that such data exists or could be extrapolated from existing data. As a starting point, however, the contributions of all three services in terms of sorties and tonnage dropped is available.

As can be seen in Table 3, Marine tactical aircraft contributed a smaller portion of the total tactical sorties than the Air Force, but delivered a higher proportion of the ordnance. The Marines were able to deliver more ordnance with fewer sorties for several reasons. To begin with, they had heavy attack aircraft, like the A-6A, which could carry more ordnance that the Air Force F-100s or F-4s that composed the majority of their strike aircraft. Second, 1st MAW's bases were all located nearby in the ICTZ, allowing the Marines to carry more ordnance because they did not need to carry as much fuel on these shorter range missions. In addition, a significant number of Air Force tactical missions were not even intended for Khe Sanh in the first place. Only 30 percent of the Air Force effort at the time was devoted to the direct support of ground troops,[477] but diversions from other missions often increased this number. In January 1968, the Navy and Air Force were using tactical aircraft to try and isolate Haiphong in North Vietnam by severing the transportation lines that lead inland from the port. During this campaign, the weather was very poor, becoming prohibitively so in February. Navy and Air Force aircraft unable to bomb their primary targets in North Vietnam were diverted to assist with the massing of air power in Operation Niagara. In February, Task Force 77 diverted 77 percent of its strike sorties from North Vietnam, followed by another 67 percent in March.[478] Despite the high number of FACs and targets around Khe Sanh, the Air Force and Marine systems had a hard time managing the extra sorties that materialized on a daily basis without warning. Bernard Nalty specified that Navy aircraft were sometimes forced to jettison their ordnance and return home when they ran low on fuel,[479] but the Air Force experienced the same problem.

Trends in the Use of CAS During the Siege: A Free-For-All?

The narrative discussion of the Hill Fights, siege, and relief of Khe Sanh has already shown that close air support was an integral and vital

Table 3. Total sortie and ordnance contributions to the defense of Khe Sanh, from Prados and Stubbe, Valley of Decision, *297.*

	Sorties	Sortie Percentage	Bomb Tonnage	Ordnance Percentage
1st Marine Air Wing	7,078	28.7%	17,015	17.2%
Navy Aircraft	5,337	21.6%	7,941	8.0%
7th Air Force Tactical Aircraft	9,691	39.3%	14,223	14.4%
B-52s	2,548	10.3%	59,542	60.3%

part of Marine operations. During the Hill Fights and the prelude to the siege, for example, CAS was used as a readily available fire support asset for maneuver units once they located and established contact with the enemy. No one, however, has identified the largest patterns to which close air support was put in the defense of the combat base and its outposts, despite the fact that so many authors have written about the siege. It is easy to overlook the big picture when confronted with the apparent chaos of daylight operations, described by the 26th Marines' Target Information Officer (TIO) as

> a vulgar free-for-all, with air and artillery under the control of local forward observers and tactical air controllers, who attacked anything and everything that looked peculiar. Targets were taken under fire as they appeared. Repeated checkfires [cease fires for safety reasons], caused by the presence of resupply aircraft and helicopters, prevented a systematic approach to target reduction.[480]

In the nighttime, when darkness prevented visual observations and visually-directed CAS missions, the TIO was able to bring B-52s, TPQ-10 missions, and artillery fires together in carefully orchestrated packages to maximize the firepower directed at a relatively limited number of high priority targets. In the daytime, on the other hand, visual observations produced a high number of "targets of opportunity" which were dealt with as quickly as possible by the individual supporting arms in their most responsive modes. This responsiveness was maximized by engaging each target separately, eliminating the coordination time required by integration with other fire support assets.[481] This "free-for-all," which proved so disturbing to the Target Information Officer who was responsible for developing a whole picture of the enemy so that air power could be applied systematically, was in fact a very effective decentralized method of employing air power. The very fact that FACs and FAC(A)s were finding valuable targets that the TIO had not been aware of added a new dimension to the air battle by allowing the Marines to rapidly use responsive CAS to destroy targets that would otherwise have gone unharmed. Compared to Captain Baig's targeting of B-52s, this decentralized battle certainly must have seemed chaotic because it was the units that were in contact with the enemy, not an intelligence officer in a bunker far underground, who were identifying the targets. If the TIO and other members of the FSCC had attempted to more carefully orchestrate supporting arms against these fleeting targets, they could not have successfully engaged so large a number. Furthermore, it was misleading for Baig to call the effort a free for all, since the FACs and FAC(A)s had to coordinate requests for air support through the DASC, which acted according to the FSCC's targeting priorities. No attacks could be made in the three zones closest to KSCB without the consent of the FSCC. Even if a FAC(A) found a promising target outside these zones, he still had to work through ABCCC to get strike aircraft to prosecute that target. ABCCC was supposed to be in contact with the 26th Marines FSCC it was supporting, and certainly had to coordinate with the Marines any time it wanted to divert a significant number of sorties destined for Khe Sanh to more promising targets in the outer zones. In summary, the FSCC was managing this decentralized battle by exercising oversight over what targets were permitted to be attacked, and what air assets were devoted to their destruction.

An examination of the week-by-week uses to which CAS was put also shows that the defensive use of CAS was by no means an unmanaged effort. Instead, over the course of the battle, the FSCC modulated the locations and targets on which it concentrated CAS. Early in the campaign, the enemy launched his largest assaults at night. CAS was sometimes used to break up the remnants of these attacks that remained at daybreak, but on the whole aircraft were kept looking for targets in the immediate vicinity of KSCB. While FAC(A)s were controlling fixed-wing strikes every 5-10 minutes near Khe Sanh during daylight hours, I/3/26 was reporting the presence of large caliber NVA artillery firing at KSCB over Hill 881S. These reports were not considered credible by the 26th Marines intelligence section, so CAS and aerial observation missions by FAC(A)'s remained concentrated around KSCB for the first two or three weeks.[482] When I/3/26 did find targets of opportunity near the hill outposts, it didn't even have a radio to direct air support, and had to call for the services of a FAC(A) who had been working closer to the combat base.

On 7 February, the sudden NVA attack on Lang Vei made that outpost the highest priority for CAS support. Once the Special Forces camp was overrun, the tanks that had attacked there remained a threat to KSCB itself. The 26th Marines reacted by devoting a portion of their sorties to finding and destroying this threat. The anti-armor effort quickly paid off when the NVA tank company was destroyed in less than 10 days. With the armor threat to KSCB eliminated, the Marines were free to reconcentrate their CAS first on NVA troop buildups, then on the artillery, rockets, and mortars that were causing the base so much distress on a daily basis. After more than two weeks of continued bombardment, the FSCC changed it priorities. As the enemy effort intensified, Hill 881S was recognized as a vital outpost not only because it prevented the NVA from setting up anti-aircraft guns directly on the aircraft approach corridors into KSCB, but also because it provided early warning for long-range artillery passing overhead on its way to the combat base. Its location eight kilometers from Khe Sanh along the combat base's long axis also put the hill in the heart of the region where the NVA wanted to set up their rocket launchers. Once the Marines on 881S found a number of rocket positions within two kilometers of the outpost, a radio was sent out for the terminal control of CAS in early February. After that, the Marines of I/3/26 found that the targets of opportunity they located were never turned down, and the company employed over 300 air strikes without the aid of a FAC(A).[483]

The day of peak bombardment was 23 February, and as time wore on, what Marines described as "A-number one" air support was given the credit for earning some breaks from the bombardment up to 48 hours long.[484] Even as the FSCC began to focus on defeating the enemy's artillery, however, an NVA trench complex was detected approaching KSCB. General Westmoreland himself, worried by the precedent established by the NVA siege trenches at Dien Bien Phu, ordered that CAS be concentrated on this immediate threat. The 26th Marines FSCC needed no urging, and had already begun to concentrate CAS on the new trenches threatening from just a few hundred meters away. Once the NVA abandoned their attempt to invest KSCB and Operation Pegasus was initiated in March, the Marines devoted the bulk of their CAS assets to the westward movement of the relief force. Each of these changes in the focus of the CAS effort at Khe Sanh shows that while CAS was executed through decentralized targeting, this effort was deliberately managed by the FSCC according to its changing operational priorities.

Forward Air Controllers

The lynchpin that connected air and ground power in close air support was the Forward Air Controller (FAC). This was the individual who submitted requests for air support once suitable targets had been identified, integrated the use of that air support into the ground unit's scheme of maneuver, assisted the air crew in locating the targets they needed to hit, and provided terminal control for the safe and effective engagement of those targets. There were two general types of FACs employed at Khe Sanh. The first type was the ground FACs, who were co-located with the units they supported on the ground. The second type was the forward air controllers who flew above the battlefield directing attack aircraft, which will collectively be referred to as Forward Air Controllers (Airborne), or FAC(A)s. This group included controllers of various sources, including Air Force Airborne FACs (AFACs), Marine Aerial Observers (AOs), Marine Tactical Air Controllers (TACs), and true Marine airborne FACs. Significantly, while Bernard Nalty described the important contribution of these controllers, he overlooked the role of ground FAC's in his Air Force-oriented analysis of Khe Sanh.

It has already been shown that the Air Force de-veloped the FAC(A) as its primary control agent for directing attack aircraft in CAS and DAS missions alike, the Marine Corps started with FACs on the ground, and later added FAC(A)s as an extension of the ground Tactical Air Control Parties. The reason for this was that in the Marine Corps the FAC was not considered merely a more accurate set of eyes to find targets for aircraft. Instead, a FAC was the primary agent for coordinating the synergistic combination of air and ground power to accomplish objectives on the ground. It therefore made the most sense to position the FAC on the ground where he could be in close communication with the supported unit commander, and develop an awareness of that unit's situation and priorities. He was then able to advise that commander and plan the integration of air power in the ground scheme of maneuver, and communicate the essential elements to the CAS aircraft, culminating in an attack under the FACs terminal control. Ideally, FACs were aviation officers temporarily assigned to duty with ground units, but combat casualties and an inability to provide enough FACs to serve with every company, platoon, and patrol out in the field meant that well-trained ground Marines often had to do the job. In cases where a fully-qualified FAC was injured, one of his radio operators would step forward, and often proved quite capable. On Hill 881S, for example, the FAC was wounded and evacuated during the first days of the siege. Since his radio operator, Corporal Robert J. Arrotta, did such a fine job, the company commander never asked for a replacement.[485] Ground FACs were especially critical because tactical aircraft engaged in CAS could not carry the immense bomb loads of B-52s, nor could such an indiscriminate weapon be employed in close proximity to friendly troops. For both reasons, tactical aircraft engaged in CAS had to be very precise in the delivery of their ordnance. This was a problem against carefully camouflaged positions, some of which could not even be seen by slow and low-flying FAC(A)s in O-1s. A ground FAC was able to see any target that

A typical Tactical Air Control Party assigned to a Marine battalion, which was usually broken up into several smaller teams supporting the rifle companies in contact with the enemy. The TACP consisted of roughly a dozen radiomen, and was ideally led by several aviators who had been trained as Forward Air Controllers. In reality, combat casualties and a shortage of aviators meant that the radiomen often had to serve as FACs, sometimes with little or no formal training for the task. Despite that problem, many performed admirably under the harshest combat conditions.

could be identified as a threat by the ground unit he supported, and mark it for attack by aircraft with highly visible cues like white smoke rounds fired by artillery and mortars, and even rounds fired from recoilless rifles. Without FACs on the ground, the Air Force was completely dependant on Marine FACs to locate and mark such targets for destruction. Even when FAC(A)s were used to support ground units, the ground FAC remained a vital link for integrating the attacks with ground operations by serving as the FAC(A)s main conduit to the supported unit.[486]

At Khe Sanh, FAC(A)s generally came from a detachment of Headquarters and Maintenance Squadron-16 at Quang Tri, or the Air Force's 20th Tactical Air Support Squadron at Da Nang. These FAC(A)s flew O-1 Bird Dogs, and were augmented by FAC(A)s in UH-1s from Marine Observation Squadron-6 at Quang Tri airfield. At least five FAC(A)s roamed the skies over Khe Sanh during daylight hours, either assisting ground units or independently searching for targets.[487] This ultimately translated to about 30 of them working the area on a daily basis, for a total of almost 1,600 FAC(A) sorties over the course of the campaign.[488] Earlier in the battle some of these light observation aircraft were based at Khe Sanh itself to maximize their responsiveness, and to minimize the fuel and flight time wasted in transit to and from the coastal bases. Although these FAC(A)s had the added benefit of face-to-face communication with the ground units at Khe Sanh, the regular bombardment of the airstrip prohibited a continuation of such operations.[489]

FAC(A)s could locate targets and control tactical aircraft to attack them independent of maneuver units, but their primary purpose in Marine operations was to control CAS attacks which were truly integrated into the fire and movement of friendly units. To do so, they would contact the unit they were supporting by radio, find out what that unit's mission, objectives, priorities, and loca-

Corporal Robert J. Arrotta of I Company, 3d Battalion, 26th Marines, dubbed "The Mightiest Corporal in the Marine Corps" by his company commander on Hill 881S. Corporal Arrotta had been in Vietnam almost a year when the battle for Khe Sanh began, and had learned the skills of a Forward Air Controller through on-the-job training in combat, including at Con Thien the previous spring. When the officer FAC was wounded on his first day on Hill 881S, Corporal Arrotta took over, and was so good at his job that the company commander never asked for a replacement. Corporal Arrotta controlled several hundred air strikes from this critical outpost over the more than two months he spent there.

tion were. Often working through a ground FAC, the FAC(A) would then assist with acquiring targets that could not be seen from the ground, such as NVA hidden on the reverse slopes of hills.[490] The FAC(A) could then facilitate the request and routing of CAS aircraft, and control them in these attacks. One example of this occurred near Hill

881S, where an observer was posted as part of the effort to locate and destroy the NVA artillery just across the Laotian border. After several weeks of searching with heavy binoculars, he located the NVA artillery by spotting the muzzle flashes on a hillside more than six miles away. The artillery was much too far away for the FAC on Hill 881S to see attacking aircraft or provide proper control, so the company contacted a FAC(A) who was in the area. The target was described to the FAC(A), who began controlling the delivery of ordnance in the general vicinity of the earlier spotting. After the first attack he received a correction from the observer on 881S to get the strikes closer to the observed enemy positions, and the second attack uncovered a hidden artillery emplacement. Once that occurred, the FAC(A) was able to control numerous flights of CAS aircraft in the area to destroy the hidden guns.[491] The Marines on Hill 881S could no longer see what was going on, but this FAC(A) was obviously conducting attacks under their guidance according to their tactical priorities.

It was critical for FAC(A)s to be familiar with the area in which they were working and the units operating there if they were to have enough situational awareness to destroy the enemy without endangering friendly troops. The Marine Corps recognized this need for familiarity, and assigned its FAC(A)s to work in specific areas on a regular basis. There were two primary FAC(A)s, for example, who supported I/3/26 on Hill 881. According to Captain Dabney, he regularly worked with Tom O'Toole operating under the call sign "Southern Oscar," and Bob Happy, known as "Southern Hotel."[492] Both of these men came from the same squadron, allowing them to share information on the latest tactical situation between flights. The fact that the company commander leading the Marines on Hill 881S knew them on a first-name basis is a testament to the teamwork and close relationships inherent in the Marine air-ground team.

The Air Force's FAC(A)s were equipped much the same as the Marine FAC(A)s, although there was no distinction about what portion of the battle they were truly meant to fight. Like the Marines, Air Force FAC(A)s ranged as far as Laos searching for targets and controlling missions, but they sometimes controlled missions right outside of friendly lines. Although the Air Force FACs were often not trained to call in artillery and mortar missions, as a pragmatic matter of survival they had to learn how to deconflict aircraft attacks from these fires, most often by demanding that they cease when air operations were in progress. This required the monitoring of radios, and the development of a good deal of situational awareness when working close to active ground operations. At times, the experience gained in this process paid off. On 8 February 1968, for example, an Air Force FAC(A) was monitoring an artillery mission being coordinated on enemy troops moving toward Lang Vei. Although only enemy forces were expected to be moving toward the hamlet after the Americans had lost Lang Vei, he acted on a hunch and sought permission to investigate before the mission was fired, and discovered that the target had been misidentified. He radioed back to the Marines that the target was actually a column of refugees, thereby saving them from destruction.[493]

Regardless of where the FAC(A)s came from and what their purpose was, Nalty is correct in his assertion that they were essential to the successful defense of Khe Sanh.[494] This is because the conduct of visual CAS procedures under the control of ground-based and airborne FACs provided a responsive, accurate, and lethal capability to bridge a gap left by strategic bombers and radar-controlled missions. It has already been shown that the NVA sought to move as close as possible to the Marine positions to take advantage of the safety restrictions imposed on B-52 and other radar-controlled air missions. The fact that they were doing so was dramatically il-

Two Marines of C Battery, 1st Battalion, 13th Marines, stand near the breech of a 105mm howitzer. It appears that they have just fired a white smoke round to mark a target close to the combat base perimeter for attack by aircraft. The dark spot at the top of the picture may be the CAS aircraft, just after releasing its ordnance.

lustrated by the discovery of NVA trenches approaching the perimeter of KSCB in the last days of February. Westmoreland himself grew anxious about the indications, and told General Momyer, "It is imperative that any opportunity be taken of weather breaks to obtain FAC coverage and directed…strikes against these [emphasis added]." MACV's Deputy for Air Operations was told to plan a "concentration of maximum controllable tactical air into the area immediately surrounding Khe Sanh."[495] It is unclear whether this decision was a defensive move to stop the NVA who had eluded the bombs of the B-52s, or an offensive move designed to use air power to capitalize on the newly-found concentrations of NVA close to the Marines' lines. Either way, the statement was an open admission by Westmoreland that the favored B-52 was unsuitable for conducting this dangerously close portion of his fight.

CAS Tactics at Khe Sanh

While controlling aircraft in their attacks on targets in close proximity to ground troops, the Marines had developed a set of procedures familiar to both their ground forces and the aviators who supported them. Upon approaching Khe Sanh, aircraft would contact the FAC to get an update on the tactical situation and receive instructions on how to find the target area. The FAC would issue those instructions by describing the desired holding position using a direction and distance from the TACAN radio navigation station at KSCB. The aircraft would then proceed to that location and orbit in a manner which allowed the aircrew to see the target area described by the FAC. If directed by a FAC(A) they would wait for a rocket or smoke grenade to be delivered near the target, get instructions on the location of the target relative to that mark, and attack, waiting for the FAC(A)s "cleared hot" before dropping their ordnance. With ground FAC's the procedure was more complicated. The ground FAC would arrange for a white phosphorus smoke round, typically fired by artillery or a mortar, to mark the target. This required some measure of trust on the part of the aviators, since these marking rounds were often fired through the altitudes where they were orbiting. Safety was usually assured by lateral deconfliction, in which the aircraft was directed to orbit on one side or the other of the marking round trajectory. Once the mark appeared and the FAC radioed a correction to the pilot, the actual attack would begin, and the pilot would get clearance to drop only when he was pointed at the target. This final authorization to drop was a vital responsibility of the FAC, since it assured not only that the bombs would impact close to that target, but also that they would not endanger any friendly troops.

On Hill 881S, these procedures were refined to allow the aircraft to attack the target immediately after the smoke round impacted near the target. Aircraft orbited in an oblong pattern over the outpost, and a mark was fired as the aircraft turned back toward the target, so that the marking round would fly in front of the aircraft and impact just as the pilot began his dive to attack. This technique took skill, and even though the Marines put a safety observer on each mortar tube to stop it from firing if an aircraft was in danger of being hit, they found that the process was just too complicated to earn pilots' confidence.[496] To enable the aircraft to continue using the responsive overhead pattern, the infantry Marines switched to direct fire weapons to mark the target. Using equipment like the 3.5-inch rocket, 106mm recoilless rifle, or 105mm howitzer fired directly at the target, produced a smaller, less-easily distinguished grey explosion, but the projectiles did not conflict with the aircraft's flight path. Aircrew, however, remained apprehensive about the risk. As the company commander on Hill 881S said, "it took some convincing for the Marine pilots, and some outright arguments for the Navy pilots. The Air Force pilots would often fly away as soon as they saw an HE [High Explosive] or WP [white phosphorus] impact beneath them, and we rarely could convince them they were in no danger."[497] He went on to relate one instance in which an angry Air Force pilot claimed that he was endangered by artillery, when in fact the Marines were marking with a recoilless rifle. Dabney explained, "We told him so, but apparently he didn't know what a recoilless rifle was."[498]

It can be seen then, that in an effort to maximize the effectiveness of CAS support, the Marines at Khe Sanh innovated techniques to improve those that had been developed and practiced before the battle. The Marine aviators proved more flexible in executing these procedures because of they had a basic understanding of the ground commander's equipment, and because of the mutual trust that existed between Marines on the ground and in the air. These were both by-products of a service which preached and practiced cooperation between air and ground forces, in direct contrast to the Air Force, which was tentative about applying its air power in support of ground operations.

The Super Gaggle: Innovation in Marine CAS

The innovative nature of the Marine air-ground

A UH-34 Seahorse from Marine Medium Helicopter Squadron-163 that crash-landed just outside the perimeter on Hill 881S. The helicopter's tail section broke off, and it was abandoned there for the duration of the 1968 battle, a constant reminder of the lethality of NVA antiaircraft fire.

A TA-4F Skyhawk of Marine Aircraft Group-11 lands at Da Nang Air Base. As a Tactical Air Controller (Airborne), the two-seat Skyhawk was used to coordinate the activities of large strike packages, including the "Super Gaggles" needed to resupply the Marines on Hill 881S.

team was manifest in other unique procedures. Even though the tactical situation at Khe Sanh was relatively static, Marine aviators' experience with true close air support—integrating air attacks with the fire and movement of friendly forces—still paid off. One of the most dramatic examples was the "Super Gaggle." This technique was developed in response to the increasing anti-air threat around Khe Sanh over the course of the siege. From the start, the NVA had used antiaircraft guns and heavy machine guns to try and shoot down resupply aircraft landing at KSCB, and helicopters moving supplies to the outposts. Even when the aircraft survived the descending approach to the landing zone, they were almost always hit by mortar fire once on the ground, and they were subjected to additional machine gun fire as they lifted off again. For this reason, antiaircraft weapons identified around Khe Sanh were prime targets when they could be identified by ground observers or by FAC(A)s. In February, the NVA took advantage of the concealment offered by the poor crachin weather to set up more automatic weapons around the base and its outposts.[499] When the weather broke enough to allow helicopter resupply missions of Hill 881S, almost every attempt resulted in some casualties.[500] By mid-February, the situation reached its worst point. When three helicopters were shot down in a single day, the Marine leadership decided something innovative had to be done.

It is not clear who came up with the idea, since several senior officers, including General Cushman himself, claimed credit for the concept. The technique was formally published in 1st MAW Op Plan 3-68. Informally it came to be known as the "Super-Gaggle," suggesting a beefed-up version of a large formation of helicopters, known as a "gaggle" in Marine slang. The plan was designed to use aviation assets to put a protective wall of smoke, fire, and flying steel around the helicopters as they conducted their resupply missions to Khe Sanh's outposts. The first mission was flown on 24 February, and with its success the technique became a regularly scheduled package of aircraft which could be summoned by the Khe Sanh DASC whenever a break in the weather was forecast.[501]

In the typical Super Gaggle, a flight of two FAC(A)-qualified TA-4s would take off from Da

Corporal Robert J. Arrotta, the FAC on Hill 881S, coordinates with aircraft. While the "Super Gaggle" was a flexible package under the control of a TAC(A), and therefore could have been used on any hilltop outpost, the first step for the TAC(A) was to coordinate with the ground unit being supported, and the FAC was the primary agent of that communication.

A KC-130 Hercules of Marine Refueler/Transport Squadron-152 provides in-flight refueling to two A-4 Skyhawks of Marine Attack Squadron-311. The Super Gaggle was a very complex evolution, integrating large numbers of both fixed-wing aircraft and helicopters with ground fires, often under tenuous weather conditions. Dedicated additional support like in-flight refueling was a costly use of resources, but it ensured that the package was flexible enough to be successful for the Marines who depended on it.

Nang and conduct a reconnaissance of the objective area to determine if the weather was indeed good enough to allow a resupply attempt. If it was, the FAC(A) would direct the DASC to launch of the rest of the package, and would remain on station as the mission commander to coordinate the effort. The helicopter formations took off next, since they flew slower, and had to stop at Dong Ha to pick up their loads,[502] therefore taking longer to reach Khe Sanh. Finally, the remaining jet aircraft took off, so that all aircraft arrived at a rendezvous point near Khe Sanh more or less simultaneously. Once the entire package was checked in and ready to go, the FAC(A) mission commander began by directing a flight of two A-4s in attacking known and suspected antiaircraft guns along the helicopters' approach path, while two more A-4s laid down smoke screens on either side of the helicopter approach corridor. As the helos entered the corridor and made their approach, the A-4s would continue to strafe on either side of the corridor to keep the heads of enemy gunners down, and delivered napalm around the perimeter of the outpost to be resupplied. The final approach of the helos was covered not only by the A-4s, which were ready to react to any unforeseen threats, but by also a renewed smoke screen and UH-1 gunships which could provide more immediate fire support around the landing zone. The withdrawal of the resupply helicopters was accompanied by similar smoke screens and suppressive fires. A small group of helicopters was incorporated into the package for immediate combat rescue operations in case any of the other aircraft was shot down, allowing the downed aircrew and passengers to be recovered before the enemy had time to capitalize on the shoot-down. Each package also contained KC-130 tankers for in-flight refueling, increasing the endurance and flexibility of the jet aircraft supporting the package.[503]

The Super Gaggle was enormously effective.

A division of four A-4 Skyhawks from Marine Attack Squadron-311 heads for Khe Sanh. Such a division would provide the heavy firepower for a Super Gaggle, delivering its bombs either on preplanned CAS targets to suppress the enemy antiaircraft gunners or as on-call CAS, attacking new threats that suddenly developed.

133

A smoke screen deployed from a low-flying aircraft as it begins to blossom and shield the landing zones on Hill 881S from enemy view.

Once the plan was put in regular practice four times a day, only two CH-46s were lost to enemy fire, and in both cases the recovery aircraft immediately rescued the aircrews. The hit rate on resupply helos was cut in half from 10 per 1,000 sorties to less than five.[504] Captain Dabney on Hill 881S later described it as "a massive, complex, well-rehearsed, gutsy, and magnificent performance and only the Marines could have pulled it off,"[505] adding, "And do you think the Army and the Air Force together could have run a super gaggle?"[506] He later elaborated, "If nothing else, [the Marines] all talked the same lingo! I used Air Force CAS and Army helos on my second tour, and my limited observation of the differences convinced me that they could never have pulled

A smoke screen as it begins to blossom, hiding the friendly positions from enemy view as seen from a high-flying aircraft.

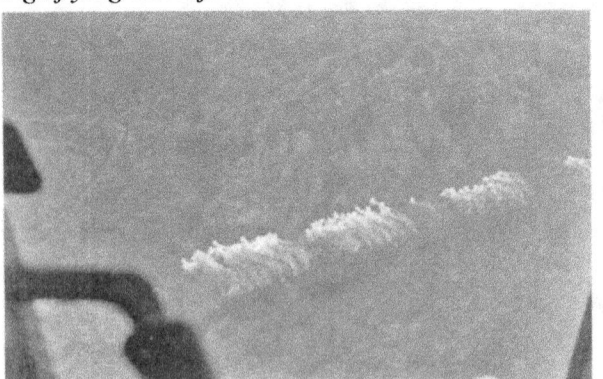

it off. Precision comes from discipline, and in my experience, both lacked the necessary discipline."[507]

Perhaps unknown to Dabney, the Air Force was attempting a similar technique to protect the

The workhorse of the Super Gaggle, a CH-46D Sea Knight of Marine Medium Helicopter Squadron-364, delivers a sling-load of supplies to Hill 881S.

transports delivering supplies to KSCB, and were enjoying about as much success as he predicted. When weather permitted, Air Force FACs directed fighters in flak suppression attacks alongside cargo planes making their final approach to the combat base. Ideally, a rendezvous was arranged by ABCCC for the FAC, attack aircraft, and transport aircraft at a higher altitude about 18 miles from Khe Sanh. As the transport descended in its approach, a FAC flew on either side, and fighter aircraft orbited overhead. This enabled the FACs

A CH46D Sea Knight of Marine Medium Helicopter Squadron-364, known as the Purple Foxes, starts to climb out after dropping its load on Hill 881 South.

to quickly call the fighters in on any antiaircraft guns which fired and gave their positions away. This ideal, package, however, was rare. Even though by the first week of March the danger of AAA was so great that flak suppression was deemed vital for all transports going into Khe Sanh, 7th Air Force failed to schedule such missions as dedicated, preplanned packages. As a result, many transports decided to brave the flak rather than wait for ABCCC to try to coordinate an ad hoc escort mission from whatever aircraft might be available.[508] This reality contrasts starkly with the priority, care, and forethought 1st MAW put into the Super Gaggle. The technique was published in a Wing operations order, and four full Super Gaggle packages were scheduled on a daily basis, just in case the weather permitted an attempt. The tactic had many supporters among the senior officers of 1st MAW, and squadron commanders personally served as the flight leaders for many of the missions.[509] Clearly, the Marines were unwilling to trust the execution of such a complex and dynamic mission to an ad hoc collection of aircraft hastily scraped together by the DASC from whatever happened to be airborne in the area. The Super Gaggle was likely developed from techniques the Marine air-ground team had already put in practice. The FSCC, for example, had already been providing suppressive fires timed to cover aircraft approaches to KSCB at the airfield manager's request.[510] Even if this was not the idea that germinated the Super Gaggle, both demonstrate the very effective results that the culture of close air-ground fire support cooperation was yielding.

Balancing Risk and Accuracy

The Super Gaggle was a superior product of the Marine culture of close air-ground cooperation. Another product of this culture was an increased willingness of aviators and their commanders to

Ordnancemen ready the 500-pound high-drag bombs hung under the wing of an A-6A Intruder from Marine All-Weather Attack Squadron-242. The "snake-eye" fins on the back of each bomb would open once the bomb was dropped off the aircraft, decelerating the ordnance enough to allow the aircraft to fly out of the fragmentation pattern created when the bomb detonated. Such devices were only necessary when tactics called for low-altitude deliveries. Marine aircraft usually carried these bombs because they got "down in the weeds" where it was easier to pick out the target designated by the FAC. Such attacks were more precise, but exposed the aircrew to greater danger of enemy fire, and required greater deconfliction with other supporting arms, like artillery and mortars. To Marine aviators, the improved performance in support of their fellow Marines on the ground was well worth the extra risk and effort.

An F-8E Crusader of Marine All-Weather Fighter Squadron-235 delivers two snake-eye bombs on a target close to one of Khe Sanh's hilltop outposts.

take risks to improve the support provided to the ground Marines. At times, individual Air Force aviators proved willing to take extreme risks. Two Air Force FAC's, for example, flew beneath a 1,000 to 1,200-foot cloud layer to guide fighters in the final defense of Lang Vei on 7 February 1968, temporarily reversing the course of the battle.[511] Institutionally, however, the 7th Air Force was not tempted by such payoffs to allow its aircrew to take these risks, even though they were routine for the 1st MAW. The Air Force insisted on carrying general purpose bombs which could be dropped from high altitude, rather than napalm or high-drag snake-eye bombs which were delivered in more precise low altitude attacks. The corresponding loss of accuracy meant that point targets, like the bunkers which provided the NVA with protection from other air attacks, could rarely be hit. During General Momyer's only visit to Khe Sanh, the 26th Marines Air Officer told him that the effectiveness of Air Force tactical aircraft were limited because they did not carry the appropriate ordnance. Momyer's response to this Marine concern was bemusement, and a refusal to risk his planes "down in the weeds." He told the Marines to depend on their own aviators for high accuracy high-drag bombing.[512] This attitude is in stark contrast with the can-do approach of Marine aviators, who often flew in valleys below Marine positions like Hill 881S.[513] Since the 7th Air Force was apparently unwilling to compromise on its tactics, the 26th Marines FSCC subsequently tried to use Air Force aircraft on radar-guided TPQ missions further from friendlies, and saved the Marines, with their more effective CAS ordnance and accurate, low-altitude attacks, for close-in targets.[514]

The Marines occasionally had to pay for the risks they took by flying at such altitudes. One F-4 was sent to destroy a tenacious .51-caliber machine gun that had been shooting at transport aircraft from a position just 200 meters off the end of the combat base's runway. During the attack the NVA gunner engaged the aircraft in a duel and actually shot the Phantom down.[515] The loss of aircraft even in such horribly inefficient exchanges, however, did not persuade the Marines to change their tactics. Apparently, they felt that the value of accurate low-altitude attacks to ground operations justified such losses in the long run.

Precision

Marine aviation's service-oriented support also produced superior results in the individual performance of its aviators. One area in which superior results were manifest was in precision. Marine aviators were willing and able to attack targets in much closer proximity to friendly positions than their peers in other services. Captain Dabney, who was supported by approximately 300 CAS missions over the course of the siege, stated, "Overall, the Marines were the most accurate." He went on to explain that the Marines were equipped with more appropriate ordnance and more suitable CAS aircraft like the A-4, "but even given these factors, the Marines were the most accurate."[516] Dabney was able to make that statement with confidence because he sometimes saw the other services conduct attacks with identical aircraft. He observed, for example, "the Navy A-4s we got were nowhere near as precise."[517] Based on his observations of the qualitative difference between the services, Dabney imposed a rule on how close to his Marines he would allow the different pilots to drop ordnance.

> We'd give them targets appropriate for their ordnance, with the rule (mine) that any targets closer than 1000 meters were for USMC birds only. The reasons for the rule were several; first, that the Navy/AF ordnance was generally low-drag, which meant they had to fly high to drop it, which meant more chance of error/miss; second, that they were probably not well-trained for CAS, if only because they were flying "up north" missions; third, they were in 'mushy' aircraft like Phantoms and F-101's which can made their bombing passes either too fast or too high for the accuracy we needed to destroy AA in caves and the like; and fourth, they were not Marines. [emphasis added]518

Here Dabney acknowledged practical limitations, but also revealed a strong belief in the superior capabilities of Marine aviators. Significantly, Dabney felt that his judgments on the accuracy of Marine CAS were widely shared. As he said,

> The Army infantry CO's I've talked to who served in I Corps or northern II Corps in Vietnam, where they could get Marine CAS, always preferred it to Air Force CAS. They knew CAS was central to our combat power, and that TAC [Air Force Tactical Air Command] has always been a poor cousin in the Air Force. The difference was obvious at Khe Sanh, where the grunt's rule was "Marine CAS for danger close, Navy at least one click out, and Air Force in the next country.519

Lieutenant Colonel Wayne C. Andersen, who commanded the Marine O-1's detachment at the time of Khe Sanh but also had extensive experience flying with Army and Air Force O-1 and

An F-4 Phantom drops six "snake-eye" bombs. The aircraft is very low, and the angle at which the photographer was holding the camera indicates that the target was very close to friendly positions.

O-2 crews, agreed. Of his experiences he summarized,

> I do not fault the Navy or Air Force pilots in their capability as their training just didn't provide them the skills to place ordnance or napalm in on targets that needed truly close air support… When it had to be truly tight support I ALWAYS sought out Marine aircraft because I knew they could lay it in tight…. The other services were good at high altitude stuff, and I and my fellow pilots just never felt comfortable laying them in truly close. While I flew with Air Force and Army observers that still was true.520

Anecdotal evidence to support these judgments on the matter of precision is plentiful. Each of the most dramatic descriptions of successful close-in attacks on enemy targets which can be traced to a particular service turns out to be the work of Marine aviators. During I/3/26's 20 January 1968 attack on Hill 881N, for example, the close air support of two Marine A-4s was critical to beating off repeated enemy counterattacks. Napalm was dropped 100 meters from the friendlies, so close that the Marines could see the pilots' heads within their cockpits, and several Marines had their eyebrows singed.521 Just the next morning, a Marine A-6 was credited with finally breaking the back of an NVA force that had been attacking Lang Vei all night. The Marines dropped all 28 of their 500-pound bombs directly on top of the enemy formation, and the few NVA who survived rapidly melted into the jungle.[522]

In the previous two examples, Marine aviators executed very accurate and effective attacks in support of relatively dynamic ground situations. Even in very static situations, Marines proved more confident in their skills than Air Force aviators. Toward the end of the siege, for example, the Marines suspected that the NVA were attempting to dig tunnels under their defenses. Near Hill 861A, a suspected tunnel was located just 15 or 20 meters from E/2/26's defensive perimeter. This target was particularly risky because it was located between two Marine positions, Hill 861 and its outpost on 861A, leaving it untouchable until the right combination of a Marine forward air controller and four attack pilots from VMFA-232 arrived on the scene.[523] As Prados and Stubbe tell it,

> For almost two weeks they begged the forward air controllers to direct fixed-wing strikes at this target. The controllers consistently refused. It happened that virtually all of these cases involved either Air Force controllers or strike aircraft or both, and the Air Force rigidly adhered to the restrictions set on distance from friendly forces at which various sizes of ordnance could be used. Then one day a Marine forward air controller was on station with Marine air coming in and the controller was talking on the radio with Captain Breeding. Told of the seriousness of the tunnel threat, the air controller agreed to buzz the target himself to judge whether it could be safely hit. After that the controller agreed to take on the target, asked Breeding to get his men under cover, and sent in a flight of four fighter-bombers

one by one. There were secondary explosions on the very first pass and before it was over the target was belching yellow smoke and finally blew up with a tremendous explosion.[524]

An even more dramatic example of Marine aviators' willingness to take on difficult and dangerous targets occurred a year earlier in the same area. During the Hill Fights a Marine patrol was ambushed near Hill 861, and the staff sergeant in charge of the patrol called in a Marine F-4 for support. He was forced to hand the radio off to his mortar forward observer, a lance corporal who had never controlled aircraft before. The extreme difficulty of the task, especially when the Marines were in such a dynamic close-contact situation and lacked an experienced FAC, resulted in two aborted attacks. On the third pass, however, the F-4 dropped napalm which impacted just 50 meters away from the patrol, breaking the ambush when the few remaining NVA ran away.[525] The patience of the Marine pilot, motivated by an understanding of the urgent situation and confidence honed by frequent work with ground troops, saved the day.

Fratricide

Attacks so close to friendly forces came at a cost. At Khe Sanh, dropping bombs closer to friendly lines reduced the NVA sanctuary from air attack and helped win close fights, but it also increased the risk of inadvertently injuring friendly troops. Stories exist of air attacks made so close that shrapnel landed in Marine trenches, apparently without creating injuries,[526] but there were also a number of cases where the defenders were not so lucky to avoid the effects of friendly fires. Here again, the evidence shows a clear difference in the results obtained by the two services. Appendix C delineates the fratricide and near-fratricide incidents which occurred in the Khe Sanh area over the course of the Hill Fights of 1967 and the events surrounding the siege of 1968. Of these 18 cases, 9 cannot be positively traced to one service or another, largely due to the fact several aircraft types were flown by more than one service. Of the remaining six cases attributable to aircrew error, two were caused by Marine helicopters and four were known to involve Air Force aircraft. At first glance, this data shows that of the entire period from May 1967 to May 1968, the Marines were involved in 50 percent fewer fratricide incidents than the Air Force, despite the fact that they provided a much higher percentage of sorties, and despite the fact that the Marines engaged targets in much closer proximity to friendly forces. Of note, the two Marine incidents that occurred took place during the fluid, chaotic Hill Fights, and were helicopter-related accidents that occurred while engaging enemy in dynamic ground combat with the supported Marines. As a comparative measure of effectiveness, it would be more appropriate rule these out in order to compare only "apples to apples": Marine fixed-wing aircraft to Air Force fixed-wing aircraft. Although four fratricide incidents can be positively traced to the Air Force, not a single one of the 18 incidents can be tied to aircrew error by Marine fixed-wing pilots. Furthermore, during the static situation that surrounded the NVA siege of 1968, which is the only time that Marine and Air Force performance can be truly considered side-by-side, there was not a single documented case of a Marine fratricide. This was the same period when at least half the Air Force fratricides occurred.

With respect to CAS, the difference between the dynamic tactical situation of 1967 and the static defensive operations of 1968 is important. The fratricide rate increased dramatically in dynamic situations. Fratricides were very rare during the siege itself because the Marines were in static positions whose elaborate trench systems made them easily visible from the air, as seen in Figure 9. Twelve of the 18 fratricide incidents occurred either during the dynamic Hill Fights of 1967, during the chaotic night when the NVA overran Lang Vei, or during the "break out" from Khe Sanh.

A closer look at the fratricide incidents of the two services is revealing. Two of the four Air Force incidents involve cases where pilots misidentified their targets. In these missions the pilots were operating independently, and were not under the control of a forward air controller. On these deep air missions which did not require FAC(A) control, the pilots failed to properly identify their targets, and wound up dropping their ordnance on villages full of civilians. Their errors were significant. In the first incident, the Air Force pilots attacked the friendly-held hamlet of Lang Vei, thinking they were attacking a target 20 miles across the border in Laos.[527] Although those missions would be more properly classified as DAS, the Air Force was the only service to experience such problems around Khe Sanh, demonstrating the danger of that service's willingness to apply air power without careful discrimination.

In the two fratricide cases traced to Air Force planes in CAS missions, the aircrew were guilty of overconfidence, and a gross misunderstanding of both CAS procedures and the caution required when attacking targets in close proximity to friendly forces. In the first incident, during an assault on Hill 861 during the Hill Fights, two Marine jets were called in to attack NVA that were interfering with a Marine company's withdrawal. After bombing and strafing runs by the Marines, an Air Force jet was brought in, but fired its rockets less than 100 meters from the Marines, wounding at least one of them. The Marines apparently perceived the aircraft to be an even greater threat than the NVA, and began firing at it.[528] In the second incident, a group of three Air Force F-100s were directed to hold and wait for control by a FAC working some Marine A-4s close to the perimeter of Hill 881S, which was clearly defined and visible from the air. Observing those attacks and perhaps mistaking some grass being burned off on another part of the hill for a target, one F-100 pilot commenced his attack without direction from the FAC and without even notifying the FAC of his intentions. The pilot dropped his bombs 50 meters away from the company command post, showering the position with dirt, rocks, shrapnel, and tree stumps. A bunker was caved in and several Marines required medical evacuation. Enraged that the pilot would even attempt to drop in such close proximity without a "cleared hot," the company commander told the F-100's to leave the area or risk being shot down by his Marines. Apparently, he decided that this was the type of support he could do without.[529] In both incidents Air Force aircrews had watched Marine jets attacking targets in close proximity to friendlies and tried to replicate the results, but got in dangerously over their heads. They also lacked an understanding of the absolute authority a FAC had to have when bombs were dropped in close proximity to friendly forces. Of the Air Force's performance in CAS, Dabney stated,

> A bird would come wings level oriented on the wrong target, we would not clear hot, and he would drop anyway…I do recall one mission where a bird took fire and his wingman rolled in and dropped on the gun position without our clearance. Air Force mission. We raised hell with the flight leader because the wingman could just as well have rolled in on us, since we were often firing machine guns from the hill during CAS.
> The Lesson here is simple. If you are executing a CAS mission, you do NOTHING that is not cleared by the ground FAC/TAC(A) first.[530]

The incidents involving Marine fratricides follow a different pattern. Both of these cases involved helicopters intentionally trying to deliver ordnance in close proximity to friendly forces they had positively identified. In these extreme situations, friendly and enemy troops were essentially intermixed so that any fire delivered to protect the Marines had a danger of hurting them as well. These two fratricide cases were the unfortunate costs of preventing the Marine positions from being completely overrun.[531] Again, not a single case of fratricide can be traced back to the Marine tactical jet aviators performing visual close air support missions. The reason for that is that the Marines understood the danger implicit in these missions, and were simply too disciplined and careful to drop unless they absolutely knew friendlies would not be hit. When queried about fratricides, the commander of the Marine O-1 detachment stated that even though he had controlled Marine jets attacking targets just 50 meters from defensive perimeters with napalm, "I never received a complaint from being too tight on target."[532] As Captain Dabney put it, they were guilty only of "being too careful."[533]

In summary, statistics show that a higher percentage of fratricide incidents were committed by Air Force pilots. In these cases, pilots most often deliberately conducted attacks on friendlies which had been mistakenly identified as enemy. This did not happen with Marine aviators, whose culture of close coordination and fear of fratricide dictated firing only on targets positively identified as enemy. Marine fratricides tended to be the result of intentional attacks under very exceptional dynamic circumstances when positively identified enemy forces had approached too close to the Marines on the ground, and the situation called for extreme risks to be taken in order to avoid much greater catastrophes.

Limitations of Close Air Support: Visual Acquisition

The several fratricide incidents at Khe Sanh illustrate the first of a number of limitations of close air support conducted by tactical aircraft in visually guided and visually controlled attacks—

the accuracy and danger of conducting such missions was highly dependant on the skill of the aircrew conducting the attack. Another factor which limited effectiveness was the need to see the target. This was especially important with tactical aircraft because they did not carry the huge volume of munitions that a B-52 could, nor could they drop bombs so indiscriminately in close proximity to friendly lines. As a result, bombs had to be placed very close to the target for the desired effects were to be achieved. The NVA realized this, and as Robert Pisor pointed out, the NVA had "truly perfected the art of camouflaging bunkers and defensive works." In essence, the best way to avoid the hammering of American air power was to avoid detection, and this became their primary defense.[534] The case of two NVA 120mm mortars that harassed Hill 881S throughout the entire siege is illustrative. Crater analysis and limited observations lead the Marines to conclude that the mortars were hidden in a bowl just a mile and a half away. A various times the target area was worked over with hundreds of tons of high explosives, including napalm and 1,000-pound bombs, but the mortars could never be located and silenced.[535]

Hill 861 was also constantly harassed by a sniper ensconced in a cave. This cave was repeatedly bombed, but the sniper always managed to clear away the dirt until a Marine FAC(A) was able to fly an extremely slow approach in the face of NVA fire to shoot a smoke rocket into the cave mouth. Once the target was finally marked accurately, an F-4 made a similar slow approach (with his flaps halfway down, in the landing configuration), and put two 500-pound snake eye bombs inside the cave. The sniper threat was permanently eliminated as a result of that attack.[536]

Limitations of Close Air Support: Ordnance

Another limitation was the unsuitability of the various types of aviation ordnance for the targets engaged. The military-industrial complex of the United States developed a wide arsenal of munitions which could be delivered by its aircraft. The various munitions were developed with different purposes in mind. Some munitions, such as cluster bombs, were designed to cover large areas with small fragments of shrapnel in order to destroy enemy troop formations. Other antipersonnel munitions, like napalm, were designed to accomplish a similar purpose with a suffocating and burning effect. Other weapons were developed with the intent of destroying the enemy in well-protected strongpoints, like bunkers and armored vehicles. General-purpose bombs could be used for any of these purposes, depending on how they were fused. Instantaneous fusing would cause the bombs to burst as soon as they hit the ground, devastating unprotected troops with above-ground fragmentation patterns. Putting a delayed fuse on the same bomb would cause it to penetrate the first object it hit before exploding. This was ideal for concentrating their destructive effects inside bunkers and tanks if a direct hit could be achieved.

The wide variation in ordnance types was not, however, instantaneously available to the pilot as he prepared to engage any of the various targets he encountered on the battlefield. Because munitions had to be loaded before takeoff, and could not be changed in flight, there were times when the ordnance carried was not appropriate for the targets encountered during the flight. This proved to be a problem several times during the battle of Khe Sanh. Early in the siege, before the NVA revealed their presence in force, the 26th Marines had requested aircraft to support Khe Sanh by carrying time-delay fused bombs. These were general-purpose bombs which would be dropped along likely avenues of approach, and would sit on the side of the trail for several hours before exploding. This ordnance was being used as part of the blind harassment and interdiction fires, rather than a precisely targeted air effort.

This created a problem on 21 January when the enemy finally revealed himself in force. Major Jim Stanton, a member of the FSCC, was flying an aerial observer mission when he located what he believed to be an NVA regiment in an open area. He assembled eight flights of aircraft, including Air Force, Navy, and Marine planes, but every one of them was equipped with the time-delay bombs. As a result, when the enemy regiment was attacked, the bombs hit the ground and did not explode. It is doubtful that the NVA obligingly waited in the area until the bombs blew up.[537]

After the siege began, the American aviators began carrying antipersonnel cluster bombs to prevent a repetition of such incidents, which worked fine until the NVA attack on Lang Vei on 7 February. During that attack the sudden appearance of a company of PT-76 tanks caught the defenders of Khe Sanh completely off guard since this was the NVA's first use of tanks inside South Vietnam for the entire war. The cluster bombs proved ineffective in stopping the tank attacks, which were decisive in the fall of Lang Vei. In reaction to that event, some tactical aircraft were directed to carry anti-tank rockets to meet the threat when it materialized again.[538] Fortunately, shortly after the fall of Lang Vei, a FAC(A) located eight of the amphibious PT-76's tied up along the bank of a river in Laos. The contact was reported to the 26th Marines FSCC, which wisely identified the tanks as a high priority target and sent a flight of Marine A-4s to attack. Their attack destroyed the tanks as well as an ammunition stockpile which had been camouflaged nearby. Intelligence analysts assessed that the threat presented by enemy armor in the region had been eliminated,[539] freeing the CAS aircraft to switch back to a heavy concentration of antipersonnel ordnance.

In some cases, the targets the Marines wanted destroyed proved impossible to reduce. In discussing the enemy trenching effort that approached KSCB at the end of February 1968, Bernard Nalty shows that General Westmoreland himself ordered the concentration of tactical aircraft against trenches right outside the Marine perimeter. Nalty goes on to describe some attacks by Navy aviators which collapsed 50 meters of trenchline and killed at least two NVA, noting that "the enemy soon abandoned the building of assault trenches."[540] The reality, however, was that the Marines experienced considerable frustration in trying to apply air power against the NVA trenches. At first, they tried destroying the NVA trenches using rockets, napalm, and high explosive bombs as large as 2,000 pounds in combination with artillery. Despite the fact that fighters and bombers were continually working over the trenches in the daytime, the NVA kept getting closer as the digging continued every night.[541] Next, the Marines applied the innovation that yielded several other effective solutions. Aircraft dropped full fuel tanks on the trenches so the jet fuel would have a chance to fill the trenches, and then lighted it off with rocket or cannon fire in "napalm baths."[542] NVA sources show that each night they had to repair between 40 percent and 70 percent of their siege work,[543] but unfortunately for the Americans, the particularly persistent nature of the NVA ultimately did prevent air power from stopping the approach of the siege trenches. The joint staff even considered aerial deliveries of wet concrete to fill the trenches, but this was far beyond the logistical capabilities of the already-stressed air bridge. Coming to the final conclusion that the siege trenches could not be destroyed by air power, General Cushman decided that the only way to prevent their use against the Marines was to request that C-47 "Spooky" gunships remain overhead to continually cover the trenches with fire.[544] The C-47 gunships had the advantage of much longer loiter times than tactical jets. As long as the threat of antiaircraft fire to these vulnerable, slow-flying aircraft was reduced (as it had by the later stages of the siege), and the targets could be effectively engaged solely with gunfire (as personnel in open trenches could), the gunships had good potential. The Marines had already developed a good appreciation for these weapons, and had placed 55-gallon drums filled with a mix of gasoline and diesel fuel just outside their perimeter. The defenders planned to light these drums on fire in case of an enemy assault at night, making it easy for "Spooky" to see the friendly lines. While the expected assault never materialized and made this necessary,[545] the gunships nonetheless proved their worth in countering NVA trenching efforts. Filling in the gap left by fast-moving tactical jets, such gunships had the well-earned respect of Marines in the defense of Khe Sanh.[546]

While the unsuitability of the various types of aviation ordnance could be a distinct limitation for tactical aircraft engaged in close air support, it is important to note that this same limitation was shared by the other air support techniques used at Khe Sanh, such as strategic bomber strikes and radar guided tactical attacks. When a Stratofortress formation laid waste to several square kilometers of distant jungle real estate, for example, little attention was paid to whether or not a particular bunker was destroyed. Tactical aircraft, on the other hand, engaged point targets in locations where the effects of their attacks could be immediately observed. When those effects fell short of the desired destruction, it was readily observable. It is important to remember, therefore, that ordnance limitations were shared by all aircraft to a large degree. It was merely more apparent with tactical aircraft engaged in the precision delivery of smaller ordnance loads.

The Effectiveness of Massed Close Air Support

Service distinctions and limitations aside, as a whole, the conduct of close air support at Khe Sanh did have a significant effect on the enemy. In addition to the numerous examples already cited throughout this work, there are some general observations demonstrating the NVA's respect for tactical air. The NVA appreciated and exploited the limitations of the B-52, stating in the 304 Division's official history that once the Americans were "forced" to use B-52s, "Our forces clung to the enemy's barbed wire, and for that reason, the enemy didn't dare attack indiscriminately because many times their bombs and ground fire caused casualties to their own troops. [emphasis added]"[547] While the enemy clearly understood the nature of the B-52 as a blunt force weapon, the NVA also knew that they would find no such sanctuary from tactical air attacks, observing that as they dug trenches right up to the Marine perimeter "There were even [air] strikes into the third [innermost] fence line."[548]

Additionally, because the high-altitude B-52 gave no warning to the NVA,[549] its deterrent effects were less direct than those of tactical aircraft. The NVA learned the presence of a tactical jet meant death for the soldier who exposed himself. On Hill 881S, for example, the Marines found themselves under constant sniping by an NVA recoilless rifle. Every time they brought in some tactical aircraft to destroy this point target, the enemy stopped firing and concealed himself until the aircraft left.[550] Even if the aircraft could not destroy this hidden position, its deterrent effect may have prevented casualties, and at a minimum bought the harried Marines some respite. Another testament to the effectiveness of tactical jets occurred when an NVA soldier decided to surrender to the Marines on 881S. There were no targets being prosecuted at the time the prisoner was on the hilltop being interrogated, so a Marine jet made a low pass over the hill as a gesture of support for the infantrymen. Hearing the approaching aircraft and finding himself exposed in the open, the NVA soldier became so terrified he defecated on himself, standing right in front of the Marines.[551] Clearly, the tactical aviation whose effects the NVA could observe on a daily basis struck them with a terror not unlike that inspired by the massive B-52 bombardments.

Conclusions

Visual CAS missions played an unquantifiable, but nonetheless valuable role in the battle for Khe Sanh by complementing the heavy, blunt firepower of the B-52. Bernard Nalty downplays the differences in the various services' contributions to the close air support battle, stating that, "pilots occasionally complained of unfamiliar procedures used by another service, but this was a minor annoyance that did not hamper air support of the Khe Sanh Marines."[552] This statement, however, overlooks the complications that were experienced, and it does not reflect the different results produced by two services with distinct approaches to close air support. Although Air Force tactical aircraft made great contributions to the close fight, the culture of the Marine air-ground team allowed an innovative and more aggressive employment of CAS with superior results.

CONCLUSIONS

Prior to the 1968 battle of Khe Sanh, the U.S. Air Force and U.S. Marine Corps were distinct institutions with distinct approaches to close air support. The Air Force was responsible for the application of air power to win wars from the tactical through the strategic levels, but chose to focus on strategic missions in the early Cold War, its formative period as a separate service. As a result, it viewed tactical ground support missions as a distraction from its strategic orientation, and from more vital tactical air missions like air superiority. Close air support became a tertiary capability, which the Air Force chose to maintain only when threatened in interservice turf battles, and even then only with multi-role aircraft which could be put to other uses. When the Vietnam War erupted, the Air Force found itself ill-prepared for low intensity conflict. As the war escalated it was constantly struggling to meet the nation's needs for tactical air support of ground forces in Southeast Asia. The Marine Corps, by comparison, was a distinctly infantry-oriented force which had developed a tactical air arm purely as a tool for supporting ground forces. For this reason, close air support was central to the Marines' conception of how to win wars, and the Corps found itself much better prepared to support ground operations in Vietnam.

When two NVA divisions surrounded the 26th Marine Regiment at the remote outpost of Khe Sanh From January to March 1968, and General Westmoreland initiated Operation Niagara, the Air Force and Marine Corps found themselves united in their operational objectives, even if their reasons for fighting there and the means by which they fought were very different. Many historians of the battle have lauded it as a victory of air power, and they are probably correct to do so. Although the primary NVA objective at Khe Sanh and the casualties they suffered in its pursuit remains unclear, there can be little doubt that General Giap would have been pleased by the fall of Khe Sanh, and that he lost a horrific number of men in the hills around the combat base. Accepting this, air power, which delivered 96 percent of the ordnance against the NVA for an average of about five tons of bombs for every NVA attacker (by conservative estimates),[553] has to be given the lion's share of the credit. NVA sources confirm the conclusion that the Communist troops feared air power above all else. While historians have therefore been correct to describe the battle as a victory of air power, they have not taken advantage of the opportunity for a comparative analysis of the U.S. Air Force's and Marine Corps' contributions to determine what these two very different institutions brought to the battle.

The Air Force attempted to fight an interdiction battle at Khe Sanh, using a variety of sensors to locate the enemy as the NVA closed in on the bait offered by the Marines at Khe Sanh Combat Base. Once located, they sought to annihilate the NVA by the application of massive air power weapons like the B-52 Stratofortress, applied against targets identified by a highly sophisticated electronic surveillance system. While Arc Lights undoubtedly demoralized the NVA and contributed to the American success at Khe Sanh, it is also clear that participants in the battle were overawed by its destructive potential, and there is little definitive evidence to show that this weapon was the decisive tool for winning the battle. Closer examination in fact reveals that the B-52 was subject to a number of limitations, including very limited responsiveness and an inability to attack targets in close proximity to friendly forces. Rather than applying innovative solutions to such problems, General Momyer placed limitations on the risks to which his aircrews could be exposed, and focused his efforts on using the battle as justification to finally win control of Marine air assets, ultimately producing a diluted version of the single management system which only further slowed the responsiveness of air forces. By failing to critically develop these limitations and errors, historians of the battle have not been motivated to examine the contributions of tactical air forces, which were more responsive and precise than the B-52s. These characteristics are exactly what made such them suitable for the true close air support of ground forces.

In this matter a clear difference between the air support provided by the Marine Corps and Air Force is apparent. The Marine Corps was better equipped for the tactical support of ground forces in Vietnam, with purpose-designed aircraft like the A-4 Skyhawk and A-6 Intruder, and an all-weather bombing capability enabled by the ground-based TPQ-10 radar direction system. The Marine Corps had an air command and control system which was more responsive, and specifically designed to foster close communications between the air ground team which had been carefully prepared according to Marine doctrine for combat deployment to Vietnam. That preparation included training which yielded superior results in terms of the quality of support rendered: it was closer, more accurate, and less deadly to the Marines who depended on it. If Khe Sanh was a victory of air power, then this tactical air power was a vital complement to the heavy firepower at which the Air Force excelled.

This conclusion should not be construed as a postulation that Marine Corps aviation is superior to that of the Air Force. In fact, they were different types of air forces, and as a combined arms team the Marine Corps was merely better suited for the war the nation faced in the jungles of South Vietnam. The Air Force, on the other hand, deserves the lion's share of the credit for the strategic deterrence provided to the nation in the Cold War, a service the Marine Corps was neither suited for nor interested in providing. It is important, however, to recognize that these two services are today perhaps just as deeply entrenched in their own approaches to close air support as they were during the battle of Khe Sanh. The Marine Corps has been recognized as the Department of Defense's senior agency for the development of close air support doctrine, yet Air Force officers have naturally served as the Joint Force Air Component Commanders (JFACC's) for all joint operations in the recent past. As a result, even as the importance of close air support has increased and deep air missions have decreased in operations like Enduring Freedom in Afghanistan and Iraqi Freedom II, the Air Force is the agency which develops the procedures and control systems for the application of air power. To many Marine participants in such CAS operations, it seems as if the U.S. military is reinventing the wheel every time, only to learn the same lessons. Air force supporters have responded to such criticism by predicting that new, hyper-precise joint service GPS-guided weapons like the Joint Direct Attack Munition have invalidated the need for such intense close air support training and single-minded focus as is advocated by Marine doctrine. This study, however, suggests that even if these predictions are true, there are many other benefits to the Marine approach, like command and control structures which are more responsive, and aviation forces which keep in closer touch with the objectives of ground commanders. If the battle of Khe Sanh is considered a single data point in a longer history of institutional disputes about close air support, it reinforces the idea that setting aside institutional parochialism in war planning to incorporate the strengths of both services will yield superior results, as these air forces complement each other in pursuit of joint objectives.

APPENDIX A: GLOSSARY OF ACRONYMS AND TERMS

AI—Air Interdiction, air attacks with the mission of denying enemy forces the resources to win a battle by attacking those resources or their means of transportation enroute to the battlefield. Interdiction is traditionally viewed as a mission falling between CAS and strategic attacks on enemy industrial resources or morale bases.

AO—Aerial observer, an artillery or infantry officer trained for aerial observation who flew in O-1s, OV-10s, and sometimes UH-1s to assist the pilot in forward air control by coordinating with ground combat units.

ASRT—Air Support Radar Team, a detachment of Marines who provided terminal guidance to aircraft using a ground based TPQ-10 radar to guide them to the proper release point to drop bombs on designated target coordinates at night or in poor weather conditions.

ALO—Air Liaison Officer, an aviation officer on temporary duty with a ground unit to advise on the integration of air and ground operations, and to coordinate such operations.

ASOC—Air Support Operations Center, an Air Force command and control agency similar to a Marine Corps DASC. An ASOC was designed to be attached to an Army corps headquarters, and to coordinate the application of close air support within that corps' area of operations.

ATO—Air Tasking Order, the daily listing or aircraft sorties flown in a theatre published by an upper command echelon to direct which units were to provide aircraft to meet various missions, including specific call signs, mission types, mission times, and targets and supported units when appropriate.

BDA—Bomb Damage Assessment, an estimation of the effectiveness of an air strike based on the observed destruction of enemy weapons, material, and personnel.

CAP—Combined Action Program or Combined Action Platoon, the U.S. Marine Corps pacification effort in the I Corps Tactical Zone.

DAS—Deep Air Support or Direct Air Support attacks upon the enemy that do not require detailed integration with the fire and movement of friendly forces. These attacks generally occur at expended ranges from friendly troops, such as deep air strikes on the enemy's strategic resources, or interdiction missions designed to stop enemy resources from reaching the battle area.

DASC—Direct Air Support Center, a subordinate operational component of a tactical air control system designed for the control and direction of close air support and other tactical air support operations. This term was used in the Marine Air Command and Control System and within the combined air command and control system in Vietnam, although Air Force doctrine used the term Air Support Operations Center (ASOC).

Direct fire—attacks upon the enemy using weapons with very flat trajectories, like rifles and tank guns. This term is used to distinguish these weapons from indirect fire weapons, like artillery and mortars. In emergency situations, some artillery can be used in direct fire modes to engage targets at close ranges.

Fixed-wing aircraft—Conventional airplane designs consisting of a fuselage and stationary wings which provide lift, in contrast to a helicopter, or rotary-wing aircraft.

FSCC—Fire Support Coordination Center, a group of personnel in a single location with centralized communication assets required for the coordination of all forms of fire support a unit may employ. Located at the command post of battalion and larger-sized ground combat units, and FSCC monitors and prioritizes requests for air, artillery, mortar, and naval gunfire support, then deconflicts and approves needed missions, and facilitates their rapid execution. With regard to air support, the FSCC works closely with the DASC, serving as its primary link to supported ground units.

FSCL—Fire Support Coordination Line, also known as the "bombline" during the Vietnam War. This fire support coordination measure is a line drawn in enemy or disputed territory beyond the region where friendly forces are operating. Beyond the FSCL there are no friendly forces, so air power can be applied permissively in air interdiction. Short of this line friendly forces are in danger of inadvertent attack by aircraft, so a forward air controller's permission is generally required to employ ordnance, typically in the form of close air support.

FAC—Forward Air Controller, a person who coordinates and directs the attacks of strike aircraft. Although a FAC may be airborne or on the ground, in this paper the term "FAC" will generally be used to indicate ground-based controllers, while airborne controllers will be referred to as FAC(A)s. FAC's are vital to close air support because they have a much closer perspective of events on the ground, and can identify targets which might not be visible to attacking aircraft. Because of the danger of fratricide when engaging in close air support, an aircraft may not drop its bombs until given a "cleared hot" by the FAC.

FAC(A)—Forward Air Controller (Airborne), a specifically trained and qualified aviator or aerial observer who performs the dual duties of visual reconnaissance/surveillance and controlling aircraft involved in close air support and deep air support missions. The U.S. Air Force tended to use FAC(A)s independent of ground operations, while Marine Corps doctrine specified that the FAC(A) was an extension of the ground unit's tactical air control party, assisting its FACs be providing control to strike aircraft as required by the ground commander.

FO—Forward Observer, a person who serves as a spotter to direct artillery and mortar missions, submitting calls for fire and observing their effects to correct the fire mission for better results.

Frag—A warning order, or preparatory order given in advance of an official operations order. In aviation units. Higher echelon commands generated a daily Air Tasking Order (ATO) with specific information on each sortie flown by its subordinate units. A Frag Order was issued roughly one day in advance so that plans and preparations could begin before the specific mission details were finalized.

Friendly—forces of one's own military or its allies. The opposite of enemy forces.

H&I Fires—Harassment and Interdiction Fires, artillery, mortars, or other supporting arms blindly targeted on probably enemy locations when the enemy's actual location is unknown. This "shot in the dark" method of targeting was largely recognized as a waste of ammunition.

ICTZ—I Corps Tactical Zone, the northernmost of South Vietnam's four zones of military authority, each organized around a combined South Vietnamese Corps headquarters and U.S. military command echelon.

Indirect fire—attacks upon the enemy using weapons with a very high trajectory, generally artillery or mortars.

KBA—Killed By Air, an estimate of enemy deaths inflicted by enemy air attacks.

KIA—Killed In Action, an estimate of friendly or enemy deaths resulting from a combat engagement.

KSCB—Khe Sanh Combat Base, the main combat base at Khe Sanh, consisting of everything within the perimeter protecting the runway, but not the hill outposts.

MAG—Marine Aircraft Group, the Marine aviation command echelon composed of two or more squadrons. Typically, a MAG operates a single type aircraft, or a collection of aircraft with similar missions operating from a single airfield. During the period covered by this paper MAG-11 was a group composed of fighter and attack jet squadrons operating from Da Nang. An additional jet group focused more closely on close air support was MAG-12, operating A-4 and A-6 aircraft from Chu Lai. That base was also shared by MAG-13, composed of three fighter/attack F-4 squadrons. MAG-16 was a rotary wing, or helicopter group, operating H-34, CH-46, and UH-1 aircraft from Marble Mountain. Further to the north at Phu Bai was another rotary wing group, MAG-36 which operated a similar collection of aircraft. These five aircraft groups, combined with a Marine Air Control Group, made up flying units of the 1st Marine Aircraft Wing.

MAW—Marine Aircraft Wing, or Marine Air Wing, the highest aviation-specific command echelon within the Marine Corps. Commanded by a major general and designed to support the aviation demands of a single Marine division, a MAW typically contained the full spectrum of aircraft types and mission capabilities within the Marine Corps arsenal, as well as the tactical air control, air traffic control, and air defense units needed for self sufficient operations. During the period covered by this paper the 1st Marine Aircraft Wing was deployed to Vietnam, where it supported the 1st Marine Division, 3d Marine Division, and at times the army units attached to III MAF in the I Corps area of operations.

MSQ-77 Combat Skyspot—The Air Force ground-based radar system used to guide aircraft in attacks on targets at night or in poor weather conditions. A less accurate system similar to the Marine TPQ-10.

PAVN—People's Army of Vietnam, the North Vietnamese title for the NVA.

Rotary-wing aircraft—helicopters.

SAC—Strategic Air Command, the U.S. Air Force major command responsible for the employment of B-52s, primarily in nuclear deterrence missions.

Sortie—a single flight of an aircraft

TAC(A)—Tactical Air Controller (Airborne), an aviation officer similar to a FAC(A) who coordinated air attacks in high risk missions. Although TAC(A)s were trained to perform FAC duties in support of ground units, they typically operated in air interdiction missions over enemy-held territory. In this role they did not have to coordinate with ground forces, and flew more survivable jet aircraft.

TACP—Tactical Air Control Party, a group of Forward Air Controllers and radiomen assigned to support a ground battalion or similar sized unit by controlling the attacks of aircraft engaged in CAS.

Targeting—the process by accurately locating and identifying possible and definite enemy forces and things that might be of value to them, prioritizing them for attack, allocating supporting arms for this purpose, and directing assets for their neutralization or destruction.

TASE—Tactical Air Support Element, a group of army personnel assigned to an Air Force or combined DASC in order to verify and prioritize air requests in accordance with the ground unit's needs before the DASC assigned aircraft to this mission. In the Marine Crops, these function was carried out by frequent contact between the DASC and the supported unit's FSCC.

TOT—Time on Target—the desired time for an air attack to deliver ordnance on a target.

TPQ-10—The Marine ground-based radar system used by an Air Support Radar Team (ASRT) to guide aircraft in attacks on targets at night or under poor weather conditions.

WIA—Wounded In Action, an estimate of surviving friendly casualties resulting from a combat engagement.

APPENDIX B: AIR ORDERS OF BATTLE

1st Marine Air Wing

15,000 Marines, 199 fixed-wing aircraft, 273 helicopters

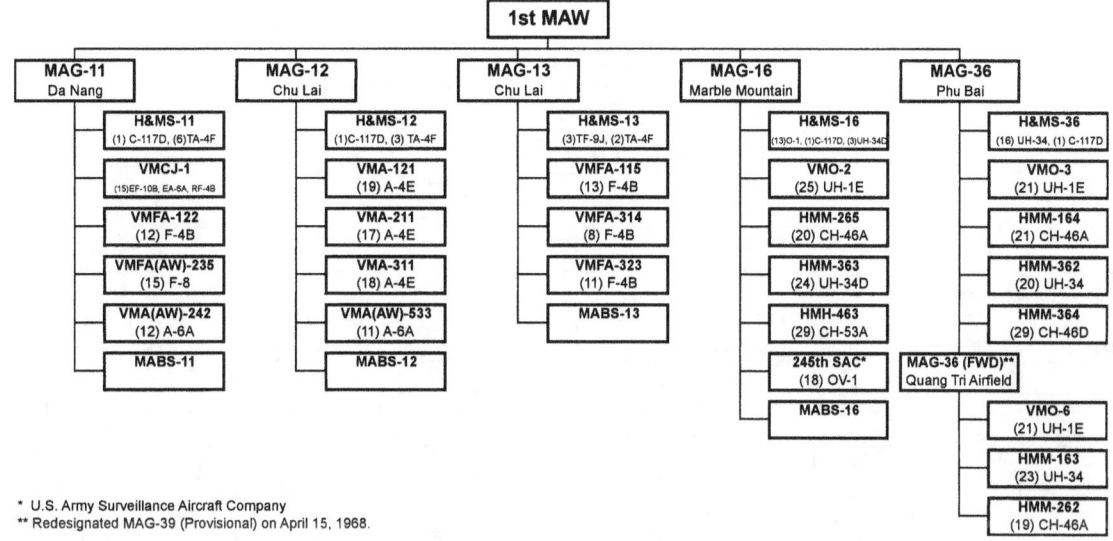

* U.S. Army Surveillance Aircraft Company
** Redesignated MAG-39 (Provisional) on April 15, 1968.

7th Air Force

58,000 airmen, 1,085 aircraft

Note: 7th Air Force could also exercise operational control of 13th Air Force units in Thailand (35,000 airmen, 523 aircraft), which it began to employ in South Vietnam in the last week of January 1968.

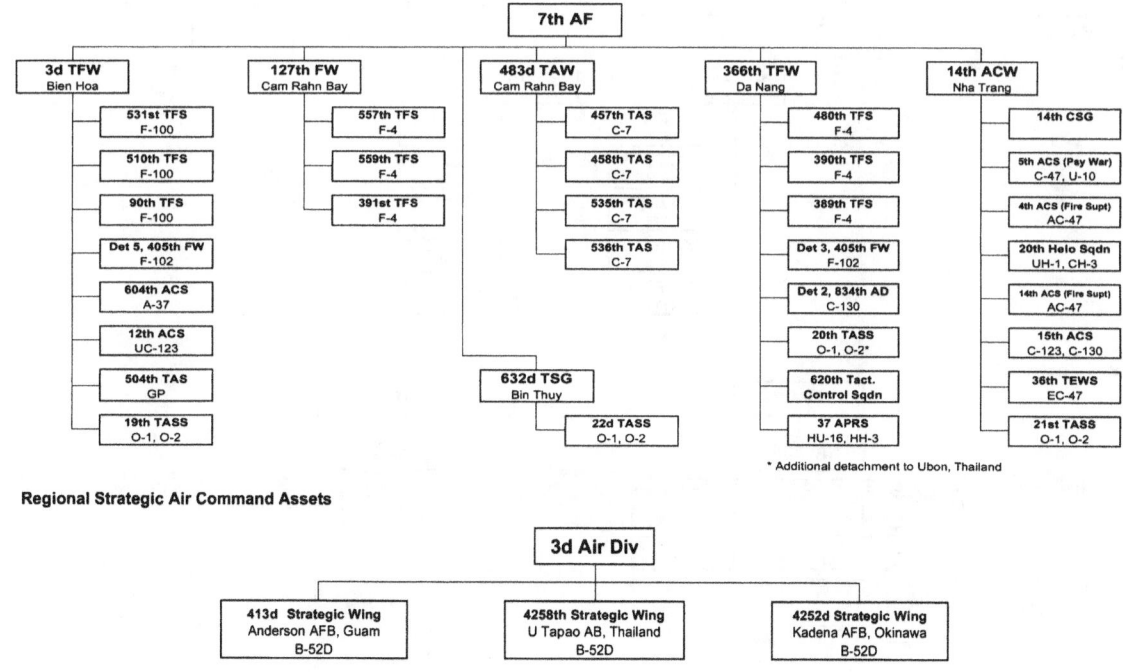

U.S. Navy

The number of personnel and aircraft varied with the constant rotation of carriers into the carrier task groups on Yankee Station.

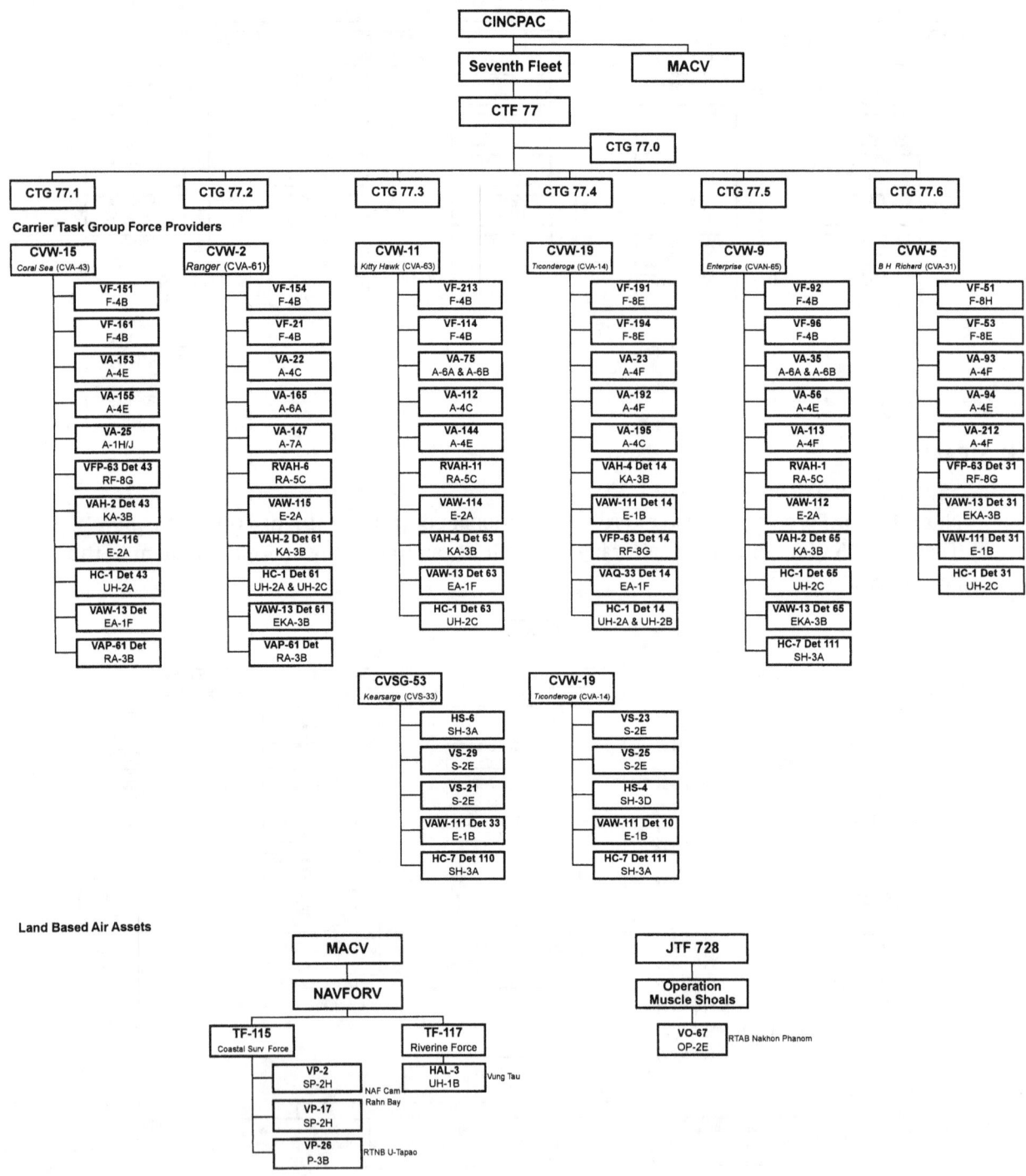

APPENDIX C: FRATICIDE AND NEAR FRATICIDE AVIATION INCIDENTS AT KHE SANH

Date	Aircraft	Location	Incident	Cause	Results	Source
2-Mar-1967	2 USAF F-4C	Lang Vei	Bombs, cluster bombs, and rockets dropped on Bru civilians	Misidentified target	112 civilians killed 213 civilians wounded	Murphy, 29; Telfer, 33; Prados and Stubbe, 73; Stubbe, *Battalion of Kings*, 28-29.
8-Mar-1967	USAF C-123 flareship	Laos	Laotian village strafed during DAS mission	Misidentified target	No casualties	Prados and Stubbe, 74.
24-Apr-1967	USMC UH-1E	Hill 861	Marine hit by stray machine gun round fired by UH-1 providing suppression for CH-46 medical evacuation	Poor fire discipline in close proximity to friendly forces	1 Marine killed	Murphy, 59; Stubbe, *Battalion of Kings*, 35.
24-Apr-1967	F-4	Hill 861	Marines bombed with two 250-pound bombs by aircraft under FAC(A) control during 3/B/1/9 withdrawal	Unknown	6 Marines killed, more than 12 wounded	Prados and Stubbe, 86; Murphy, 61; Stubbe, *Battalion of Kings*, 35.
26-Apr-1967	USAF tactical jet	Hill 861	Marine position hit by fragments from stray rocket during CAS attack	Poor fire discipline in close proximity to friendly forces	At least 1 Marine wounded	Murphy, 93.
2-May-1967	USMC UH-1	Hill 881N	Marine position hit by rockets during CAS attack	Pilot failed to follow saftey restriction imposed on attack in close proximity to friendlies	1 Marine killed 2 Marines wounded	Murphy, 201.
Summer 1967	UH-1	Unknown	Marine reconnaissance patrol fired upon with rockets when pursued to evacuation site by NVA	Misidentified target	No casualties	Prados and Stubbe, 182.
7-Feb-1968	Unknown	Lang Vei	Bomb dropped inside Laotian position	Unspecified mistake	No casualties	Prados and Stubbe, 325.
7-Feb-1968	A-1	Lang Vei	Napalm canister landed "just feet" from U.S. soldier	Pilot dropped on large group of NVA surrounding friendly forces	Soldier survived, otherwise unknown	Prados and Stubbe, 335.
7-Feb-1968	Unknown	Lang Vei	4 U.S. soldiers and 40 CIDG caught in cluster bomb attack while attempting to flee U.S. compound	Unknown	Unknown	Pisor, 194.
10-Feb-1968	A-1E	KSCB	"Gravel" antipersonnel mines dropped on Marine position	Unknown	1 Marine wounded	Nalty, 94-95, but not in 1/26 Command Chronology as cited.
26-Feb-1968	Navy F-4	KSCB	Two rockets fired into FOB-3 compound during CAS attacks on enemy in close proximity	Unknown	1 Marine killed	Stubbe, *Final Formation*, 70-71; Stubbe, *Battalion of Kings*, 221; Stubbe, to Callahan, 12 Dec 2006.
Feb/Mar 1968	USAF F-100	Hill 881S	Four 500-pound bombs dropped on Marine perimeter during CAS attack	Pilot misidentified target and dropped without clearance	Several Marines injured	Dabney, to Callahan, Part 2.
Feb/Mar 1968	F-4	Hill 881S	Four 250-pound bombs dropped on Marine perimeter during CAS attack	Pilot mistook smoke on the hill for a mark and attacked without clearance	2 Marines wounded	Dabney, to Colandreo; Arrotta, 2.
Feb/Mar 1968	A-4	Hill 881S	Following successful CAS rocket attack, pilot strafed Marine position without clearance to attack	Pilot violated FAC's instructions by using inaccurate guns on a close target.	Unknown	Dabney, to Colandreo, and to Callahan, Part 2; Arrotta.
7-Mar-1968	Unknown	KSCB	"Second incident of bomb dropping inside ARVN perimeter"	Unknown	Unknown	Donaghy, to Callahan, Part 6.
5-Apr-1968	Marine F-4	Hill 471	Twenty-six unarmed 500-pound bombs dropped on 1/9 by aircraft under TPQ-10 control	Target cancellation not received by TPQ-10 crew, due to delays in new single management system.	1 Marine wounded	Prados and Stubbe, 434-435; Donaghy, to Callahan, Part 2; Stubbe, *Battalion of Kings*, 276.
April 1968	Navy A-4	Unknown	Ordnance dropped on an advancing 1st Air Cavalry Division unit by aircraft under TPQ-10 control	Target cancellation not received by TPQ-10 crew due to Army unit unfamiliar with MACCS.	No casualties	Shulimson, 479.

BIBLIOGRAPHY

Books

Camp, Colonel Richard D., Jr. *Lima-6: A Marine Company Commander in Vietnam, June 1967 - January 1968*. New York: Atheneum, 1989.

Corbett, John. *West Dickens Avenue: A Marine at Khe Sanh*. New York: Ballantine Books, 2003.

Drez, Ronald J., and Douglas Brinkley. *Voices of Courage: The Battle for Khe Sanh, Vietnam*. New York: Bulfinch Press, 2005.

Drury, Richard S. *USAF Close Air Support*. Singapore: Motorbooks International, 1991.

Hammel, Eric. *Khe Sanh: Siege in the Clouds, An Oral History*. Pacifica, California: Pacifica Military History, 1989.

Krulak, Lieutenant General Victor H. *First to Fight: An Inside View of the U.S. Marine Corps*. Annapolis: Naval Institute Press, 1999.

MacIssac, David. "Voices from the Central Blue: The Air Power Theorists." In *Makers of Modern Strategy from Machiavelli to the Nuclear Age*, ed. Peter Paret, 624-647. Princeton: Princeton University Press, 1986.

Murphy, Edward F. *Semper Fi Vietnam: From Da Nang to the DMZ, Marine Corps Campaigns, 1965-1975*. New York: Ballantine Books, 1997.

———. *The Hill Fights: The First Battle of Khe Sanh*. New York: Ballantine Books: 2003.

Pisor, Robert. *The End of the Line: The Siege of Khe Sanh*. New York: W.W. Norton & Company, 1982.

Prados, John, and Ray W. Stubbe. *Valley of Decision: The Siege of Khe Sanh*. New York: Houghton Mifflin, 1991. Reprint, Annapolis: Naval Institute Press, 2004.

Rottman, Gordon L. *Khe Sanh 1967-68: Marines Battle for Vietnam's Vital Hilltop Base*. New York: Osprey Publishing, Ltd., 2005.

Spencer, Ernest. *Welcome to Vietnam, Macho Man: Reflections of a Khe Sanh Vet*. Walnut Creek, California: Corps Press, 1989.

Stubbe, Ray W. *Battalion of Kings: A Tribute to our Fallen Brothers who Died Because of the Battlefield of Khe Sanh, Vietnam*. Milwaukee: Khe Sanh Veterans, Inc., 2005.

———. *The Final Formation: Those Who Died Because of Khe Sanh*. Wauwatosa, Wisconsin: by the author, 1995.

———. *Khe Sanh and the Mongol Prince*. Wauwatosa, Wisconsin: by the author, 2002.

Windrow, Martin. *The Last Valley: Dien Bien Phu and the French Defeat in Vietnam*. Cambridge: Da Capo Press, 2004.

U.S. Government Publications

Condon, Major General John P. *Corsairs to Panthers: U.S. Marine Aviation in Korea*. Washington, D.C.: History and Museums Division, Headquarters Marine Corps, 2002.

Cooling, Benjamin Franklin, ed. *Case Studies in the Development of Close Air Support*. Washington, D.C.: Office of Air Force History, U.S. Air Force, 1990.

Davis, Richard G. *The 31 Initiatives: A Study in Air Force-Army Cooperation*. Washington, D.C.: Office of Air Force History, U.S. Air Force, 1987.

Holloway, Admiral James L., III. "Tactical Command and Control of Carrier Operations." In *Command and Control of Air Operations in the Vietnam War: Colloquium on Contemporary*

History, January 23, 1991, No. 4, 5-16. Washington, D.C.: Naval Historical Center, Department of the Navy, 1991.

Johnson, Lieutenant Colonel Edward C. *Marine Corps Aviation: The Early Years, 1912-1940*. Washington, D.C.: History and Museums Division, Headquarters U.S. Marine Corps, 1977.

Kohn, Richard H., and Joseph P. Harahan, eds. *Air Interdiction in World War II, Korea, and Vietnam: An Interview with General Earl E. Partridge, General Jacob E. Smart, and General John W. Vogt, Jr.* Washington, D.C.: Office of Air Force History, U.S. Air Force, 1986.

Lester, Gary Robert. *Mosquitoes to Wolves: The Evolution of the Airborne Forward Air Controller*. Maxwell AFB, Alabama: Air University Press, 1977.

Momyer, General William W. *Air Power in Three Wars.* Washington, D.C.: U.S. Government Printing Office, 1978.

Mrozek, Donald J. *Air Power and the Ground War in Vietnam: Ideas and Actions.* Maxwell AFB, Alabama: Air University Press, 1988.

Nalty, Bernard C. *Air Power and the Fight for Khe Sanh*. Washington, D.C.: Office of Air Force History, U.S. Air Force, 1973.

———. "Operation Niagara: Air Power and the Siege of Khe Sanh." In *Command and Control of Air Operations in the Vietnam War: Colloquium on Contemporary History, January 23, 1991*, No. 4, 39-48. Washington, D.C.: Naval Historical Center, Department of the Navy, 1991.

Sbrega, John J. "Southeast Asia." *In Case Studies in the Development of Close Air Support*, ed. Benjamin Franklin Cooling, 411-490. Washington, D.C.: Office of Air Force History, U.S. Air Force, 1990.

Schlight, John. *A War Too Long: The USAF in Southeast Asia, 1961-1975*. Washington, D.C.: Air Force History and Museums Program, 1996.

———. *The United States Air Force in Southeast Asia: The War in South Vietnam, The Years of the Offensive, 1965-1968*. Washington, D.C.: Air Force History and Museums Program, 1999.

Shore, Captain Moyers S., II. *The Battle for Khe Sanh*. Washington, D.C.: History and Museums Division, Headquarters U.S. Marine Corps, 1969.

Shulimson, Jack, Lieutenant Colonel Leonard A. Blaisol, Charles R. Smith, and Captain David A. Dawson. *U.S. Marines in Vietnam: The Defining Year, 1968*. Washington, D.C.: History and Museums Division, Headquarters U.S. Marine Corps, 1997.

Sunderland, Riley. *Evolution of Command and Control Doctrine for Close Air Support*. Washington, DC: Office of Air Force History, U.S. Air Force, 1973.

Telfer, Major Gary L. and Lieutenant Colonel Lane Rogers. *U.S. Marines in Vietnam: Fighting the North Vietnamese, 1967*. Washington, D.C.: History and Museums Division, Headquarters Marine Corps, 1984.

U.S. Department of Defense. Joint Chiefs of Staff. Joint Publication 1-02: *Department of Defense Dictionary of Military and Associated Terms*. Washington, D.C.: Government Printing Office, 2001 (amended through 2005).

U.S. Congress. House. Committee on Armed Services. *Special subcommittee on Tactical Air Support. Close Air Support*. 89th Cong., 2d sess., 1966. Committee Print 44.

U.S. Marine Corps, Landing Force Manual 22: *Coordination of Supporting Arms*. Quantico, Virginia: Marine Corps Landing Force Development Activity, 1960.

———. MCS-77E: *Air Support Operations*. Quantico, Virginia: Marine Corps Educational Center, Marine Corps Schools, 1955.

———. Operational Handbook 5-4: *Close Air Support (CAS) Handbook*. Quantico, Virginia: Marine Corps Development and Education Command, 1979.

———. *Small Wars Manual*. Washington, D.C.: Government Printing Office, 1940.

Articles

Anderson, Brigadier General Norman J. "Marine Aviation Ready for Any Emergency: Air-Ground Team Concept is Hailed." *Army Navy Air Force Journal and Register* 100, no. 10 (3 November 1962): 18-19.

Bolt, Lieutenant Colonel J.F. "Goodbye Able Dog." *Marine Corps Gazette* 41, no. 10 (October 1957): 28-31.

Beckett, Major W.H. "The L2VMA: Light CAS Needs Boondockers." *Marine Corps Gazette* 47, no. 3 (March 1963): 20-23.

Cole, Bernard D. "A Noglow in Vietnam, 1968: Air power at the Battle of Khe Sanh." *Journal of Military History* 64, no. 1 (January 2000): 141-158.

Dabney, Colonel William H. "Under Siege." *The Elite* 2, no. 13 (1985): 241-254.

Keller, Lieutenant Colonel R.P. "Trained For Support." *Marine Corps Gazette* 38, no. 5 (May 1954): 28-31.

McCutcheon, Lieutenant General Keith. "Marine Aviation in Vietnam, 1962-1970." *U.S. Naval Institute Proceedings: Naval Review* 1971 (97), no. 819 (May 1971): 122-155.

———. "Air Support for III MAF." *Marine Corps Gazette* 51, no. 8 (August 1967): 18-23.

———. "Marine Corps Aviation: An Overview." *Marine Corps Gazette* 52, no. 5 (May 1968): 22-27.

Nikele, First Lieutenant S. Joseph, Major Karl S. Smith, and Major George E. Constantino. "Pilot Retention: Three Views." *Marine Corps Gazette* 52, no. 5 (May 1968), 55-57.

Sabia, Captain Robert V. "The AO and the Field Commander." *Marine Corps Gazette* 52, no. 5 (May 1968): 45-49.

Standish, Colonel Anthony. "Infantry-Air Support Single Command." *United States Army Combat Forces Journal* 2, no. 12 (July 1952): 31-34.

Steinkraus, Colonel Robert F. "Air/Ground Coordination." *Marine Corps Gazette*, v. 50, no. 5 (May 1966): 29-31.

Tutton, Lieutenant Colonel Marshall R. "Marine Corps Aviation." *United States Naval Institute Proceedings* 87, no 5 (May 1961): 48-53.

Verdi, Captain J.M. "The Case for Jet CAS." *Marine Corps Gazette*, v. 45, no. 6 (June 1961), 32-35.

"Weakness in Air Force." *U.S. News & World Report*, 3 November 1950, 17-19.

Interviews

Anderson, Major General Norman J. Interview by Benis M. Frank, 3 March 1981, transcript. Marine Corps Oral History Collection, Gray Research Center Archives, Quantico, Va.

Alexander, First Lieutenant James M. Interview by Corporal Norman R. Carlson, 26 April 1968. Interview 2934, digital audio file. Marine Corps Oral History Collection, Gray Research Center Archives, Quantico, Va.

Baig, Mirza M. Interview by Ernest W. Bivans, circa May 1968. Dialog notes contained in MACV (J332) letter "Muscle Shoals and the Siege of Khe Sanh" to the Defense Communications Planning Group, Washington, D.C., 7 May 1968. Transcript in the Records of the U.S. Marine Corps, History and Museums Division Publication Background Files: USMC in Vietnam, 1967-69, National Archives, College Park, Maryland.

Bergstrom, Major Carl F. Interview by Corporal Norman R. Carlson, 11 March 1968. Interview 2832, digital audio file. Marine Corps Oral History Collection, Gray Research Center Archives, Quantico, Va.

Dabney, Colonel William H. Interview by Benis M. Frank, 20 May 1982, transcript. Marine Corps Oral History Collection, Gray Research Center Archives, Quantico, Va.

Danielson, Major Darrell C. Interview by 3d Mar Div, 7 July 1967. Interview 1264, transcript. Records of the U.S. Marine Corps, History and Museums Division Publication Background Files: USMC in Vietnam, 1967-69, National Archives, College Park, Maryland.

Delorean, First Lieutenant Andrew C. Interview by Corporal Norman R. Carlson, 19 April 1968. Interview 2667, digital audio file. Marine Corps Oral History Collection, Gray Research Center Archives, Quantico, Va.

Dowling, Captain Bobby G. Interview by Corporal Norman R. Carlson, 26 April 1968. Interview 2836, digital audio file. Marine Corps Oral History Collection, Gray Research Center Archives, Quantico, Va.

Dougal, Captain Robert J. Interview by Corporal Norman R. Carlson, 10 April 1968. Interview 2664, digital audio file. Marine Corps Oral History Collection, Gray Research Center Archives, Quantico, Va.

Loftus, Major William E. Interview by Corporal Norman R. Carlson, 12 March 1968. Interview 2835, digital audio file. Marine Corps Oral History Collection, Gray Research Center Archives, Quantico, Va.

McCutcheon, Lieutenant General Keith B. Interview by Major Thomas E. Donnelly, 22 April 1971, transcript. Marine Corps Oral History Collection, Gray Research Center Archives, Quantico, Va.

Post, Captain Gary L. Interview by Corporal Norman R. Carlson, 19 April 1968. Interview 2665, digital audio file. Marine Corps Oral History Collection, Gray Research Center Archives, Quantico, Va.

Regan, Major Frank C. Interview by Corporal Norman R. Carlson, 12 March 1968. Interview 2834, digital audio file. Marine Corps Oral History Collection, Gray Research Center Archives, Quantico, Va.

Shaver, Major Glen J., Jr. Interview by Corporal Norman R. Carlson, 10 April 1968. Interview 2663, digital audio file. Marine Corps Oral History Collection, Gray Research Center Archives, Quantico, Va.

Sullivan, Major William J. Interview by Corporal Norman R. Carlson, 26 April 1968. Interview 2935, digital audio file. Marine Corps Oral History Collection, Gray Research Center Archives, Quantico, Va.

Wilcox, Major Kenneth H. Interview by Gunnery Sergeant Charles V. Marquez, Jr., 3 April 1968. Interview 2661, digital audio file. Marine Corps Oral History Collection, Gray Research Center Archives, Quantico, Va.

Lumsden, Major J.L. Interview by Corporal Norman R. Carlson, 24 April 1968. Interview 2830, digital audio file. Marine Corps Oral History Collection, Gray Research Center Archives, Quantico, Va.

Miscellaneous Sources

Andersen, Lieutenant Colonel Wayne C., Venice, Florida, letter to Shawn P. Callahan, Annapolis, 11 July 2005. Shawn P. Callahan Papers, Archives and Special Collections, Marine Corps University Library, Quantico, Virginia.

Arrotta, Robert J., Comments on Shawn P. Callahan, draft ms, "Close Air Support and the Battle for Khe Sanh: A Study in Institutional Approaches to Air Power." 28 April 2007. Transcript in the hand of Shawn P. Callahan, Annapolis.

"B-52 at War." Available from http://www.faqs.org/docs/air/avb52_2.html; accessed 11 August 2005.

"Battle of Khe Sanh," Available from http://en.wikipedia.org/w/index.php?title=Battle_of_Khe_Sanh& oldid=139552467; accessed June 27, 2007.

Carr, Colonel Richard W., Hampstead, North Carolina, letter to Shawn P. Callahan, Annapolis, 14 July 2005. Shawn P. Callahan Papers, Archives and Special Collections, Marine Corps University Library, Quantico, Virginia.

Chapman, General Leonard F., Jr., Washington, D.C., letter to General William C. Westmoreland, Washington, D.C. regarding comments on draft monograph of Captain Moyer S. Shore, The Battle for Khe Sanh, circa 1968. Transcript in the Records of the U.S. Marine Corps, History and Museums Division Publication Background Files: USMC in Vietnam, 1967-69, National Archives, College Park, Maryland.

Cushman, Lieutenant General Robert E., Jr., Da Nang, Vietnam, letter to Brigadier General W.D. Sawyer, Washington, D.C. regarding comments on draft monograph of Captain Moyer S. Shore, The Battle for Khe Sanh, 26 December 1968. Transcript in the Records of the U.S. Marine Corps, History and Museums Division Publication Background Files: USMC in Vietnam, 1967-69, National Archives, College Park, Maryland.

———, Da Nang, Vietnam, letter to Lieutenant General V.J. Van Ryzin, Washington, D.C. regarding comments on draft monograph of Captain Moyer S. Shore, The Battle for Khe Sanh, 23 March 1969. Transcript in the Records of the U.S. Marine Corps, History and Museums Division Publication Background Files: USMC in Vietnam, 1967-69, National Archives, College Park, Maryland.

Dabney, Colonel William H., Comments on Shawn P. Callahan, draft ms, "Close Air Support and the Battle for Khe Sanh: A Study in Institutional Approaches to Air Power." 7 December 2006. Transcript in the hand of Shawn P. Callahan, Annapolis.

———, Lexington, Virginia, letter to Major Biagio Colandreo, Jr., Naval Amphibious Base Little Creek, Virginia, circa 1999. Transcript in the hand of Shawn P. Callahan, Annapolis.

———, Lexington, Virginia, letter to Shawn P. Callahan, Annapolis, circa 1999. Transcript in three parts in the hand of Shawn P. Callahan, Annapolis.

Democratic Republic of Vietnam, General Directorate for Rear Services. Rear Service Operations: 1968 Spring-Summer Khe Sanh Route 9 Campaign, 1988. Transcript in the hand of Ray W. Stubbe, Wauwatosa, WI.

―――, Military History Institute of Vietnam. Victory in Vietnam: The Official History of the People's Army of Vietnam, 1954-1975. Translated by Merle L. Pribbenow. Lawrence, Kansas: University Press of Kansas, 2002.

Donaghy, Lieutenant Colonel Richard, Irvine, California, letter to Shawn P. Callahan, Annapolis, 22 November 2004. Transcript in six parts in the hand of Shawn P. Callahan, Annapolis, Maryland.

Director, Historical Division, Headquarters, U.S. Marine Corps comments on Director of Information Press Query #41, "'Air Delivery' by First Lieutenant Barney Halloran, USMC" of 20 March 1970. Records of the U.S. Marine Corps, History and Museums Division Publication Background Files: USMC in Vietnam, 1967-69, National Archives, College Park, Maryland.

Egen, Lieutenant Colonel Bill, Havelock, North Carolina, letter to Shawn P. Callahan, Annapolis, 10 July 2005. Shawn P. Callahan Papers, Archives and Special Collections, Marine Corps University Library, Quantico, Virginia.

Ellis, John W., Jr. *The Airborne Forward Air Controller: Past Accomplishments and Future Opportunities*. Santa Monica: The Rand Corporation, 1978.

Finch, George A., III, Santa Rosa, California, letter to Shawn P. Callahan, Annapolis, 11 July 2005. Shawn P. Callahan Papers, Archives and Special Collections, Marine Corps University Library, Quantico, Virginia.

Krulak, Lieutenant General Victor H., CG FMFPAC message 2621112Z 67, exclusive to CMC, General Wallace M. Greene, Jr,. Camp Lejuene, NC, 26 December 1967. Transcript in the Records of the U.S. Marine Corps, History and Museums Division Publication Background Files: USMC in Vietnam, 1967-69, National Archives, College Park, Maryland.

Moriarty, Robert J., Miami, letter to Shawn P. Callahan, Annapolis, 5 July 2005. Shawn P. Callahan Papers, Archives and Special Collections, Marine Corps University Library, Quantico, Virginia.

Ronald Osborne, Camp Pendleton, letter to Shawn P. Callahan, Annapolis, 5 July 2005. Shawn P. Callahan Papers, Archives and Special Collections, Marine Corps University Library, Quantico, Virginia.

Pacey, Van C., St. Charles, Minnesota, letter to Shawn P. Callahan, Annapolis, 6 July 2005. Shawn P. Callahan Papers, Archives and Special Collections, Marine Corps University Library, Quantico, Virginia.

Prentice, Glen, Comments on Shawn P. Callahan, draft ms, "Close Air Support and the Battle for Khe Sanh: A Study in Institutional Approaches to Air Power." 26 April 2007. Transcript in the hand of Shawn P. Callahan, Annapolis.

Smith, Lieutenant Colonel Clinton A., Tampa, letter to Shawn P. Callahan, Annapolis, 8 July 2005. Shawn P. Callahan Papers, Archives and Special Collections, Marine Corps University Library, Quantico, Virginia.

Shulimson, Jack. "The Marine War: III MAF in Vietnam, 1965-1971." Available from http://www.vietnam.ttu.edu/vietnamcenter/events/1996_Symposium/96papers/ marwar.htm; accessed 14 May 2004.

Steele, Lieutenant Colonel David L., Kirkland, Washington, letter to Shawn P. Callahan, Annapolis, 11 July 2005. Shawn P. Callahan Papers, Archives and Special Collections, Marine Corps University Library, Quantico, Virginia.

Stubbe, Ray W., Wauwatosa, Wisconsin, letter to Shawn P. Callahan, Annapolis, 12 December 2006. Shawn P. Callahan Papers, Archives and Special

Collections, Marine Corps University Library, Quantico, Virginia.

Westmoreland, General William C., Washington, D.C., letter to General Leonard F. Chapman, Washington, D.C. regarding comments on draft monograph of Captain Moyer S. Shore, The Battle for Khe Sanh, 29 March 1969. Transcript in the Records of the U.S. Marine Corps, History and Museums Division Publication Background Files: USMC in Vietnam, 1967-69, National Archives, College Park, Maryland.

———, Washington, D.C., letter to General Leonard F. Chapman., Washington, D.C. regarding comments on draft monograph of Captain Moyer S. Shore, The Battle for Khe Sanh, 21 April 1969. Transcript in the Records of the U.S. Marine Corps, History and Museums Division Publication Background Files: USMC in Vietnam, 1967-69, National Archives, College Park, Maryland.

Wilkinson, Lieutenant Colonel James B., Comments on Shawn P. Callahan, draft ms, "Close Air Support and the Battle for Khe Sanh: A Study in Institutional Approaches to Air Power." 22 November 2006. Transcript in the hand of Shawn P. Callahan, Annapolis.

U.S. Department of Defense, *The Battle of Khe Sanh*. Videotape, 15 min., Washington D.C.: Aerospace Audio Visual Service, circa 1968.

———, Military Assistance Command, Vietnam. Military Assistance Command Office of Evaluations. An Analysis of the Khe Sanh Battle, Memorandum for COMUSMACV, Saigon, RVN, 1968.

———, U.S. Marine Corps. 1st Marine Air Wing. 1st Marine Air Wing Command Chronology, 1 January to 31 January 1968. Da Nang, RVN, 1968.

———, 1st Marine Air Wing. 1st Marine Air Wing Command Chronology, 1 February to 29 February 1968. Da Nang, RVN, 1968.

———, 1st Marine Air Wing. 1st Marine Air Wing Command Chronology, 1 March to 31 March 1968. Da Nang, RVN, 1968.

———, 1st Marine Air Wing. 1st Marine Air Wing Command Chronology, 1 April to 30 April 1968. Da Nang, RVN, 1968.

———, Marine Aerial Refueler Transport Squadron-152, Marine Aerial Refueler Transport Squadron Command Chronology, 1 January to 31 January 1968. Futenma, Japan, 1968.

———, Marine Aerial Refueler Transport Squadron-152, Marine Aerial Refueler Transport Squadron Command Chronology, 1 February to 29 February 1968. Futenma, Japan, 1968.

———, Marine Aerial Refueler Transport Squadron-152, Marine Aerial Refueler Transport Squadron Command Chronology, 1 March to 31 March 1968. Futenma, Japan, 1968.

———, Marine Observation Squadron-2. Marine Observation Squadron-2 Command Chronology, 1 January to 31 January 1968. Da Nang, RVN, 1968.

ENDNOTES

1. Department of Defense, Military Assistance Command, Vietnam, Military Assistance Command Office of Evaluations, "An Analysis of the Khe Sanh Battle," memorandum for COMUSMACV (Saigon, DRV, 1968), 2, places the total quantity of air ordnance at 96,000 tons, while the total quantity of ground ordnance, including artillery, at only 3,600 tons.

2. U.S. Department of Defense, Joint Chiefs of Staff, Joint Publication 1-02: *Department of Defense Dictionary of Military and Associated Terms* (Washington, D.C.: Government Printing Office, 2001 [amended through 2005]), 90.

3. Lieutenant General Keith McCutcheon, "Marine Aviation in Vietnam, 1962-1970," *U.S. Naval Institute Proceedings: Naval Review* 1971 (97), no. 819 (May 1971): 146. The U.S. Army began operating AH-1G's in Vietnam in November 1967. These aircraft did support the withdrawal from Khe Sanh, but the scale was very limited, and generally confined to Army air cavalry units.

4. John J. Sbrega, "Southeast Asia," in *Case Studies in the Development of Close Air Support,* ed. Benjamin Franklin Cooling (Washington, D.C.: Office of Air Force History, U.S. Air Force, 1990), 414-415.

5. Donald J. Mrozek, *Air Power and the Ground War in Vietnam: Ideas and Actions* (Maxwell AFB, Alabama: Air University Press, 1988), 24-27.

6. Sbrega, 439.

7. Mrozek, 6.

8. Richard H. Kohn and Joseph P. Harahan, eds., *Air Interdiction in World War II, Korea, and Vietnam: An Interview with General Earl E. Partridge, General Jacob E. Smart, and General John W. Vogt, Jr.* (Washington, D.C.: Office of Air Force History, U.S. Air Force, 1986), 2.

9. David MacIssac, "Voices from the Central Blue: The Air Power Theorists," in *Makers of Modern Strategy from Machiavelli to the Nuclear Age,* ed. Peter Paret (Princeton: Princeton University Press, 1986), 639.

10. Benjamin Franklin Cooling, ed., *Case Studies in the Development of Close Air Support* (Washington, D.C.: Office of Air Force History, U.S. Air Force, 1990), 8.

11. Richard G. Davis, *The 31 Initiatives: A Study in Air Force-Army Cooperation* (Washington, D.C.: Office of Air Force History, U.S. Air Force, 1987), 11.

12. Kohn and Harahan, 49.

13. MacIssac, 644.

14. Mrozek, 123.

15. Sbrega, 413, shows that in joint plans drawn up in 1960, the planned level of Air Force support for Army operations was fixed at five daily sorties per battalion.

16. Mrozek, 21.

17. Sbrega, 420.

18. John Schlight, *A War Too Long: The USAF in Southeast Asia, 1961-1975* (Washington, D.C.: Air Force History and Museums Program, 1996), 5-6.

19. Kohn and Harahan, 60.

20. Sbrega, 413.

21. Ibid., 455-456.

22. Sbrega, 418.

23. Mrozek, 17.

24. Sbrega, 414.

25. Ibid., 416.

26. Davis, 17.

27. Sbrega, 415.

28. Davis, 16.

29. Sbrega, 416.

30. General William W. Momyer, *Airpower in Three Wars* (Washington, D.C.: U.S. Government Printing Office, 1978), 261.

31. Sbrega, 428-430. Davis, 19, shows that the Army responded to this significant compromise on the part of the Air Force by reducing its number of Caribou and Mohawk aircraft, returning to the Air Force a portion of the transport and observation territory which had been infringed upon. The Army also decreased its air mobility plan from five divisions to just one, but it was determined to protect this new concept. In 1965 the Army pressed ahead with the 1st Air Cavalry Division, and likewise proceeded with the development of an aerial fire support system. These efforts were critical to the production of an attack helicopter.

32. Sbrega, 422.

33. Gary Robert Lester, *Mosquitoes to Wolves: The Evolution of the Airborne Forward Air Controller* (Maxwell AFB, Alabama: Air University Press, 1977), 125.

34. Schlight, 23.

35. Momyer, 265.

36. Sbrega, 454.

37. Momyer, 277.

38. Sbrega, 469.

39. Cooling, 1.

40. Sbrega, 445.

41. Lester, 109.

42. John W. Ellis Jr., *The Airborne Forward Air Controller: Past Accomplishments and Future Opportunities* (Santa Monica: The Rand Corporation, 1978), 13.

43. Lester, 109.

44. House Committee on Armed Services, Special Subcommittee on Tactical Air Support, Close Air Support, 89th Cong., 2d sess., 1966, Committee Print 44, 4862-4864.

45. Riley Sunderland, *Evolution of Command and Control Doctrine for Close Air Support* (Washington, D.C.: Office of Air Force History, U.S. Air Force, 1973), 54, and House Committee on Armed Services, 4861-4862.

46. Ellis, 14.

47. Lester, 121-122, 124, 142.

48. Schlight, 26-27.

49. Lester, 114.

50. House Committee on Armed Services, 4861-4862.

51. Lester, 118-119.

52. Ibid., 114-115.

53. Ibid., 120.

54. Lester, 116-118.

55. Ibid., 177, shows that the 23d Tactical Air Support Squadron, composed of O-1 and O-2 aircraft, was established in Nakhon Phanom, Thailand, in April 1966, having begun operations there as a subset of another unit in January.

56. Momyer, 269.

57. Schlight, 27-28.

58. Lester, 25.

59. Momyer, 269.

60. Sunderland, 54.

61. Sbrega, 418.

62. House Committee on Armed Services, 4867.

63. Momyer, 32, 274.

64. Momyer, 270; and Sbrega, 441.

65. Sbrega, 418.

66. House Committee on Armed Services, 4867.

67. Davis, 21.

68. House Committee on Armed Services, 4864.

69. Richard S. Drury, *USAF Close Air Support* (Singapore: Motorbooks International, 1991), 7-8.

70. Kohn and Harahan, 46.

71. Mrozek, 125.

72. Ibid., 125.

73. Sbrega, 444.

74. Ibid., 415.

75. Mrozek, 127-128.

76. Sbrega, 444; and Schlight, 31-32.

77. Mrozek, 128.

78. Momyer, 282.

79. Sbrega, 438. These aircraft were both replaced by the OV-10 by June 1969, which began service in Veitnam with the Marine Corps and Air Force in July 1968.

80. House Committee on Armed Services, 4865.

81. Schlight, 40.

82. Major General Keith McCutcheon, "Air Support for III MAF," *Marine Corps Gazette* 51, no. 8 (August 1967): 19-23.

83. Lieutenant Colonel Edward C. Johnson, *Marine Corps Aviation: The Early Years, 1912-1940* (Washington, D.C.: History and Museums Division, Headquarters U.S. Marine Corps, 1977), 35.

84. Johnson, 56.

85. Lieutenant Colonel Marshall R. Tutton, "Marine Corps Aviation," *United States Naval Institute Proceedings* 87, no. 5 (May 1961): 48.

86. Johnson, 79.

87. U.S. Marine Corps, *Small Wars Manual* (Washington, D.C.: Government Printing Office, 1940), Chapter X, 17.

88. Ibid., Chapter X, 19.

89. Colonel Anthony Standish, "Infantry-Air Support Single Command," *United States Army Combat Forces Journal* 2, no. 12 (July 1952): 32-33.

90. "Weakness in Air Force," *U.S. News and World Report*, 3 November 1950, 17-19.

91. U.S. Marine Corps, *Landing Force Manual 22: Coordination of Supporting Arms* (Quantico, Virginia: Marine Corps Landing Force Development Activity, 1960), 37. The phrase "and with supporting forces" had been excluded from the definition of CAS in U.S. Marine Corps, *MCS-77E: Air Support Operations* (Quantico, Virginia: Marine Corps Educational Center, Marine Corps Schools, 1955), 10.

92. Captain Robert V. Sabia, "The AO and the Field Commander," *Marine Corps Gazette* 52, no. 5 (May 1968): 46.

93. Lieutenant Colonel R.P. Keller, "Trained For Support." *Marine Corps Gazette* 38, no. 5 (May 1954): 30.

94. Keller, 30.

95. "Weakness in Air Force," 19.

96. Tutton, 53.

97. McCutcheon, "Marine Aviation in Vietnam," 130.

98. Lieutenant Colonel J.F. Bolt, "Goodbye Able Dog." *Marine Corps Gazette* 41, no. 10 (October 1957): 30.

99. Tutton, 50.

100. Bolt, 29-30.

101. Brigadier General Norman J. Anderson. "Marine Aviation Ready for Any Emergency: Air-Ground Team Concept is Hailed," *Army Navy Air Force Journal and Register* 100, no. 10 (3 November 1962): 18.

102. Major General Keith McCutcheon, "Marine Corps Aviation: An Overview," *Marine Corps Gazette* 52, no. 5 (May 1968): 24.

103. McCutcheon, "Marine Corps Aviation: An Overview," 27.

104. Lieutenant Colonel Richard Donaghy, Irvine, California, letter to Shawn P. Callahan, Annapolis, 22 November 2004, Shawn P. Callahan Papers, Archives and Special Collections, Marine Corps University Library, Quantico, Virginia, Part 1 (letter in six parts).

105. Sabia, 47.

106. Robert J. Arrotta, Comments on draft ms, 28 April 2007, transcript in the hand of Shawn P. Callahan, Annapolis, 1.

107. Arrotta, 1.

108. Donaghy, Part 1.

109. Sbrega, 459; and McCutcheon, "Marine Aviation in Vietnam," 141.

110. Major General John P. Condon, *Corsairs to Panthers: U.S. Marine Aviation in Korea* (Washington, D.C.: History and Museums Division, Headquarters Marine Corps, 2002), 6-8.

111. U.S. Marine Corps, *Operational Handbook 5-4: Close Air Support (CAS) Handbook* (Quantico, Virginia: Marine Corps Development and Education Command, 1979), 5.

112. Tutton, 53; and Anderson, 18.

113. Major W. H. Beckett, "The L2VMA: Light CAS Needs Boondockers." *Marine Corps Gazette* 47, no. 3 (March 1963), 20-23.

114. Sabia, 47; McCutcheon, "Marine Corps Aviation: An Overview," 24, and Colonel Richard W. Carr, Hampstead, North Carolina, letter to Shawn P. Callahan, Annapolis, 14 July 2005, Shawn P. Callahan Papers, Archives and Special Collections, Marine Corps University Library, Quantico, Virginia.

115. Lieutenant Colonel Wayne C. Andersen, Venice, Florida, letter to Shawn P. Callahan, Annapolis, 11 July 2005, Shawn P. Callahan Papers, Archives and Special Collections, Marine Corps University Library, Quantico, Virginia.

116. Andersen; Lieutenant Colonel Bill Egen, Havelock, North Carolina, letter to Shawn P. Callahan, Annapolis, 10 July 2005, Shawn P. Callahan Papers, Archives and Special Collections, Marine Corps University Library, Quantico, Virginia; Van C. Pacey, St. Charles, Minnesota, letter to Shawn P. Callahan, Annapolis, 6 July 2005, Shawn P. Callahan Papers, Archives and Special Collections, Marine Corps University Library, Quantico, Virginia; and Robert J. Moriarty, Miami, letter to Shawn P. Callahan, Annapolis, 5 July 2005, Shawn P. Callahan Papers, Archives and Special Collections, Marine Corps University Library, Quantico, Virginia.

117. Pacey.

118. Carr and Pacey.

119. Lieutenant Colonel Clinton A. Smith, Tampa, letter to Shawn P. Callahan, Annapolis, 8 July 2005, Shawn P. Callahan Papers, Archives and Special Collections, Marine Corps University Library, Quantico, Virginia.

120. Moriarty.

121. Ronald Osborne, Camp Pendleton, letter to Shawn P. Callahan, Annapolis, 5 July 2005, Shawn P. Callahan Papers, Archives and Special Collections, Marine Corps University Library, Quantico, Virginia.

122. McCutcheon, "Marine Aviation in Vietnam," 141.

123. House Committee on Armed Services, 4872-4873.

124. Jack Shulimson et al., *U.S. Marines in Vietnam: The Defining Year, 1968* (Washington, D.C.: History and Museums Division, Headquarters U.S. Marine Corps, 1997), 501.

125. Sbrega, 460.

126. Shulimson, 58-59.

127. Ibid., 58.

128. John Prados and Ray W. Stubbe, *Valley of Decision: The Siege of Khe Sanh* (New York: Houghton Mifflin, 1991; reprint, Annapolis: Naval Institute Press, 2004), 16 (page citations are to the reprint edition).

129. Edward F. Murphy, The *Hill Fights: The First Battle of Khe Sanh* (New York: Ballantine Books, 2003), 8; and Prados and Stubbe, 22-23.

130. Murphy, 9; and Prados and Stubbe, 19-21.

131. Prados and Stubbe, 37.

132. Ibid., 46.

133. Murphy, 3.

134. Ibid., 10-12

135. Murphy, 14.

136. Major Gary L. Telfer and Lieutenant Colonel Lane Rogers, *U.S. Marines in Vietnam: Fighting the North Vietnamese, 1967* (Washington, D.C.: History and Museums Division, Headquarters Marine Corps, 1984), 31.

137. In March 1966, the A Shau Special Forces Camp, 55 kilometers southeast of Khe Sanh, was attacked and overrun by the NVA when the low cloud ceilings created by seasonal monsoon weather prevented air support. After a hurried evacuation on 9 March, only about 150 of the approximately 400 camp members escaped, most by fleeing into the jungle. Murphy, 7. After 1/3 arrived at Khe Sanh for Operation Prairie, Westmoreland visited the battalion commander and told him, "Well, I'm not going to have another A Shau Valley up here. That's why you're here." Murphy, 17.

138. Murphy, 18-19, 44.

139. Ibid., 19.

140. These soldiers attempted to maintain their isolated position until it was too late. During the fateful attacks of January 1968 that placed the Khe Sanh Combat Base under siege, the Green Berets and CIDG were overrun by the NVA. The commander of the 26th Marines at Khe Sanh determined any relief force would be walking into an ambush, and was therefore futile. Most historians of the battle agree that this was a very wise but unfortunate decision.

141. Telfer and Rogers, 203.

142. Murphy, xiv.

143. Prados and Stubbe, 70-71.

144. Telfer and Rogers, 34.

145. Prados and Stubbe, 83.

146. Murphy, 44.

147. Ibid., 45.

148. Telfer and Rogers, 36-37.

149. Murphy, 58.

150. Prados and Stubbe, 87-88.

151. Telfer, 38.

152. Murphy, 112, states that 382,000 pounds of bombs were dropped on 27 April alone. Prados and Stubbe, 91, totals the aviation ordnance of 28 April at 382,700 pounds.

153. Telfer and Rogers, 39, states that 1st MAW dropped 518,700 pounds of ordnance, or nearly 68 percent of the total. Subtracting the total payload of two B-52's (120,000 pounds) from the two-day total, Marine tactical aircraft dropped close to 80 percent of the remaining ordnance.

154. Telfer and Rogers, 39.

155. Murphy, 112.

156. Telfer and Rogers, 39.

157. Prados and Stubbe, 62.

158. Enemy KIA from Telfer and Rogers, 40-41. Friendly losses from Ray W. Stubbe, *The Final Formation: Those Who Died Because of Khe Sanh* (Wauwatosa, Wisconsin: by the author, 1995), 17-18.

159. Prados and Stubbe, 99; and Telfer and Rogers, 229-231.

160. Murphy, 150.

161. Robert Pisor, *The End of the Line: The Siege of Khe Sanh* (New York: W.W. Norton & Company, 1982), 19.

162. Telfer and Rogers, 41.

163. Pisor, 19.

164. Telfer and Rogers, 41.

165. Ibid., 42.

166. Pisor, 18.

167. Telfer and Rogers, 41.

168. Pisor, 18.

169. Telfer and Rogers, 42-43.

170. Murphy, 191; and Telfer and Rogers, 43-44.

171. Prados and Stubbe, 98-99.

172. Murphy, 211-212.

173. Prados and Stubbe, 95-97.

174. Telfer and Rogers, 44-45.

175. Murphy, 215.

176. Murphy, 221-222.

177. Telfer and Rogers, 45.

178. Prados and Stubbe, 102; and Telfer and Rogers, 45.

179. Telfer and Rogers, 45.

180. Telfer and Rogers, 45.

181. Pisor, 20.

182. Shulimson, 61, and Prados and Stubbe, 155.

183. Pisor, 40-41.

184. Prados and Stubbe, 216.

185. Mrozek, 73.

186. Prados and Stubbe, 195.

187. Pisor, 94.

188. Pisor, 95.

189. Shulimson, 64.

190. Prados and Stubbe, 203.

191. Pisor, 103.

192. Colonel William H. Dabney, Interview by Benis M. Frank, 20 May 1982. Transcript. Marine Corps Oral History Collection, Marine Corps Historical Center, Washington, D.C., 17-18.

193. Ibid., 21.

194. Pisor, 23.

195. Prados and Stubbe, 214.

196. Pisor, 17.

197. Prados and Stubbe, 198.

198. Pisor, 77-78.

199. Prados and Stubbe, 361-363.

200. Shulimson, 67.

201. Pisor, 135.

202. Telfer and Rogers, 21-22.

203. Ibid., 95.

204. Ibid., 102-103.

205. Ibid., 103.

206. Telfer and Rogers, 203.

207. Pisor, 70.

208. Ibid., 69-70.

209. Prados and Stubbe, 159.

210. Pisor, 70.

211. Mrozek, 73.

212. Pisor, 122-124, 133-136, 138.

213. Pisor, 70-71.

214. Ibid., 138.

215. Bernard C. Nalty, *Air Power and the Fight for Khe Sanh* (Washington, D.C.: Office of Air Force History, U.S. Air Force, 1973), 42; Lieutenant General Victor H. Krulak, *First to Fight: An Inside View of the U.S. Marine Corps* (Annapolis: Naval Institute Press, 1999), 216; and Pisor, 211.

216. U.S. Marine Corps, Marine Aerial Refueler Transport Squadron-152, Marine Aerial Refueler Transport Squadron Command Chronology, 1 January to 31 January 1968 (Futenma, Japan, 1968), 3; and U.S. Marine Corps, Marine Aerial Refueler Transport Squadron-152, Marine Aerial Refueler Transport Squadron Command Chronology, 1 February to 29 February 1968 (Futenma, Japan, 1968), 3; and U.S. Marine Corps, Marine Aerial Refueler Transport Squadron-152, Marine Aerial Refueler Transport Squadron Command Chronology, 1 March to 31 March 1968 (Futenma, Japan, 1968), 3; The 1st Marine Air Wing kept its KC-130 squadron based in Okinawa, and rotated aircraft through a five-plane detachment in Da Nang, in order to avoid inflating the apparent number of aircraft based in Japan.

217. Shulimson, 66, and Pisor, 139. Martin Windrow, *The Last Valley: Dien Bien Phu and the French Defeat in Vietnam* (Cambridge: Da Capo Press, 2004), 268-272 and 556-561, presents an excellent analysis of the additional factors which hampered the full application of air power at Dien Bien Phu.

218. Pisor, 37.

219. Shulimson, 471.

220. Prados and Stubbe, 220.

221. Pisor, 103.

222. Pisor, 37-38.

223. Ibid., 124.

224. Shulimson, 473.

225. Prados and Stubbe, 236.

226. Pisor, 27.

227. Prados and Stubbe, 237.

228. Ibid., 224.

229. Pisor, 17.

230. Murphy, 235.

231. Pisor, 104.

232. Prados and Stubbe, 228.

233. Dabney, 77-78.

234. Pisor, 29-31.

235. Shulimson, 71.

236. Prados and Stubbe, 231.

237. Hammel, 55-56; Prados and Stubbe, 231.

238. Pisor, 56.

239. Pisor, 109.

240. Ibid., 113-114.

241. Eric Hammel, *Khe Sanh: Siege in the Clouds, An Oral History* (Pacifica, California: Pacifica Military History, 1989; reprint, New York: ibooks, inc., 2004), 81-82 (page citations are to the reprint edition).

242. Hammel, 77.

243. Pisor, 115-118.

244. Hammel, 84-85.

245. Hammel, 87.

246. Hammel, 70, 170.

247. Pisor, 131. In addition to the normal tension between regular and irregular forces, and forces of different nations, the Americans had the memory of the attack on the Lang Vei Special Forces Camp during the Hill Fights. On May 4, 1967, enemy agents infiltrated the CIDG unit and killed some perimeter guards, enabling the entry of another force which caused significant damage and killed the American CO and XO of the Special Forces Team.

248. Hammel, 123, Pisor, 137.

249. Hammel, 148, 276; and Prados and Stubbe, 296.

250. Shulimson, 265; and Nalty, 25.

251. Shulimson, 270-272; and Nalty, 93.

252. Prados and Stubbe, 265.

253. Murphy, 239.

254. Prados and Stubbe, 327; and Shulimson, 275.

255. Pisor, 197.

256. Prados and Stubbe, 336-337; and Shulimson, 276.

257. Pisor, 197.

258. Shulimson, 278.

259. Hammel, 200, and Shulimson, 277-278.

260. Hammel, 200.

261. Prados and Stubbe, 280.

262. Pisor, 213.

263. Prados and Stubbe, 443.

264. Colonel William H. Dabney, Lexington, Virginia, letter to Major Biagio Colandreo Jr., Naval Amphibious Base Little Creek, Virginia, circa 1999, transcript in the hand of Shawn P. Callahan, Annapolis.

265. Hammel, 271-272.

266. Shulimson, 279. Prados and Stubbe quote estimates that the NVA may have fired as many as 1,700 rounds that day.

267. Nalty, 38.

268. Prados and Stubbe, 398. Colonel Dabney insists that 130mm guns actually began firing from positions in Laos on 21 January, when heavy artillery was observed shooting over Hill 881S toward the combat base. This continued regularly afterwards, and was reported by Dabney, but he states that the 26th Marines probably did not accept this assessment because the artillery fire was often mixed with rocket fire, which masked its effects when they arrived at KSCB. From 881S, it was much easier to distinguish between heavy artillery passing overhead and rockets being fired from the immediate vicinity of the hill. Colonel William H. Dabney, Comments on draft ms, 7 December 2006, transcript in the hand of Shawn P. Callahan, Annapolis.

269. Glen Prentice, Comments on draft ms, 26 April 2007, transcript in the hand of Shawn P. Callahan, Annapolis.

270. Hammel, 354.

271. Ibid., 112.

272. Keller, 77.

273. Prados and Stubbe, 53-54.

274. Nalty, 62.

275. Nalty, 35-38, 45.

276. Shulimson, 481.

277. Prados and Stubbe, 377-378, and Hammel 244-245.

278. Nalty, 50, 58.

279. Ibid., 63-64.

280. Prados and Stubbe, 391.

281. Mrozek, 83.

282. Mrozek, 83; and Nalty, 42-59.

283. 8,120 tons of supplies were delivered by Air Force parachute drops and low altitude delivery systems, and another 4,310 tons were delivered by Air Force aircraft landing at the base. 1,926 tons were delivered by Marine Corps fixed-wing aircraft landing at the combat base, while marine helicopters delivered another 3,000 tons, predominantly to the hill outposts. Director, Historical Division, Headquarters, U.S. Marine Corps comments on Director of Information Press Query #41, "'Air Delivery' by 1stLt Barney Halloran, USMC" of 20 March 1970. Records of the U.S. Marine Corps, History and Museums Division Publication Background Files: USMC in Vietnam, 1967-69, National Archives, College Park, Maryland.

284. Prados and Stubbe, 395, Hammel, 290-291.

285. Hammel, 249.

286. Pisor, 232.

287. Shulimson, 281; and Nalty, 96.

288. Nalty, 96; and Shulimson, 281.

289. Hammel, 315.

290. Ibid., 355-356.

291. Nalty, 96.

292. Prados and Stubbe, 424-425.

293. Dabney, interview transcript, 22; and Pisor, 32.

294. Dabney, interview transcript, 4-5.

295. Prados and Stubbe, 177.

296. Krulak, 217.

297. Ibid., 218-219.

298. Edward F. Murphy, *Semper Fi Vietnam: From Da Nang to the DMZ, Marine Corps Campaigns, 1965-1975* (New York: Ballantine Books, 1997), 183.

299. Dave Richard Palmer, *Summons of the Trumpet: U.S.-Vietnam in Perspective* (San Rafael, California: Presidio Press, 1978), 172.

300. Dabney, interview transcript, 27.

301. Military History Institute of Vietnam, *Victory in Vietnam: The Official History of the People's Army of Vietnam, 1954-1975*, trans. Merle L. Pribbenow (Lawrence, Kansas: University Press of Kansas, 2002), 216-230.

302. Sedgwick D. Tourison Jr., *B5-T8 in 48 QXD: The Secret Official History of the North Vietnamese Army at the Siege of Khe Sanh, Vietnam, Spring, 1968* (Wauwatosa, Wisconsin: Khe Sanh Veterans, Inc., 2006), 3-4.

303. Tourison, 5.

304. Tourison, 5.

305. Tourison, 5-7, 16.

306. Tourison, 14, 34.

307. General Directorate for Rear Services, Rear Service Operations: 1968 Spring-Summer Khe Sanh Route 9 Campaign, 1988, transcript in the hands of Ray W. Stubbe, Wauwatosa, WI.

308. Tourison, 27-28, 13.

309. Tourison, 10.

310. Tourison, 14.

311. Toursion, 34.

312. Tourison, 78, 67.

313. Tourison, 30.

314. Department of Defense, *An Analysis of the Khe Sanh Battle*, 4.

315. Tourison, 92.

316. Tourison, 37.

317. Tourison, 79.

318. Tourison, 37.

319. Tourison, 81.

320. Tourison, 39.

321. Tourison, 93, 95.

322. General Directorate for Rear Services.

323. Tourison, 92.

324. Prados and Stubbe, 2; Shulimson, 476-477; and Westmoreland as quoted in Department of Defense, *The Battle of Khe Sanh*, videotape, 15 min., (Washington D.C.: Aerospace Audio Visual Service, circa 1968), and in "B-52 at War," available from http://www.faqs.org/docs/air/avb52_2.html; accessed 11 August 2005.

325. Tourison, 44. Note the NVA use of the word "siege" to describe phase II operations.

326. Krulak, 215.

327. Nalty, 96; and Pisor, 176.

328. Pisor, 241.

329. General William C. Westmoreland, Washington, D.C., letter to General Leonard F. Chapman, Washington, D.C., regarding comments on draft monograph of Captain Moyer S. Shore, The Battle for Khe Sanh, 29 March 1969, transcript in the records of the U.S. Marine Corps, History and Museums Division Publication Background Files: USMC in Vietnam, 1967-69, National Archives, College Park, Maryland, 3.

330. Lieutenant General Robert E. Cushman Jr., Da Nang, Vietnam, letter to Brigadier General W.D. Sawyer, Washington, D.C. regarding comments on draft monograph of Captain Moyer S. Shore, The Battle for Khe Sanh, 26 December 1968, transcript in the records of the U.S. Marine Corps, History and Museums Division Publication Background Files: USMC in Vietnam, 1967-69, National Archives, College Park, Maryland.

331. Prados and Stubbe, 418.

332. Jack Shulimson, "The Marine War: III MAF in Vietnam, 1965-1971," available from http://www.vietnam.ttu.edu/vietnamcenter/events/1996_Symposium/96papers/marwar.htm; accessed 14 May 2004.

333. Pisor, 240.

334. Prados and Stubbe, 420-421.

335. Ibid., 444.

336. Ibid., 428-429.

337. Shulimson, *The Defining Year*, 284; and Nalty, 99.

338. Prados and Stubbe, 439-440; and Colonel Richard D. Camp Jr., *Lima-6: A Marine Company Commander in Vietnam, June 1967 - January 1968* (New York: Atheneum, 1989), 283.

339. Lieutenant General Robert E. Cushman Jr., Da Nang, Vietnam, letter to Lieutenant General V.J. Van Ryzn, Washington, D.C. regarding comments on draft monograph of Captain Moyer S. Shore, The Battle for Khe Sanh, 23 March 1969, transcript in the records of the U.S. Marine Corps, History and Museums Division Publication Background Files: USMC in Vietnam, 1967-69, National Archives, College Park, Maryland, 2.

340. Shulimson, 285; and Prados and Stubbe, 436.

341. Prados and Stubbe, 440-441.

342. Cushman, to Van Ryzn, 2-3.

343. Prados and Stubbe, 440.

344. Nalty, 100.

345. Murphy, 241.

346. Prados and Stubbe, 448.

347. Shulimson, *The Defining Year*, 312.

348. Hammel, 416-417.

349. Ibid., 422.

350. Hammel, 425-434; and Murphy, 240.

351. Nalty, 102.

352. Hammel, 436.

353. Shulimson, *The Defining Year*, 317-319.

354. Ibid., 320.

355. Shulimson, *The Defining Year*, 321-324.

356. Prados and Stubbe, 448.

357. Murphy, 241.

358. Prados and Stubbe, 448; and Shulimson, *The Defining Year*, 326.

359. Shulimson, *The Defining Year*, 467-468.

360. U.S. Marine Corps, 1st Marine Air Wing, 1st

Marine Air Wing Command Chronology, 1 January to 31 January 1968 (Da Nang, RVN, 1968), 2-4.

361. Shulimson, *The Defining Year,* 508

362. Shulimson, *The Defining Year*, 508. On page 498, Shulimson mentions USAF planning a sustained sortie rate of 1.2, but this was still considerably less than the Marines' 2.0 sortie rate.

363. Shulimson, *The Defining Year*, 472.

364. Sunderland, 46. Lester, 115-116, presents additional evidence that Momyer had fixated on the single management issue more than the massing of air power for a battle of annihilation at Khe Sanh by examining his decisions with regard to Air Force assets in Thailand. Since the 7th Air Force was formed in April 1966, its commander had operational control of Air Force units in Thailand as well, but Momyer did not chose to use these assets in Vietnam until the Tet offensive began, after the "destroy" phase of Niagara had begun.

365. Ray W. Stubbe, *Battalion of Kings: A Tribute to Our Fallen Brothers Who Died Because of the Battle of Khe Sanh, Vietnam* (Milwaukee: Khe Sanh Veterans, Inc., 2005), 276.

366. Ibid.

367. Telfer, 202.

368. Mrozek, 41, shows that technically, a third DASC existed for the control of Vietnamese Air Force aircraft, I DASC, but the volume of traffic and air support requests handled by this DASC was so small compared to the other DASC's that it had no adverse effects.

369. McCutcheon, "Marine Aviation in Vietnam," 140.

370. Prados and Stubbe, 295.

371. Shulimson, *The Defining Year*, 474.

372. Ibid.

373. Hammel, 157.

374. Ibid., 325.

375. Hammel, 155.

376. U.S. Marine Corps, Marine Observation Squadron-2, Marine Observation Squadron-2 Command Chronology, 1 January to 31 January 1968 (Da Nang, RVN, 1968), 6.

377. Nalty, 90.

378. Pisor, 105-106.

379. Ibid., 106-107.

380. Pisor, 217.

381. Hammel, 177.

382. Prados and Stubbe, 301-302.

383. Hammel, 177-178; and Ray W. Stubbe, *Khe Sanh and the Mongol Prince* (Wauwatosa, Wisconsin: by the author, 2002), 23. Colonel Dabney affirms a general suspicion of Muscle Shoals information created by the paradoxical system of collecting tactical intelligence data and sending it to the highest levels of command for analysis, far from the battlefield and people most affected by that intelligence. By doing so, the information was subjected to the bureaucratic politics of multiple intelligence agencies sometimes working at cross-purposes. Each agency tended to overvalue the importance of its own contributions and undervalue the observations of other agencies, including units engaged with the enemy, ultimately at the expense of providing combat units with a better multi-source intelligence picture. Colonel William H. Dabney, Comments on draft ms, 7 December 2006, transcript in the hand of Shawn P. Callahan, Annapolis.

384. Hammel, 179, 301; and Prados and Stubbe; 415-416.

385. Prados and Stubbe, 301.

386. Hammel, 301.

387. Hammel, 451-452.

388. Prados and Stubbe, 297, is the most authoritative source on statistics for the battle, having integrated numerous sources. This work totals the contribution of B-52s at 59,542 tons of bombs dropped, compared to 39,179 dropped by tactical aircraft.

389. Shulimson, *The Defining Year*, 475.

390. Murphy, 18.

391. Sbrega, 445.

392. Mrozek, 40-41.

393. Mrozek, 23.

394. Shulimson, *The Defining Year*, 476; and Hammel, 150.

395. Shulimson, *The Defining Year*, 476, and Hammel, 150.

396. Shulimson, *The Defining Year*, 476.

397. Ronald J. Drez and Douglas Brinkley, *Voices of Courage: The Battle for Khe Sanh, Vietnam* (New York: Bulfinch Press, 2005), 168.

398. Hammel, 149.

399. Shulimson, *The Defining Year*, 68.

400. Pisor, 105.

401. Pisor, 141-143.

402. Tourison, 53.

403. Nalty, 83; and Pisor, 216.

404. Shulimson, *The Defining Year*, 476.

405. Prados and Stubbe, 297-298.

406. Ibid., 416.

407. Hammel, 291.

408. Prados and Stubbe, 304.

409. Dabney, interview transcript, 79.

410. Prados and Stubbe, 407.

411. Prados and Stubbe, 406.

412. Dabney, interview transcript, 25-26.

413. Hammel, 152.

414. Prados and Stubbe, 409.

415. Ibid., 411.

416. Tourison, 37.

417. "B-52 at War."

418. Department of Defense, *The Battle of Khe Sanh*.

419. Prados and Stubbe., 2.

420. Tourison, 79.

421. Shulimson, *The Defining Year*, 476-477.

422. Hammel, 150.

423. Hammel, 151.

424. Mrozek, 82.

425. Pisor, 247-248.

426. Shulimson, *The Defining Year*, 270.

427. Prados and Stubbe, 458.

428. Tourison, 92. Examining the casualty statistics of one regiment which was involved in both the encirclement of Khe Sanh Combat Base and in the mobile operations which followed, the official campaign history reports 62.3 percent casualties from air strikes, 24.6 percent from artillery

and mortars, and 11.0 percent from direct fire during the static encirclement. Comparing this to the 37.8 percent sustained due to air strikes, 47.5 percent due to indirect fires, and 13.1 percent ue to direct fires during the mobile phase, it is apparent that the unpredictable and fleeting contacts created by the more dynamic mobile phase decreased the effectiveness of air power compared to the other, more responsive weapons organic to the ground combat element.

429. Dabney, interview transcript, 83.

430. Prados and Stubbe, 297, 411. Out of the 2,548 B-52 sorties flown during Operation Niagara, 589 were classified as close-in missions.

431. Ibid., 457.

432. Tourison, 92.

433. Shulimson, *The Defining Year*, 476.

434. Shulimson, *The Defining Year*, 486.

435. Hammel, 303.

436. Shulimson, *The Defining Year*, 476.

437. Hammel, 452-453.

438. Hammel, 454-455.

439. "B-52 at War."

440. Momyer, 309.

441. Pisor, 217.

442. Shulimson, *The Defining Year*, 63.

443. Krulak, 114-119.

444. McCutcheon, "Marine Aviation in Vietnam," 139.

445. U.S. Marine Corps, 1st Marine Air Wing Command Chronology, 1 January to 31 January 1968, 2-4..

446. Prados and Stubbe, 223-224.

447. Ibid., 406.

448. Shulimson, *The Defining Year*, 477.

449. Ibid., 477.

450. Shulimson, *The Defining Year*, 477.

451. Ibid., 477-478.

452. Pisor, 185.

453. Mrozek, 81.

454. Hammel, 156.

455. Ibid., 185-186.

456. Shulimson, *The Defining Year*, 477.

457. Ibid., 477.

458. Captain Moyers S. Shore II, *The Battle for Khe Sanh* (Washington, D.C.: History and Museums Division, Headquarters U.S. Marine Corps, 1969), 103.

459. Krulak, 119.

460. Ibid., 119.

461. Ibid., 216.

462. Momyer, 178.

463. Nalty, 66-67.

464. Prados and Stubbe, 42, 48, and 194.

465. Sbrega, 451; and Nalty, 67.

466. McCutcheon, "Marine Aviation in Vietnam," 139.

467. Momyer, 178-179.

468. Schlight, 30.

469. Sbrega, 449-500.

470. Shulimson, *The Defining Year*, 469.

471. Shore, 104.

472. Nalty, 66.

473. Nalty, 67.

474. Nalty, 67.

475. Pisor, 216.

476. Arrotta, 2.

477. Momyer, 293.

478. Nalty, 61-62.

479. Ibid., 62.

480. Hammel, 153. Egen notes that the apparent chaos was magnified by an insufficient number of air control frequencies. This resulted in confusion between air strikes in different locations being simultaneously coordinated on the same frequency.

481. Hammel, 153-154.

482. Ibid., 295.

483. Ibid., 204-205.

484. Ibid., 355.

485. Dabney, to Colandreo.

486. Shulimson, *The Defining Year*, 469.

487. Ibid., 478.

488. Lester, 133-134. Of note, this source follows the Air Force tendency to overlook the role of the ground FAC at Khe Sanh, erroneously giving these FAC(A) sorties credit for controlling all the ordnance dropped in Operation Niagara.

489. Nalty, 60-65; Shulimson, *The Defining Year*, 478; and Andersen.

490. Shulimson, *The Defining Year*, 266.

491. Pisor, 220.

492. Hammel, 297.

493. Nalty, 66.

494. Ibid., 64.

495. Nalty, 62.

496. Colonel William H. Dabney, Lexington, Virginia, letter to Shawn P. Callahan, Annapolis, 21 August 2004, transcript in three parts in the hand of Shawn P. Callahan, Annapolis, Part 3.

497. Dabney, to Colandreo.

498. Dabney, to Callahan, Part 3.

499. Nalty, 56.

500. Hammel, 207.

501. U.S. Marine Corps, 1st Marine Air Wing, 1st Marine Air Wing Command Chronology, 1 February to 29 February 1968 (Da Nang, RVN, 1968), 2-3.

502. Mrozek, 84.

503. McCutcheon, "Marine Corps Aviation: An Overview," 27.

504. Shulimson, *The Defining Year*, 485.

505. Ibid., 485.

506. Dabney, interview trancript, 87-88.

507. Dabney, to Callahan, Part 1.

508. Nalty, 62-63.

509. Dabney, to Callahan, Part 1.

510. Prados and Stubbe, 572.

511. Nalty, 33-34.

512. Shulimson, *The Defining Year*, 475.

513. Hammel, 205.

514. Shulimson, *The Defining Year*, 475.

515. Hammel, 239.

516. Dabney to Callahan, Part 3.

517. Ibid., Part 1.

518. Ibid., Part 1.

519. Dabney, to Colandreo. The specific restriction to use Marine air support inside of 1,000 meters has been independently stated by at least one other Marine who was in Vietnam at the time, specifically George A. Finch III, Santa Rosa, California, letter to Shawn P. Callahan, Annapolis, 11 July 2005, Shawn P. Callahan Papers, Archives and Special Collections, Marine Corps University Library, Quantico, Virginia.

520. Andersen.

521. Shulimson, *The Defining Year*, 71; Hammel, 50; and Dabney, to Callahan, Part 1.

522. Prados and Stubbe, 260.

523. Drez and Brinkley, 172-173.

524. Prados and Stubbe, 391.

525. Murphy, 36.

526. Hammel, 308.

527. Prados and Stubbe, 74; and Murphy, 29.

528. Murphy, 93-94.

529. Dabney to Callahan, Part 2, and Arrotta, 2. Dabney actually describes the aircraft as F-101s, but these were not in use in Vietnam at the time, and are similar in form to the F-100s that Arrotta describes in the same incident.

530. Dabney to Callahan, Part 3.

531. Murphy, 59, 182, and 201.

532. Andersen.

533. Dabney to Callahan, Part 3.

534. Pisor, 164.

535. Ibid., 219-220.

536. Lieutenant Colonel David L. Steele, Kirkland, Washington, letter to Shawn P. Callahan, Annapolis, 11 July 2005, Shawn P. Callahan Papers, Archives and Special Collections, Marine Corps University Library, Quantico, Virginia.

537. Hammel, 83.

538. Pisor, 199.

539. Hammel, 198.

540. Nalty, 62.

541. Hammel, 292; and Prados and Stubbe, 397.

542. Shulimson, *The Defining Year*, 278.

543. Tourison, 38.

544. Prados and Stubbe, 397.

545. Lieutenant Colonel James B. Wilkinson, Comments on draft ms, 22 November 2006, transcript in the hand of Shawn P. Callahan, Annapolis.

546. Hammel, 351.

547. Tourison, 79. The stand-off requirements imposed on B-52s in fact ensured that they were not involved in any fratricide incidents at Khe Sanh, but it remains clear that the NVA understood why they had to get close to Marine positions, and did so.

548. Tourison, 82.

549. Colonel Dabney states that the first indication of an impending B-52 attack was the blank-

ing out of radio communication frequencies which occurred three to four minutes before the attack, which the Marines concluded was from the jammers the B-52s used when approaching the DMZ and North Vietnamese surface-to-air missile defenses. The Marines frequently heard NVA intrusion on American frequencies, so the NVA must have been aware of the same phenomenon. A few minutes, however, was insufficient time to take adequate countermeasures against a B-52 bombardment. Colonel William H. Dabney, Comments on draft ms, 7 December 2006, transcript in the hand of Shawn P. Callahan, Annapolis.

550. Hammel, 311.

551. Dabney, interview transcript, 35.

552. Nalty, 60.

553. Prados and Stubbe, 297.

www.ingramcontent.com/pod-product-compliance
Lightning Source LLC
Chambersburg PA
CBHW082122230426
43671CB00015B/2776